P9-DIF-918

TEENAGE
SEXUALITY
OPPOSING VIEWPOINTS®

1994

Other Books of Related Interest in the Opposing Viewpoints Series:

TEENAGE SEXUALITY

OPPOSING VIEWPOINTS®

David Bender & Bruno Leone, *Series Editors*

Karin L. Swisher, *Book Editor*
Terry O'Neill & Bruno Leone, *Assistant Editors*

OPPOSING
VIEWPOINTS
SERIES®

Greenhaven Press, Inc.   PO Box 289009   San Diego, CA 92198-9009

No part of this book may be reproduced or used in any form or by any means, electrical, mechanical, or otherwise, including, but not limited to, photocopy, recording, or any information storage and retrieval system, without prior written permission from the publisher.

Library of Congress Cataloging-in-Publication Data

Teenage sexuality : opposing viewpoints / Karin L. Swisher, book editor; Terry O'Neill, Bruno Leone, assistant editors. — [Rev. ed.]
    p.   cm. — (Opposing viewpoints series)
    Includes bibliographical references (p.) and index.
    ISBN 1-56510-103-0 (lib. bdg. : acid-free paper). — ISBN 1-56510-102-2 (pbk. : acid-free paper)
    1. Teenagers—United States—Sexual behavior. 2. Teenage pregnancy—United States—Prevention. 3. Sex instruction for teenagers—United States. 4. Gay teenagers—United States. 5. Abortion—United States. 6. AIDS (Disease) in adolescence—United States. I. Swisher, Karin, 1966-   . II. O'Neill, Terry, 1944-   . III. Leone, Bruno, 1939-   . IV. Series: Opposing viewpoints series (Unnumbered)
HQ27.T424 1994
306.7'0835—dc20   93-30962
                                          CIP
                                          AC

Copyright © 1994 by Greenhaven Press, Inc.
Printed in the U.S.A.

Every effort has been made to trace owners of copyrighted material.

"Congress shall make no law . . .
abridging the freedom of speech,
or of the press."

First Amendment to the U.S. Constitution

The basic foundation of our democracy is the first amendment
guarantee of freedom of expression. The Opposing Viewpoints
Series is dedicated to the concept of this basic freedom and the
idea that it is more important to practice it than to enshrine it.

Contents

Why Consider Opposing Viewpoints?

"The only way in which a human being can make some approach to knowing the whole of a subject is by hearing what can be said about it by persons of every variety of opinion and studying all modes in which it can be looked at by every character of mind. No wise man ever acquired his wisdom in any mode but this."

John Stuart Mill

In our media-intensive culture it is not difficult to find differing opinions. Thousands of newspapers and magazines and dozens of radio and television talk shows resound with differing points of view. The difficulty lies in deciding which opinion to agree with and which "experts" seem the most credible. The more inundated we become with differing opinions and claims, the more essential it is to hone critical reading and thinking skills to evaluate these ideas. Opposing Viewpoints books address this problem directly by presenting stimulating debates that can be used to enhance and teach these skills. The varied opinions contained in each book examine many different aspects of a single issue. While examining these conveniently edited opposing views, readers can develop critical thinking skills such as the ability to compare and contrast authors' credibility, facts, argumentation styles, use of persuasive techniques, and other stylistic tools. In short, the Opposing Viewpoints Series is an ideal way to attain the higher-level thinking and reading skills so essential in a culture of diverse and contradictory opinions.

In addition to providing a tool for critical thinking, Opposing Viewpoints books challenge readers to question their own strongly held opinions and assumptions. Most people form their opinions on the basis of upbringing, peer pressure, and personal, cultural, or professional bias. By reading carefully balanced opposing views, readers must directly confront new ideas as well as the opinions of those with whom they disagree. This is not to simplistically argue that everyone who reads opposing views will—or should—change his or her opinion. Instead, the series enhances readers' depth of understanding of their own views by encouraging confrontation with opposing ideas. Careful examination of others' views can lead to the readers' understanding of the logical inconsistencies in their own opinions, perspective on why they hold an opinion, and the consideration of the possibility that their opinion requires further evaluation.

Evaluating Other Opinions

To ensure that this type of examination occurs, Opposing Viewpoints books present all types of opinions. Prominent spokespeople on different sides of each issue as well as well-known professionals from many disciplines challenge the reader. An additional goal of the series is to provide a forum for other, less known, or even unpopular viewpoints. The opinion of an ordinary person who has had to make the decision to cut off life support from a terminally ill relative, for example, may be just as valuable and provide just as much insight as a medical ethicist's professional opinion. The editors have two additional purposes in including these less known views. One, the editors encourage readers to respect others' opinions—even when not enhanced by professional credibility. It is only by reading or listening to and objectively evaluating others' ideas that one can determine whether they are worthy of consideration. Two, the inclusion of such viewpoints encourages the important critical thinking skill of objectively evaluating an author's credentials and bias. This evaluation will illuminate an author's reasons for taking a particular stance on an issue and will aid in readers' evaluation of the author's ideas.

As series editors of the Opposing Viewpoints Series, it is our hope that these books will give readers a deeper understanding of the issues debated and an appreciation of the complexity of even seemingly simple issues when good and honest people disagree. This awareness is particularly important in a democratic society such as ours in which people enter into public debate to determine the common good. Those with whom one disagrees should not be regarded as enemies but rather as people whose views deserve careful examination and may shed light on one's own.

Thomas Jefferson once said that "difference of opinion leads to inquiry, and inquiry to truth." Jefferson, a broadly educated man, argued that "if a nation expects to be ignorant and free . . . it expects what never was and never will be." As individuals and as a nation, it is imperative that we consider the opinions of others and examine them with skill and discernment. The Opposing Viewpoints Series is intended to help readers achieve this goal.

David L. Bender & Bruno Leone,
Series Editors

Introduction

*"Fear of AIDS and furor over society's values [have]
made it hard to agree on the ethical issues and emotional
context that used to be part of learning about sex. "*
Nancy Gibbs, *Time,* May 24, 1993

Since the mid-1980s, the debate over teen sexuality has increasingly been shaped by two related problems. One is the spread of HIV/AIDS. The other is the economic and social costs of the shift in teen pregnancy away from older, married teens to younger, unmarried teenagers. The fallout from these social problems has prompted public policy experts, teachers, parents, and teenagers themselves to examine the issues of teenage sexuality more closely.

When HIV/AIDS first appeared, it seemed to be confined to gay men, intravenous (IV) drug users (many of whom were black or Hispanic), and prostitutes. The heterosexual, non-IV-drug-using population virtually ignored it until, in the mid-1980s, statistics and newspaper headlines warned that HIV/AIDS was spreading gradually among heterosexuals. In 1994 the Centers for Disease Control and Prevention (CDC) reported that between 1990 and 1991 alone, heterosexual transmissions had risen by 21 percent. As the disease gained ground, fear of AIDS escalated even faster than did the number of cases.

As HIV/AIDS began to spread beyond the original "at risk" groups, many became aware of the vulnerability of sexually active teenagers. In October 1989, a front-page *New York Times* headline warned, "AIDS Is Spreading in Teenagers, A New Trend Alarming to Experts." Andy Humm and Frances Kunreuther of the Hetrick-Martin Institute for Gay and Lesbian Youth attest that since AIDS was first identified in the United States in 1981, teenagers have constituted 20 percent of new HIV infections. CDC statistics quoted in the May 1993 *Time* show that 20 percent of all AIDS patients are under 30. The incubation period is 8 years or more, so many were infected as teenagers. *Time* also reports that three-fourths of America's youth have had sex by age 20, and every year one-fourth of sexually active teenagers contract a sexually transmitted disease. Such facts finally galvanized the public to try to prevent a teenage AIDS epidemic.

One result was nearly universal AIDS education as part of school sex education programs. In 1980, only 3 states mandated sex education. By 1993, 47 states required or recommended it, and all 50 supported AIDS education. The fear of AIDS is a powerful motivator; as Marion Howard of Grady Memorial Hospital in Atlanta warns, "It's no longer the facts of life, it's the facts of death."

The message most AIDS education programs promoted was that of "safe sex"—using a condom during intercourse to prevent the spread of HIV. Many schools also followed the lead of New York City, which began the controversial practice of providing free condoms to students, hoping to reduce the number of possible infections. But a number of health professionals and social conservatives oppose the safe sex message and condom distribution to teenagers. Pointing to studies that show condom failure rates between 12 and 27 percent for teenagers, they insist that condom use is an unreliable method for preventing the spread of HIV. They also contend that teaching explicitly about sex and handing out condoms sends the implied message that sexual activity is acceptable for teenagers. University of Kentucky professor of medicine Robert C. Noble supports this position. He writes, "Passing out condoms to teenagers is like issuing them squirt guns for a four-alarm blaze. Condoms just don't hack it. . . . *Abstinence and sexual intercourse with one mutually uninfected partner are the only totally effective prevention strategies.*"

More recently, many schools and public education programs—recognizing that high condom failure rates among teenagers preclude condom use as a panacea and that abstinence and monogamy are more reliable ways to prevent AIDS—have altered the safe sex message to saf*er* sex. In addition, in January 1994 the Clinton administration began airing television commercials as part of its AIDS reduction strategy. The commercials urge young people to abstain from sex, but caution them to use a condom if they do have intercourse. Although reaching a consensus on this emotional issue remains difficult, for now many see these changes as a sensible compromise.

Teenage Sexuality and Pregnancy

The second problem shaping the teenage sexuality debate—teenage pregnancy—is older than AIDS but is presenting a new face. Several social trends converged during the 1980s shifting teen pregnancy patterns: More and younger teenagers are having sexual intercourse more often than in previous decades. The proportion of girls aged 15-19 who had had premarital sex rose from 29 percent in 1970 to 52 percent in 1988. A 1993 *Time* magazine poll showed that 19 percent of teenagers aged 13-15 reported that they had had sexual intercourse, as had 55 percent of 16- to 17-year-olds.

The increase in teenage sexual activity is the result of a number of changes in American society. Some blame the youth rebellion of the 1960s and 1970s for eradicating long-held mores about gender and sexuality. Peter Benson, director of the Minneapolis-based research organization, Search Institute, notes:

> It used to be easy to say it's just wrong to have sex before marriage. You could expect churches to say that, adults from many walks of life to somehow communicate that. We went through a sexual revolution since the '60s that poked a major hole in that. And nothing has come along to replace it.

Other factors include the increasing trend toward households with two working parents (or a single working parent), which has provided new opportunities for privacy for teenagers to have sex. At the same time, according to *Time* magazine's Nancy Gibbs, "since the turn of the century, better health and nutrition have lowered the average age of sexual maturity." Teenage girls are now more likely to begin menstruating at age 12 instead of age 14.

The result of these trends is that more and younger unmarried teenagers are bearing children. Although the teen birthrate dropped during the 1960s and 1970s—as birth control and abortions became easier to obtain—by 1986 the rate had begun a steady rise. Out-of-wedlock births for teenagers rose from 15 percent of all births in 1960 to 67 percent in 1990. This worries many experts because the proliferation of unwed teenage mothers and their children creates a ripple effect of problems both for mother and child and for society.

Unwed teen mothers generally have more health problems than their married, older counterparts. These girls, only about half of whom are likely to seek prenatal care, have higher rates of unplanned pregnancies, are more likely to suffer complications during pregnancy, and are more likely to suffer from depression after giving birth, writes author Ann Phoenix in *The Politics of Pregnancy*. Their children share their difficulties; as writer Sarah Glazer notes, "Babies born to teen mothers are at higher risk of being born at low birth-weight, with all the attendant health problems. They generally score lower on tests [and] perform worse in school."

While such health and social problems cause serious concerns, it is the financial consequences of unwed teen pregnancy that are in the spotlight. According to the Congressional Budget Office, nearly 50 percent of unwed teenage mothers go on welfare within a year after giving birth. That percentage increases to 77 percent within 5 years after giving birth. An unwed teen mother is less likely to finish high school, making it even more difficult for her to support herself and her children. The Center for Population Options in Washington, D.C., estimates that the families of those who gave birth as teens may cost the government $25 billion a year in food stamps, Medicaid, and welfare payments.

As these soaring costs meet strapped federal and state budgets, many see the welfare system as it has grown in recent years as both cause and victim of unwed motherhood. Robert Rector of the Heritage Foundation maintains that although the availability of welfare support may not directly cause teenagers to get pregnant, it does encourage them to do so. Conversely, the American Enterprise Institute's Ben Wattenberg states baldly, "It is the growth in out-of-wedlock birth that is pushing up the welfare numbers."

Regardless of whether the large welfare expenditures are a cause of unwed teen childbearing, an effect, or both, such arguments raise serious questions. As Wattenberg's AEI colleague Douglas J. Besharov maintains, "The association between poverty, poor school performance and poor life prospects on the one side and out-of-wedlock births on the other is too obvious to ignore." When these complex issues are added to the near-panic about the possible spread of HIV/AIDS to the nation's youth, it is no surprise that debates on issues of teenage sexuality tend to be hotly argued and passionately expressed. The chapters in this newly revised edition of Greenhaven's 1988 book of the same title examine the issues in these chapters: What Affects Teenagers' Attitudes Toward Sex? What Causes Teen Pregnancy? How Can Teen Pregnancy Be Reduced? Is Sex Education Necessary? How Should Teenage Homosexuality Be Treated?

What Affects Teenagers' Attitudes Toward Sex?

TEENAGE
SEXUALITY

Chapter Preface

Teenage sexual activity is unquestionably on the rise—and the phenomenon is global in scope. According to a 1993 report by the International Planned Parenthood Federation, adolescent sexual activity and unwanted pregnancies are increasing throughout the world. In the United States, eleven out of every one hundred teenagers will become pregnant out of wedlock, bequeathing to America the dubious honor of having the highest rate in the West.

According to Planned Parenthood, the increase can be attributed largely to improved nutrition and health care, both of which contribute to an earlier onset of puberty. The report, however, goes on to suggest that sociocultural elements do influence adolescent sexual behavior and that these elements can range from peer group pressure to the accessibility and content of sex education. The following chapter offers a diversity of opinions on sociocultural factors that, the authors contend, affect the attitudes of teenagers toward sex.

"Today's parents, distraught from thinking about potential teenage catastrophes . . . capitulate on what seem like 'smaller' issues, allowing behavior they would have found shocking only a few years earlier."

Changing Family Attitudes Affect Teen Sexuality

Patricia Hersch

Writer Patricia Hersch is working on a book about the nature of the adolescent experience today. In the following viewpoint, she contends that the attitudes of teens toward sex have changed dramatically since the youthful days of their parents, the so-called baby boomers. "What most separates this age from the '60s," she writes, "is that behavior once at the fringe of late adolescent radicalism has now deeply permeated the mainstream culture of high school." Sex among teens, she maintains, has become commonplace and at younger and younger ages. Hersch concludes that the heart of the problem is an attitude of ignore and neglect prevalent in family and society today.

As you read, consider the following questions:

1. According to the author, among which group of teenage women is the greatest increase in sexual activity occurring?
2. In what ways do the lives of adolescents today differ from those of an earlier generation, in Hersch's view?
3. What does the author mean by the parental "sliding scale"?

Patricia Hersch, "Sex and the Boomers' Babies," *Family Therapy Networker*, March/April 1993. Reprinted with permission.

The adults who were part of the youth culture during the '60s, whose governing motto was "Do your own thing," could scarcely have predicted the behavior they are witnessing in their children, or their unease about it. . . . Now, the middle-aged children of that generation look with anxious uncertainty at the moral vacuum their own children seem to inhabit.

At the far extreme from this anxious, mostly liberal, middle-class cohort of parents is an aggressive and highly vocal movement of social conservatives, fueled by the religious right, who have launched a vigorous attack on moral permissiveness, emphasizing the very real consequences of uncontrolled sexuality: an epidemic of sexually transmitted diseases among adolescents, teenage pregnancy and, most frightening, AIDS. Add to these already mixed messages about sex being received by teenagers the undeniable fact that in a mass consumer culture, sex *sells*, and the result is a kind of postmodern ambiguity about the meaning and value of sexuality.

Lifelong marriage to the same person has long since stopped being regarded as an inevitable, natural or even particularly desirable human phenomenon. "The development of the singles culture in the '60s was still seen as a temporary stage before marriage," says Stephanie Coontz, author of *The Way We Never Were*. "Now, marriage seems to be a temporary interruption of the singles culture." Since there are so many more people who have never married or are divorced than in the '60s, kids have fewer visible role models for committed, longstanding intimate relationships. No wonder that for today's adolescents, uncommitted sex seems to be no big deal. "Kids today live in an environment where sex is an everyday thing between two people," explains one 16-year-old boy. "They just think it is something to pass the time, or to have fun with, so let's do it."

Changing Sexual Attitudes

What most separates this age from the '60s is that behavior once at the rebellious fringe of late adolescent radicalism has now deeply permeated the mainstream culture of high school, and is seeping into the fabric of junior high, as well. "Teenagers of the '60s began to experiment with sexuality," says sex educator Sylvia Hacker, "while today they anticipate it. The question is not, 'Should we have sex?' but 'When?'" And the when comes at younger and younger ages. The *1990 Youth Risk Behavior Surveillance Survey*, published by the Centers for Disease Control (CDC), reports that by the spring of freshman year in high school, 40 percent of all students have had sex. By senior year, almost three-quarters are sexually active.

Nor are these figures drawn from poor, inner-city neighborhoods, as many middle-class parents once comfortably supposed. Far from it. According to the Guttmacher Institute, the continual increase in the number of sexually active teenaged women was "primarily attributable" to increases among white adolescents and adolescents in higher-income families. The relative increase in births to unmarried teens, according to Children's Defense Fund figures, has been greater among white girls than blacks for the past two decades.

But adults don't seem to know about this new world. The real mysteries of adolescent life are cloaked in secrecy, in a world where nobody is at home, quite literally, but the kids. According to *A Matter of Time: Risk and Opportunity in the Nonschool Hours*, a 1992 report published by the Carnegie Council on Adolescent Development, about 40 percent of adolescents' waking hours are spent in "discretionary activities—not committed to other activities (such as eating, school, homework, chores or working for pay)." Many young people "spend virtually all of this discretionary time without companionship or supervision from responsible adults."

Among the reasons for this growing bifurcation between the two worlds of adults and adolescents is the transformation in American family life. As the Carnegie Council report points out, most children and adolescents today grow up in homes headed by single, working parents or live in two-parent households in which both parents work. Extended families—the grandparents, aunts and uncles whom parents could once count on—have become dispersed across the country, following job opportunities or retiring to distant communities. Furthermore, in the decline of close-knit communities, a "neighbor" has become a purely technical term for a stranger who lives in the immediate vicinity—not a trusted friend who watches out for the kids next door.

Finally, as the report indicates, American adolescents spend much less time in school than young people from other cultures—six to seven hours a day, 180 days a year (compared to nine hours daily, for 240 days in Japan, for example). In school or out, they spend much of the time either alone or with their friends. Nobody thinks twice about 12-year-olds navigating their own lives for several hours every day, unsupervised, free to do as they please, giving the whole notion of adolescent experimentation ominous new possibilities. "You basically have a life of your own," says one 16-year-old girl.

No Parental Supervision

Sex is clearly one of those possibilities, played out in the comfortable ambience of home. Ask teenagers today if they ever "made out" in a car and they are likely to laugh at you. Does a teenager have a parent at home after school? No prob. A friend undoubtedly has the house alone, and will happily oblige a chum or make use of the opportunity him- or herself. "My mom never gets home before 6:20," one kid told me. "My girlfriend and I can use my bed. If I have a friend and his girl over, they can use the couch." They have the time, the opportunity and a sex-saturated media to show them fairly explicitly what they could, or even should, be doing. "With a TV, nobody has to spell it out—you can just picture it happening," says one 15-year-old boy. "It's like you and the girl are alone in the house, and you have to go through with it." The pace and progression of sexual behavior is speeded up, partly because young people are intensely interested in sex anyway, but mainly because no adult is likely to walk in and interrupt the proceedings. The "dating game" has been replaced by "Just Do It." One eighth-grade girl said, "Last year at this time, it was a big deal for me to even kiss a boy, and this Halloween, I lost my virginity." Unsurprisingly, according to the CDC, by the end of senior year, 29 percent of all high school students will have had four or more sex partners.

It is hard not to be struck by the rootlessness of adolescent social life today, the lack of grounding in family and community

© Cullum/Copley News Service. Reprinted with permission.

organizations. Teenagers rove around in restless hordes, forming temporary groups, separating, regrouping in ever-changing locations. Sometimes what is going on is perfectly harmless, but the lack of organized social options removes traditional safety nets. Most of the time parents do not have a clue about what their kids are doing, whom they are with, where they are, what's really going on. Kids from every background and age group mix indiscriminately far more than did earlier generations, gravitating en masse to "where it's happening," which is often the Party—a large, usually unplanned gathering at somebody's empty house, fueled by alcohol and often out of control.

Naturally, parents do not like the idea of these parties and many, if they could, would refuse to give permission to attend just as they would not allow their kids to have sex or do drugs— if they had much control over these situations. They often do protest, warn, lecture and issue prohibitions, to not much avail. Teenagers, to avoid these hassles, universally lie about the behaviors they know their parents hate—they say they are going to a movie when they are going to a party, then they call and say they are going to a *later* movie so they can stay at the party longer, or tell their parents they are going to spend the night at a friend's house when they plan to sleep with a girl- or boyfriend or maybe just keep partying all night long. Adolescent lying to parents is not a new development, of course, but today, the behavior that the lies presumably conceal is generally a long reach beyond what their parents would have lied about when they were adolescents.

Parental Leniency

Consider drinking, for example. Many of the parents of today's adolescents probably sneaked into their own parents' liquor hoard now and then, but routine drinking (not to mention drugs and sex) was relatively rare. Today, on the other hand, drinking is a norm for kids. On average, according to the CDC, adolescents start drinking at 13, and by senior year, more than 90 percent of all high school students drink. Bored teens watching videos are easily drawn to their parents' bar. "My dad has the bottles three deep," says one. "I just tell my friends to pour from the back ones." For these teenagers, drinking and sex were made for each other.

Some parents rationalize their own acquiescence in behaviors they don't like by arguing that at least they *know* what their kids are doing, which may give them some small degree of personal influence, if not any veto power. "The only way to keep them from doing what their friends do is to lock them in the house," says one mother. "I'd rather have them do what they do now, in front of me, when I can guide them a little bit, than have them doing it behind my back or worry about them when they start college."

Today's parents, distraught from thinking about potential teen-age catastrophes (getting pregnant, contracting AIDS, dying of a drug overdose, being killed in an alcohol-related car crash or, increasingly, being the victim of drunken violence or date rape) capitulate on what seem like "smaller" issues, allowing behavior they would have found shocking only a few years earlier. This is the parental "sliding scale"—a hedge against even worse, but not uncommon, disasters in American adolescent life. The logic seems based on the parents' demoralized sense that if their kids are only drinking moderately (but not getting too drunk, too often and generally not in cars when they are), or only doing a little dope (but not completely strung out), or only sleeping with one boy at a time, they have a fair chance of making it to adulthood. . . .

In the vacuum where traditional behavioral expectations for young people used to exist has grown an anxious, but de facto consensus among parents as well as their children that anything goes. "Every signal the kids get is that everything they do is okay—it is only harmful if you get a disease," says Nancy Burke, athletic trainer and family-life educator at South Lakes High School in Reston. "Sex is not harmful just because you could get pregnant, because we can solve that. There are no penalties, no rules like we used to have. We are seeing 13- and 14-year-olds trying to live the lives of 25-year-olds without the maturity required."

So it is not surprising that we live in a culture in which the kids call the shots while the adults try desperately to catch up. Teenagers who have spent huge blocks of time either alone or with friends or taking care of siblings after school while their parents are at work have come to believe that they can handle anything. Like the 13-year-old boy who thought he could drink "responsibly," they have talked themselves into the posture that they don't *need* adults. "Usually, my parents are gone when I wake up," explains one teen, "and usually they are not there when I get home. So all that time in between I am on my own and I make it day to day using my own judgment, getting by just fine. Since I've done it this way so far, and haven't had any problems, why are you trying to interfere now?"

A Challenge to Parents

And parents have no convincing response. They neither know the parents of their children's friends, nor have the time to forge alliances with other adults; often they are embarrassed to tell their own peers about what their kids are doing. They are also afraid to push their kids too hard, for fear of making the situation worse—their children might run away, get busted, be killed.

Even parents who struggle to maintain some control have a hard lot; there are too many other parents who have capitulated to the youth culture, or pretend not to know what is going on. "Parents are confronting gigantic challenges with their children—the alcohol, the drugs, the sex—without the support of a peer group, which other generations could draw upon, either from neighbors who shared parenting values, or from society at large," says Jerry Newberry, coordinator of Family Life Education for the Fairfax County Public Schools in Virginia. "Now, the kids, unlike their parents, do have close-knit peer groups that set norms, reinforce their behaviors, while parents are isolated from one another and don't have any idea how to challenge the culture the children have created for themselves."

"Social attitudes toward the sexuality of young people become particularly important during adolescence."

Social Attitudes Affect Teen Sexuality

Catherine S. Chilman

Catherine S. Chilman is a professor of social welfare at the University of Wisconsin-Milwaukee and the author of several books on adolescents. Chilman believes that sexuality is influenced by societal and cultural values. In the following viewpoint, Chilman writes that one's social status and cultural setting largely determine one's sexual mores. Chilman believes the social upheaval of the 1960s had a great impact on how society views teenage sexuality.

As you read, consider the following questions:

1. According to the author, why do sexual values differ among various social groups?
2. Why does Chilman believe one's culture is so influential during adolescence?
3. In the author's opinion, how did the 1960s alter sexual attitudes?

From *Adolescent Sexuality in a Changing American Society* by Catherine S. Chilman. Copyright ©1983 by John Wiley & Sons. Reprinted by permission of John Wiley & Sons Inc.

Social attitudes toward the sexuality of young people become particularly important during adolescence. Until recently, concepts of sex as sinful and as a dangerous primitive drive that had to be kept under strict control (especially for girls) created large problems of repression, denial, anxiety, and secrecy for both young people and the persons considered responsible for them (parents, human service professionals, and religious leaders). These concepts still exist but are countered by others that see sex as healthy, natural, and relatively safe (now that contraceptives and abortions are available).

The late 1960s and the 1970s witnessed radical upheavals in the culture of sexuality. Sex-specific attitudes and behaviors became highly permissive, and the push for equal sex roles at home and abroad became strong and widespread. In a sexually open and stimulating climate, young people as well as older ones were almost forced to take a fairly public stand regarding their sexual identity. This was especially difficult for teenagers because of their incomplete and vulnerable stage of psychosocial sexual development. In general, the absence of clear sexual guidelines provided both freedom and confused anxiety. The culture of sexuality differed somewhat in various regions of the country and for people of differing socioeconomic status.

Social Status

The extent to which social status makes a difference to the person depends on the degree of social stratification in a society and its meaning to that society. Although American society is less stratified than most and earlier definitions of social class have wavered under the impact of recent socioeconomic upheavals in this country, social status still makes a difference in the person's total development and current life situation. The effects of social status are also mediated by race, ethnicity, religion, and regional origins. All these demographic characteristics tend to affect cultural values—values that influence the way people view themselves and are viewed by others.

Culture evolves from the life history and experiences of a group and constitutes the group's attempt (over the years) to adapt to its environment. Culture plays an important part in the way the child is reared, from birth through adolescence and youth. The values, norms, beliefs, and expectancies of a group are intricately woven into all aspects of the developing person. They constitute many of the roots of personality, and it is both difficult and sometimes dangerous to try to change them.

Cultural Influences

Culture affects all aspects of sexuality: attitudes and behaviors concerning gender and sex identities, sexual expression, sex roles,

25

mating, fertility control, and parenthood. Culture is most readily changed when the person's basic life situation is changed; when cultural leaders, with whom the individual can identify and wishes to identify, lead the way to new values and beliefs; and when the tools for change are made available.

There is considerable disagreement, at present, as to how much difference social status makes in contemporary American society. Class lines and values are not nearly so sharply defined as they were in earlier generations. The whole culture experienced such an upheaval in the 1960s that the country is witnessing pervasive "cultural confusion." The mass media (especially television) reach such an extensive audience that new ideas and beliefs are diffused much more rapidly than they formerly were.

Crumbling Social Structures

Why was it that teenagers became more sexually active in the 60s? I think anyone with an elementary sense of human psychology and anyone who can remember when he was a teenager can answer that question. When people my age and older were in high school we had hormonal drives and all of that stuff, but we also had a social structure that helped us maintain chastity. . . .

So what happened when they claimed that contraception and abortion were the answer to teenage pregnancy is that teenagers came under considerable pressure to become sexually active.

Michael Schwartz, *CCL News*, January/February 1987.

However, the life situation for the various social classes and racial groups in the United States has not changed as much as some suppose and as many desire. The distribution of national income for individuals and families has not changed for at least 25 years. About 15 percent or more of the population still lives in poverty. Although the median income of American families has risen, the cost of living has outpaced these increases for most people. A small number of minority-group people have experienced marked improvements in income, educational opportunities, and employment, but the majority still suffers disproportionately from poverty, unemployment, underemployment, and, in general, access to "the good life."

Social Subgroups

The social status of adolescents is largely determined by the educational, occupational, and income characteristics of their parents. Those who come from families near the top of the socioeconomic ladder are apt to view themselves and their world in relatively optimistic, positive terms. In times of social change, such families tend to be cultural innovators because they have a basic security that allows them the freedom to be nontraditional. This often applies to their sexual attitudes and behaviors as well as other aspects of their lives.

Persons near the middle of the socioeconomic structure (including white-collar workers and upwardly mobile skilled laborers) are often beset by anxieties about losing the security they have and about failing to achieve the upward mobility to which so many of them aspire. Less secure than those at higher levels and more hopeful than those at lower ones, they tend to be more conventional and conservative because they have so much that may be gained—and so much that may be lost. In the area of sexuality, for example, this middle group tends to be more cautious and traditional with respect to sexual freedoms and contraceptive risk taking than those either at the top of the social heap or near or at the bottom.

Members of the less upwardly mobile blue-collar class and those in the lowest socioeconomic group are often alienated from society and its norms. Feeling little hope for the future and viewing society as essentially hostile and dangerous and themselves as powerless, they tend to react to the situation of the moment and take risks because they find life basically uncontrollable anyway.

Sex Roles

The culture largely determines how people are socialized for masculine and feminine sex roles. An enormous literature has developed on this topic in recent years. Sociologists have emphasized particularly the part played by socialization for sex roles in dating, marriage, family formation, and the like. For instance, if females are socialized to believe that their major function is childbearing, child care, and homemaking, then, quite naturally, they tend to feel these are their major life functions and seek to fulfill them. On the other hand, socialization for work and community roles outside the home and for roles shared with men tends to promote the desire for no or few children. In a similar vein, socialization of males that emphasizes their functions as father-providers or, in contrast, as role-sharing partners with employed women has a pronounced effect on the male's view of his life functions and goals.

Role socialization also affects attitudes toward sexual behaviors. Traditionally, more sexual freedom has been allowed to adolescent males because of the double standard of sex morality. This standard holds that males are "naturally sexy" and will "take what they can get." It is up to females to control the situation. . . . Although these attitudes are changing, they are still prevalent, especially among blue-collar and lower-middle-class groups.

Role socialization varies by social class, religion, ethnicity, and race. In line with earlier comments, adolescents in the higher social classes are more likely to be socialized in nontraditional ways for fairly equal roles and freedoms between the sexes and for considerable sharing of interests and functions, both within and outside the home. Blue-collar youth, more traditional in their early socialization, are changing rapidly in their expressed attitudes toward more equalitarian sex roles. On the other hand . . . expressed attitudes are one thing, but the attempt to change enough to *live* these attitudes and to accept them emotionally is quite another. . . .

There is growing recognition that life situations and cultural climates can vary enormously for adolescents at different periods of history. For instance, youngsters who entered puberty in the radicalized 1960s were part of a huge population cohort that crowded the schools, created an enormous youth market and a strident youth culture, and, to a large extent, provided further fuel for the liberals in their revolt against all forms of authority, including the military. This is but one example of "times making (or helping to make) the teens." Impressive work by social scientists who are studying periods of social history and the effects of these periods on life course development are providing a broadened perspective of human attitudes and behaviors in the context of the total environment at various periods of time.

"The message of our popular culture . . . is: sex rules.*"*

Popular Culture Affects Teen Sexuality

Joy Overbeck

Many believe that popular culture, especially as exemplified in music, art, dress, and literature, historically has affected the mores of a nation's young. In the following viewpoint, Joy Overbeck illustrates why she finds this especially true today in the area of sexuality. She argues that the bawdier aspect of contemporary popular culture is exerting a negative sexual influence on youth. She concludes that society's preoccupation with sex propels young people into a premature sexualization and robs them of the joys and benefits of childhood. Overbeck is an author, playwright, and freelance writer who resides in Denver, Colorado.

As you read, consider the following questions:

1. What does the author mean when she writes that "the message of our popular culture . . . is: *sex rules*"?
2. What does the author mean by "competitive sex"? What examples does she offer?

Joy Overbeck, "Sex, Kids, and the Slut Look," *Newsweek*, July 26, 1993. Copyright © 1993, Newsweek, Inc. All rights reserved. Reprinted with permission.

The other day my 10-year-old daughter and I breached the prurient wilds of the Junior Fashion Department. Nothing in what she sneeringly calls the "little kid" department seems to fit anymore. She's tall for her age and at that awkward fashion stage between Little Red Riding Hood and Amy Fisher. She patrolled the racks, hunting the preteen imperative—a pair of leg-strangling white tights culminating in several inches of white lace. Everywhere were see-through dresses made out of little-flower-print fabric, lacy leggings, transparent tops and miniature bustiers for females unlikely to own busts. Many were garments that Cher would have rejected as far too obvious.

Lace leggings? When I went to grade school, you were sent home if you wore even normal pants. The closest we got to leggings were our Pillsbury Doughboy snow pants, mummy-padding we pulled on under our dresses and clumped around in as we braved the frigid blasts of winter. Today's high-school girls have long dressed like street-corner pros; but since when did elementary school become a Frederick's of Hollywood showroom?

Erotic Fashions

Grousing that her dumb clothes compromised her popularity, the offspring had herded me to fashion's outer limits. She appeared to be the only 10-year-old in the area: the rest were 14 or so, unaccompanied by their mothers. She pranced up, holding out a hanger on which dangled a crocheted skirt the size of a personals ad and a top whose deep V-neck yawned like the jaws of hell.

"Isn't this great! I want this!" she yodeled, sunshine beaming from her sweet face once more. "You're 10 years old," I said. "Shhh," she hissed, whipping her head around in frantic oh-God-did-anybody-hear mode. Then she accused me of not wanting her to grow up. She's 10 years old and the kid talks like a radio shrink.

It's not really that I want her to be a little girl forever. It's just that it would be nice if she were a child during her childhood. Instead, she's been bathed in the fantasy of bodies and beauty that marinates our entire culture. The result is an insidious form of premature sexual awakening that is stealing our kids' youth.

Meredith was 8 and we were in the car, singing along to some heartbroken musical lament on the radio, when she said, "Mom, why is everything in the world about sex?" I laughed and asked where she got that idea. But then, listening as she knowledgeably recited examples from music, movies, MTV and advertising, it hit me that she was right. The message of our popular culture for any observant 8-year-old is: *sex rules*. Otherwise, why would it deserve all this air time, all this agony and ecstasy, all this breathless attention?

Kids pick up on the sexual laser focus of our society, then mimic what they see as the ruling adult craze, adding their own bizarre kid twist. Recently, I read that the authors of *The Janus Report on Sexual Behavior* were shocked to find how many had sex at 10, 11 and 12. Too young to know how to handle it, kids mix sex with the brutal competitiveness they learn in the two worlds they know best: sports and the streets. Sex is grafted onto their *real* consuming passion—to be the most radical dude or dudette in their crowd. Peer pressure—what I'm seeing now in my 10-year-old's wardrobe angst—takes over. The result is competitive sex: California gangs vying for the record in number of girls bedded; teenage boys raping girls my daughter's age in a heartless sexual all-star game where all that counts is the points you rack up. In Colorado Springs, not far from where I live, gangs are demanding that kids as young as 10 have sex as a form of initiation. It's the old "chicken" game in *Rebel Without a Cause*, played with young bodies instead of cars.

Turning Back the Clock

Today's trend of accepting the idea that "everybody's doing it" originated with the 1960s sexual revolution. Extramarital sex became the norm, and the age of consent steadily decreased. The electronic media took their cue, creating movies, sitcoms and mini-series sizzling with sex. That is, sex that had no consequences nor responsibilities. Soon, teens simply had to turn on the tube to confirm their mistaken conception that "everybody's doing it.". . .

If we could turn the clock back, perhaps we wouldn't have accepted the forgone conclusion that teens are going to be sexually active and, worse yet, given them instructions on how to proceed. Perhaps we wouldn't have asked: "What can we do to prevent pregnancy and disease?" Instead, we might have asked: "What can we do to prevent teen sexual activity?" If we as parents, public health professionals and teen behavior experts had done that, perhaps we wouldn't see sexually active sixth, seventh and eighth graders or 11- and 12-year-old mothers.

Kristine Napier, *Priorities*, Summer 1993.

The adult reaction to all of this is outrage. But why should we be shocked? Children learn by example. Sex is omnipresent. What do we expect when we allow fashion designers to dress us, grown women, in garments so sheer that any passing stranger can see us nearly naked for the price of a casual glance?

Or look at Madonna on the cover of *Vanity Fair* wearing only a pink inner tube and hair done up in cutesy '50s pigtails. Here's a 34-year-old heroine to little girls—the core of her fandom is about 14—posing as innocent jailbait. Inside, she romps on a playground in baby-doll nighties, toying with big, stuffed duckies and polar bears. This is a blatant child molester's fantasy-in-the-flesh. Does kiddie porn encourage sex crimes against children? Who cares!

Rudimentary good sense must tell us that sexualizing children not only sullies their early years, but also exposes them to real danger from human predators. What our culture needs is a little reality check: in an era when sexual violence against children is heartbreakingly common—a recent study estimates that about one quarter of women have been victims of childhood sexual abuse—anything that eroticizes our children is irresponsible, at best.

It's up to adults to explode the kids-are-sexy equation. Our kids need us to give them their childhood back. But the eroticization of our girl children proceeds apace. The crop tops! The tight little spandex shorts! (Our moms wore them under their clothes and called them girdles.) My daughter's right, everybody struts her stuff. I've seen 5-year-old Pretty Babies.

As for me, I don't care anymore if my kid has a hissy fit in the junior department. She's not wearing the Slut Look. Let her rant that I'm a hopelessly pathological mom who wants to keep her in pacifiers and pinafores forever. Let her do amateur psychoanalysis on me in public until my ears fry—I've shaken the guilt heebie-jeebies and drawn the line.

"There is no question . . . that teens learn about sexuality from the media."

The Media Affect Teen Sexuality

Debra W. Haffner, Marcy Kelly, and L. Brent Bozell III

According to the Neilsen and Radio Advisory Board reports, teenagers spend more time being entertained by the media than doing anything else except sleeping. In Part I of the following viewpoint, Debra W. Haffner and Marcy Kelly, researchers at the Center for Population Options, trace the influence of the media on sexual attitudes. They believe parents and educators should use the media to positively influence teens' sexual values. In Part II, L. Brent Bozell III, a conservative syndicated columnist, addresses the effects of the media's crusade to convince teenagers to use condoms to prevent AIDS. This kind of "sex education," he believes, simply encourages teenagers to have sex.

As you read, consider the following questions:

1. What proof do Haffner and Kelly offer to show that the media's role in sex education is not new?
2. According to Haffner and Kelly, how has television's portrayal of sex changed since 1985?
3. What objections does Bozell have to Hollywood's campaign to prevent AIDS?

Excerpted from "Adolescent Sexuality in the Media" by Debra W. Haffner and Marcy Kelly, *SIECUS Report*, March/April 1987. Copyright by the Sex Information and Education Council of the United States. Reprinted with permission. "Hollywood Has Little Respect for Children's Rights" by L. Brent Bozell III, *Conservative Chronicle*, October 20, 1993. By permission of L. Brent Bozell III and Creators Syndicate.

Papa don't preach, I'm in trouble deep.
Papa don't preach, I've been losing sleep.
But I made up my mind, I'm keeping my baby.
(Sire Records © 1986)

Let's take love step by step,
Let's go step by step, Wait.
(Fuentes y Fomento Intercontinentales © 1985)

Two "number one" songs. The first, by Madonna, glorifies teenage childbearing. The second, by Tatiana and Johnny, is a hit in Mexico and Latin America that encourages young people to wait to have sexual intercourse. The second song, "Detente," has increased the number of young people in Mexico seeking information at family planning clinics. Does "Papa Don't Preach" affect American teenagers' behavior?

Did the increase in the number of explicit sexual references in teen-oriented music, television, and movies help lead to the increase in teen sexual activity, or does the portrayal of sex in the media reflect the changes American society has experienced in [recent] decades? Sexuality educators share an uneasy alliance with radically conservative groups in our concern about what our children are learning about sex from the media. Most people agree with the report of the National Academy of Sciences that the media provides "young people with lots of clues about how to be sexy, but . . . little information about how to be sexually responsible."

Media's Role in Sexuality

The media plays a pervasive role in most Americans' lives. The average American family has a television set turned on over seven hours a day. Teenagers watch approximately 24 hours of television and listen to the radio an average of 18.5 hours a week. If one adds movies, teenagers are spending more time being entertained by the media than any other activity, with the possible exception of sleeping! . . .

The media has always provided sexuality information. The first radio soap operas airing in the 1930's focused on such issues as marriage, divorce, infidelity, and standards of correct behavior for men and women. Teen-oriented music, such as "Louis Louis" in the 1950's, "House of the Rising Sun" in the 1960's and "Dancing in the Sheets" in the 1980's has titillated teens with its sexual messages while causing their parents to protest.

Television, radio, movies, and advertisements all play a role in our sexuality education. Sexuality in the media not only includes suggestive behaviors, but information about sex roles, family life, physical attractiveness, friendship, parent-child communication, pregnancy, and childbearing. The TV show *Moonlighting* not only included frequent sexual innuendos, but provided messages about body image, male-female friendships, and working relationships and roles. *The Cosby Show* taught us about family relationships and, in some ways, presented as difficult an idealized model as *Father Knows Best* and *The Brady Bunch*. Advertisements use highly attractive people in suggestive postures to encourage buying products that will somehow make us more sexually desirable. Music videos frequently feature sexual situations, sexist images, and sexual violence.

More Explicit

The media *has* become more explicit about sexual behaviors. In an analysis of specific sexual content in prime-time television, the investigators identified approximately 20,000 scenes of suggested sexual intercourse and behavior, sexual comments, and innuendos in one year of evening television. Sex on the afternoon soap operas is even more prevalent—and almost all sexual encounters on the soaps are between people who are not married to each other. During the late 1970's, there was a fourfold increase in flirtations and seductive behaviors on TV, a fivefold increase in the number of sexual innuendos, and almost a doubling of the number of implied acts of sexual intercourse. Verbal references to intercourse increased from 2 to 53 a week during this time.

Media Influence

The media is a pervasive force in all of our lives, but especially in the lives of children and adolescents. One can learn much about sexual behavior and attitudes condoned by society by looking at the Jordache jeans advertisements on television or in the *New York Times* Magazine section. Movies and other media sources are also providing clear messages about sexual behavior.

Andrea Parrot, *Human Sexuality*, 1984.

And yet, until recently, contraception was considered a taboo subject for television entertainment programs. A famous *All in the Family* episode in the 1970's was about sterilization, and in *Maude*, Maude had an abortion. These were rare exceptions. In fact, a 1970's *James at 15* episode was never aired because the network refused to allow James to refer to contraception in a scene in which he was to lose his virginity. Indeed, until 1985, neither birth control in general nor specific forms of contracep-

35

tion were mentioned on network television.

A major change has occurred. In 1985, generic terms like "birth control" and "contraception" became acceptable. By the 1986-87 season, actual methods of contraception were being discussed. For example, in "Babies Having Babies," a CBS daytime *School-Break Special*, the words "rubber," "condom," and "birth control" were used. In NBC's *St. Elsewhere*, the terms "IUD," "condoms," and "the pill" were used, and ABC's *Choices* included mention of a "diaphragm" and "birth control pills."

Further, several shows included honest portrayals of adolescent sexuality. In *Kate and Allie*, Allie counseled her daughter Jenny to postpone sexual intercourse, but to seek contraception if she didn't wait. Harvey and Mary Beth Lacey of *Cagney and Lacey* counseled 16-year-old Harv Jr. about condoms and educated early adolescent Michael about pornography. On *Fame*, *Mr. Belvedere*, *Facts of Life*, and *Growing Pains*, middle adolescent girls and boys have faced the decision to have first intercourse, and all have chosen abstinence. On the soap opera *Days of Our Lives*, a teenage couple chose to have sex, and in groundbreaking episodes, visited a clinic and a drugstore for contraception.

Media Impact

There is considerable disagreement about whether the media influences us to change our attitudes and behaviors or whether it merely mirrors the changes in our society. There has been only limited research on the impact of media messages on teen sexual behavior, and what exists has offered conflicting results.

A 1981 study indicated that there was no link between the amount of television teens watched and the likelihood that they would have intercourse. However, another study found a strong correlation between the amount of sexually oriented television watched, as a proportion of all TV viewed, and the probability that an adolescent had had intercourse. In another survey, researchers found that a preference for MTV and other music television programs was associated with increased sexual experience among middle adolescents, but not among early and late teens.

There is no question, however, that teens learn about sexuality from the media. Teens report that TV is equally or more encouraging about sexual intercourse than their friends, and high television use has been correlated with dissatisfaction about virginity among high school and college students. In fact students who think TV accurately portrays sex are more likely to be dissatisfied with their own first experiences.

Responsibility

The Center for Population Options has an office in Los Angeles that works with the entertainment media on portraying sexuality in a responsible manner. The three components of the program include a Media Advisory Service, a Media Awards Program, and a Seminars Series.

The Media Advisory Service assists media writers and producers with theme development, research, factual review, site visits, shooting locales, script review, and consultation to improve the quality and increase the impact of sexual responsibility messages. The kinds of shows needing information range from dramatic and comedy series and Casey Kasem's "American Top 40" radio show to syndicated game shows and "Nightline."

As part of the Media Advisory Service, CPO has developed guidelines for the portrayal of sexuality in the media. These guidelines were developed by CPO's Media Advisory Committee, consisting of representatives from such major entertainment organizations as the Writers' Guild, Women in Film, the Academy of Television Arts and Sciences, NBC, Carson Productions, and Warner Brothers. The guidelines have been distributed nationwide to TV and film critics, members of the TV Academy, and network and production companies.

These guidelines offer the following suggestions for the presentation of responsible sexual content:

- Recognize sex as a healthy and natural part of life.
- Parent and child conversations about sex are important and healthy and should be encouraged.
- Demonstrate that not only the young, unmarried, and beautiful have sexual relationships.
- Not all affection and touching must culminate in sex.
- Portray couples having sexual relationships with feelings of affection, love, and respect for each other.
- Consequences of unprotected sex should be discussed or shown.
- Miscarriage should not be used as a dramatic convenience for resolving an unwanted pregnancy.
- Use of contraception should be indicated as a normal part of a sexual relationship.
- Avoid associating violence with sex or love.
- Rape should be depicted as a crime of violence, not one of passion.
- The ability to say "no" should be recognized and respected. . . .

A Tool for Sex Education

Sexuality educators can use the media to help children and adolescents learn about sexuality. David Green's excellent monograph, "Sex on TV: A Guide for Parents," encourages parents to develop active viewing skills in order to understand TV's role in sexuality education. He encourages parents to initiate conversations about sexual issues by discussing TV characters and their actions.

Sexuality educators can use the media to supplement lessons. Students can be asked to clip advertisements as a springboard for a discussion of standards of physical attractiveness and sex role stereotypes. Movies such as *Killing Us Softly* and *Stale Buns* can help sensitize students about the role that sex plays in advertising. Students can dissect the lyrics of popular songs to explore their sexual messages. Parents and children can be asked to discuss what their favorite shows tell them about sex roles, family life, intimacy, and communication. Parent seminars can focus on how to use the media to stimulate discussions about sexual topics.

II

The proliferation of AIDS prevention programs in the classroom is renewing the debate over the rights of parents to shield their children—especially grade-school children—from condommania. The recent appointment of the new surgeon general, Joycelyn Elders, who has made condom distribution a priority in the school system, further fuels the controversy. The entertainment television industry, always on the lookout for hip trends, has joined the fray with an avalanche of programming supporting the condom distributors.

Asay, by permission of the *Colorado Springs Gazette Telegraph*.

Switch on your set at night, and you'll find that entertainment television's role models are never without their lucky latex. When child prodigy Doogie Howser, the title character of *Doogie Howser, M.D.*, decides to lose his virginity, his best friend Vinnie hands him a condom. On *Beverly Hills, 90210*, teens nod approvingly at prom centerpieces containing condoms, which these "responsible" seniors eagerly snatch up. *Roseanne*'s teen-age daughters, after admitting they have slept with their boyfriends, appease Mother by telling her they used their trusty condoms.

Abstinence, the best method of prevention, is not taken seriously on prime-time television. After a father talks to his son about safe sex on *Frannie's Turn*, the mother objects, "I thought you were going to talk to him about no sex." The father's response carries the moral weight of parental authority on television today: "I try. The boy is going to do what he's going to do. The only thing that we can hope is that he is responsible."

Hollywood Is on a Mission

Hollywood [is] on a mission to force America to accept condom distribution. One of the most egregious displays of this sexual agenda was ABC's special *In a New Light, '93*, a back-to-school AIDS prevention extravaganza, featuring enlightened celebrities giving their not-so-homespun advice on sex and AIDS to the young.

The show reported ways AIDS is contracted and encouraged the young to lend a compassionate hand to the suffering, but what could have been a vehicle rallying teens to choose abstinence was railroaded by a sexual ethic whose notion of self-sacrifice and love amounts to the use of prophylactics.

Actress Rosie Perez bantered, "Little Joey's out there doing it! Wake up, America!" A star from teen-age America's favorite show, *Beverly Hills, 90210*, opened his spot with: "Hi, I'm Luke Perry, and tonight I have only one thing on my mind: sex. . . . By the age of 16, over 50 percent of American teenagers have had sex at least once." The song "Silent Legacy," performed by Melissa Etheridge, blamed repressive parents for laying archaic "guilt" upon children who indulge their passions. Etheridge commented after her performance, "It is still hard to be a teenager . . . and be in this repressive society where you're just supposed to say no and abstain."

What should a young girl do when approached for sex? "If someone comes to you with . . . that macho man nonsense," Perez admonished, "you can say, 'Hey, buddy, you know, either put it on, or get out.'" Similarly, comedienne Elayne Boosler counseled, "If someone loves you, then putting on a condom is the best thing they [sic] can do to show you that." Only one celebrity, Holly Robinson, spoke for abstinence: "You don't have to have sex, it's not that important, let's wait."

The program was not complete without showcasing its version of real-world heroes. One group of birth control-advocating young teens spotlighted—"condoms and dental dams in hand"—formed an AIDS information group for their eighth-grade peers. In another example, school sex educators, advocating explicit sex education courses in schools, were depicted as modern-day Prince Valiants.

Does this approach work? The evidence is in, and overwhelmingly, the answer is "No." A 1986 Planned Parenthood/Harris poll revealed that teens undergoing comprehensive sex education emphasizing condoms were 53 percent more likely to initiate intercourse than those whose sex education did not discuss contraceptives. Before Dr. Elders introduced condoms in the school districts of Arkansas, the pregnancy rate was 6.8 percent. Six years and thousands of distributed condoms later, it had risen to 15 percent.

Hollywood demands drastic measures to combat the deadly AIDS disease but refuses to endorse the only way to stop it. It is a monumental testimony that more and more teens are rejecting Hollywood's morality and embracing virginity, joining pro-chastity campaigns such as "True Love Waits" and "Best Friends." Abstinence programs would stop the spread of the AIDS virus, reduce illegitimacy and ruin half the story plots on so-called entertainment television.

"The mixed messages being sent about the issues of 'love and sex'. . . have the potential to cause lasting harm to our children."

Sex Education Affects Teen Sexuality

Gary L. Bauer

Gary L. Bauer is president of the Family Research Council of Washington, D.C., a nonprofit advocacy group that promotes traditional family values. In the following viewpoint, Bauer maintains that a majority of parents in America are justifiably concerned about the drugs, violence, and poor academic standards they believe are prevalent in public schools today. Of even greater concern, he argues, are "the mixed messages being sent about the issues of 'love and sex.'" Many schools are now promoting the use of condoms as the path to safe sex, which, he charges, signals the young that adults have capitulated and are no longer promoting abstinence or even a sense of personal responsibility for choices made. Bauer concludes that the approach to sexual education being followed in America's schools is desensitizing teenagers to the more sublime and morally proper aspects of human sexuality.

As you read, consider the following questions:

1. What is the author's attitude toward U.S. Surgeon General Joycelyn Elders? How can you tell?
2. What is "whirlpooling"? According to the author, what is one of the primary causes of practices such as "whirlpooling"?

From Gary L. Bauer's September 1, 1993, letter to the members of the Family Research Council. Reprinted with permission.

*B*ack to School!

For me, and probably for you too, those words bring back many strong memories—most of them happy. I recall the feelings of nervous anticipation about new teachers and the sense that I had grown older. I remember the happiness of seeing friends that I missed during the summer and being able to start a new year with a clean slate. Even more, I can remember teachers who changed my life with small words of encouragement or by introducing me to great works of literature and history.

Today there are still tens of thousands of dedicated men and women who have devoted their lives to educating our young. *But in the last 30 years—in far too many of our nation's classrooms—something has gone terribly wrong.* Today, the words "Back to School" raise high anxiety and even fear for many parents and children.

That's not surprising. In fact, a new Gallup poll conducted for *Parenting* magazine shows that . . .

- 78% of parents are troubled about drugs in school;
- 68% list violence to their children as a major worry;
- 62% are concerned about low academic standards;
- 50% are worried about poor curriculum.

The behavioral problems of students today are a far cry from the 1950's when similar studies showed top concerns of teachers and parents were students chewing gum and "acting up" in class.

As you might guess, there are a lot of reasons for the decline in the classroom. Our schools have been under attack by cultural radicals beginning in the early 60's when Supreme Court decisions began limiting the right to pray or read the Bible. In the years since, the American Civil Liberties Union, People for the American Way and their allies have continued their aggressive attacks on the remaining Judeo-Christian traditions.

Add to this list budget problems, overcrowded classrooms, sexual harassment and an explosive growth in violence, then compound these problems with a sea of legal restrictions that severely limit our teachers' ability to teach.

Education Is Changing

How different from the education we once knew. In fact, during the years of our founding as a nation, most Americans believed that education should deal with the enlightenment of the whole man. Children were taught the academic basics of reading, writing and arithmetic, but they also learned the importance of understanding and practicing reliable standards of right and wrong. Education concerned itself with the moral, intellectual and physical development of each child. They seemed to understand that as a great poet once penned, "Education is not the filling of a pail, but the lighting of a fire!"

42

Sadly, educational philosophy has taken a big step backward from those early days. In today's world, American students generally perform poorly compared to those in other industrialized nations. Many textbooks have been "dumbed down" so our students can more easily understand their elementary content. Now in many cases, instead of challenging students, the academic curriculum has been lowered to meet falling student performance. The grading standards, on the other hand, have also been manipulated and are no longer a reliable indicator of one's mastery of a subject. *This intellectual deficit is serious, but it pales in comparison to the implications of our failure to treat students as morally reasoning human beings.*

Reprinted by permission: Tribune Media Services.

The mixed messages being sent about the issues of "love and sex," for instance, have the potential to cause lasting harm to our children and ultimately to our nation. School after school has fallen victim to "condom mania." Younger and younger children are being taught that condoms and birth control pills are the only ways to handle their raging hormones. Believe it or not, the New Haven, Connecticut, School District is now beginning condom distribution to students in the fifth grade!

What's more, Dr. Joycelyn Elders [has] been confirmed as Surgeon General of the United States. In her home state of

Arkansas, Dr. Elders has aggressively pushed for school-based health clinics which dispense contraceptives to children. This approach has never worked and the experience in Arkansas is no exception. The state has reported more out-of-wedlock pregnancies and the rampant spread of venereal disease among its young people.

Moral Surrender

The last thing our children need is for the adults in their lives to engage in moral surrender. Yet that is exactly what people like Dr. Elders and her allies are doing when they put clinics in the schools. They are throwing up their hands and saying, "We give up trying to tell you about abstinence, or for that matter, even trying to educate you about the true cost of your choices. Here, take these implements and try to limit the inevitable consequences of your acts."

And the consequences are even more deadly now than ever.

Consider, for example, the increasing use of explicit "AIDS education" information. Because of the understandable fear of this terrible disease, school officials have implemented widespread distribution of graphic materials to children in the classrooms.

In addition, homosexual activists have repeatedly been allowed to lecture students—often spending more time promoting the desirability of their "alternative lifestyle" than providing kids with the real facts about the spread of AIDS.

With Dr. Elders leading the charge, President Clinton throwing the weight of the White House behind her and groups like the National Education Association anxious to help her carry out her radical agenda, the debate over condom distribution and school-based clinics is likely to spread to even more schools.

This desensitizing approach to human sexuality is decadent—pure and simple. Its results can be readily seen in the increasingly barbaric behavior of many youngsters in our urban areas. In New York City, for example, where the "sex without responsibility" approach has been pushed for years, the latest "sport" for boys is "whirlpooling." The *New York Times* reports that as many as 20 to 30 boys, some as young as 12, will lock arms and surround lone girls in the city's public swimming pools. Then each girl is attacked by the group, frequently having her bathing suit ripped off while she is being repeatedly fondled. The boys reportedly have a great time—particularly if the girls can be reduced to tears of humiliation.

A Decadent New World

Even the liberal *New York Times* wondered what was really going on. They conducted an informal survey of 50 boys from a variety of neighborhoods. They discovered a new world where "romance is gone—having been replaced by easy sex and trashy language." One boy was asked for an explanation of the whirl-pooling phenomenon. His chilling response was, "It's nature. Look at a female dog and a male dog. It's the same thing. You see 20 male dogs on a female dog. It's the male nature in a way."

This young man is tragically mistaken. I don't believe for a moment that this kind of behavior is the nature of my son, or yours either. Nor should anyone's daughters have to grow up in a society where men reflect such attitudes.

My good friend and outstanding columnist Mona Charen recently wrote a piece about this phenomenon. She said:

> So much for 5,000 years of civilization insisting that human beings, creatures created in the image and likeness of God, are not mere dogs in heat and are capable of better behavior.

> The moral swamp we have allowed to emerge threatens the United States far more than high budget deficits. . . .

> In my lifetime, we have gone from a world in which men customarily rose from their chairs when a woman entered the room to a world in which a 14-year-old cannot swim in a public pool without fear of sexual assault.

> It's been a steep decline.

"Sex is . . . being taught to youngsters through the wide distribution of pornography."

Pornography Affects Teen Sexuality

Kenneth S. Kantzer

Though pornography is theoretically off-limits to teenagers under age 18, sexually explicit books, magazines, and videos are easily accessible to American youth. What effect does this material have on teenage sexuality? In the following viewpoint, Kenneth S. Kantzer argues that pornography gives teens a perverted perspective on sexuality. Kantzer, a writer for the evangelical Christian magazine *Christianity Today*, writes that the main consumers of pornography are 15- to 19-year-old males. The author believes that parents, educators, and church leaders should teach teenagers positive sexual values to counter the negative influence of pornography.

As you read, consider the following questions:

1. According to Kantzer, what lessons do teens learn from pornography?
2. What suggestions does the author make to combat pornography's negative influence?
3. In Kantzer's opinion, what myth about pornography must be overcome?

Kenneth S. Kantzer, "The Real Sex Ed Battle," *Christianity Today*, April 17, 1987. Copyright 1987 by *Christianity Today*. Used by permission.

In all the furor over whether sex ought to be taught in the public schools, one fact is often overlooked: Sex is *already* being taught to youngsters through the wide distribution of pornography. And recent findings on the effects of pornography on the young ought to mobilize an even greater groundswell of public outrage aimed at publishers of pornography.

Since 1970, pornographers have enjoyed the support of a U.S. presidential commission report downplaying the effects of pornography. That report "found no evidence to date that exposure to explicit sexual materials plays a significant role in the causation of delinquent or criminal behavior." Rather, it presented pornographic material as essentially harmless entertainment that often had a cathartic influence upon those who used it. But [in] July [1986] the U.S. Department of Justice issued a two-volume report that reverses those findings.

Harmful Influence

The Justice Department's report comes at a time when research has called into question most of the basic conclusions of the 1970 commission. Specifically, it raises questions about the "cathartic" theory espoused by the older report. Experimentation with pornography does not always lead to satiation and boredom (thus serving as a harmless fantasy outlet for those who would otherwise engage in rape or other forms of sexual abuse, so the theory goes). Quite to the contrary, viewing some kinds of hardcore pornography tends to foster imitation. The 1986 report notes that research "shows a causal relationship between exposure to material of this type and aggressive behavior towards women." Rapists interviewed in prison were 15 times more likely than nonoffenders to have been exposed to hard-core pornography during the ages of 6 to 10.

Here we are not dealing with so-called adult entertainment. Rather, we are confronted with the favorable treatment of criminal acts against children and women. What is most alarming is that this offensive material may be the most prevalent form of sex education for our nation's youth. According to Henry Boatwright, chairman of the U.S. Advisory Board for Social Concerns, 70 percent of all pornographic magazines end up in the hands of minors. One member of the commission estimated that the chief consumers of even hard-core pornography are males 15 to 19 years old.

And what lessons do young people assimilate from such instruction? The movies, magazines, and books teach these impressionable youth that women are playthings, that sex has little to do with love and need not be tied to commitment or fidelity, and that sexual activity is appropriate anywhere, with anyone, and at any time.

No wonder the number of unmarried couples living together has quadrupled; abortions among unmarried women more than doubled (500,000 to over 1,200,000 per year); and single-parent families tripled (1,900,000 to 5,600,000). Meanwhile, teenage pregnancy in the U.S. is the highest in the world—over one million each year with more than half ending in abortion.

Though Christians have admirably joined the battle to prevent the wide distribution of pornography, more must be done to combat this calculated effort to educate our youth. Few understand just how serious the purveyors of pornography are in making their message available. The Playboy Foundation, for example, underwrote the formation of the Organization for Free Press to counter efforts against the distribution of pornography. And the public relations firm of Gray and Company proposed to members of a media coalition a $900,000 annual budget to fight the strong opposition that has risen against pornography. The underlying strategy of such efforts is to portray those who oppose pornography as narrow-minded religious bigots, ultraconservative in their attitudes toward life, hopelessly outdated, and determined to destroy freedom of speech and freedom of press in all other areas of American life.

Pornography

It has become increasingly clear to us that many children who escape actual sexual abuse are nevertheless receiving their primary education in human sexuality from a graphically inappropriate source. Such a source describes sexual fulfillment as conditioned upon transience, dominance, aggression, or degradation.

Bruce Ritter, *The Wanderer*, July 24, 1986.

What do we recommend? The first line of defense against pornography's vile influence is to instruct our children in a sound and healthful view of sex. This is no time to retreat behind a false sense of biblical modesty. We must take for granted that our children will be bombarded with a hedonistic philosophy of sex, not only from publications recognized as pornographic, but from the flood of material that comes to them incessantly through public advertising, radio, and television (including the "family programs" run at the prime hours of the day). It is far better that our children receive their sex education within the framework of a biblical philosophy of sex as an honorable and treasured gift of God. The Christian home, Christian schools, Sunday schools, church youth groups, seminars, and youth retreats—these are the appropriate places for instructing our children about sex.

Second, we must speak out boldly in our neighborhoods, at parent-teacher meetings, and at local newsstands, drugstores, and bookstores. This is an issue on which evangelicals really do have a moral majority. A 1985 Gallup Poll showed that 73 percent of the American people believed explicit sexual magazines and movies influence some people to commit rape or other sexual violence. And 93 percent called for stricter control of magazines displaying sexual violence. We must take the lead in speaking out boldly and fearlessly against this festering sore in our society.

Third, we must be willing to back others who take a stand, joining them in petition drives and boycotts in the fight against stores that display or sell pornographic materials and against television programs that carry debasing sexual themes.

A Need for Education

Fourth, we must support studies so that our opposition is based on a clear understanding of the difference between opposition to pornography and opposition to freedom of speech. This, after all, is the final defense of most proponents of pornography. They warn that any laws that bar obscenity will inevitably lead to laws destroying our constitutional freedoms of press and speech. We can combat this defense by educating ourselves (and the public) regarding definitions of pornography and obscenity.

For too long, the public has accepted the myth that pornography harms no one, even the legions of minors who are frequently exposed to it. The Justice report effectively dashes that notion. If the church cares to enter the real sex-education battle, it would be wise to step up the attack on easy-to-obtain smut and accept responsibility for the sex education of our youth.

Periodical Bibliography

The following articles have been selected to supplement the diverse views presented in this chapter.

DeNeen L. Brown — "The New Age of Innocence?" *The Washington Post*, November 29-December 5, 1993.

William F. Buckley — "How to Deal with Illegitimacy," *Conservative Chronicle*, May 6, 1993. Available from PO Box 11297, Des Moines, IA 50340-1297.

Mona Charen — "Being Gay Is the Rage Among Today's Teens," *The Human Life Review*, Fall 1993.

Barbara Kantrowitz — "Breaking the Poverty Cycle," *Newsweek*, May 28, 1990.

Janice Kaplan — "Sex on TV '93: What's Taboo and What's Not," *TV Guide*, August 14, 1993.

Cardinal Mahoney — "How the Entertainment Media Influence Adolescents' Values," *Origins*, February 13, 1993.

Rick Petosa — "Does Education Deter Risky Sex?" *USA Today*, December 1992.

Deb Price — "Teaching Teens Safe Sex Ought to Be a Priority," *Liberal Opinion Week*, July 26, 1993. Available from 108 E. Fifth St., Vinton, IA 52349.

J. Rinzler — "Teens and Sex: What Every Parent Must Know," *McCall's*, July 1993.

Joseph Lee Rodgers — "Close Encounters of the First Kind," *Discover*, March 1993.

Jill Smolowe — "Sex with a Scorecard," *Time*, April 5, 1993.

Charlene Marmer Solomon — "From Sensation to Good Sense," *American Medical News*, October 19, 1990.

Richard Starr — "Sex, Lies, and Media Hype," *Insight*, August 9, 1993. Available from 3600 New York Ave. NE, Washington, DC 20002.

U.S. News & World Report — "Teenage Sex: Just Say 'Wait,'" July 26, 1993.

Utne Reader — "The New Sexual Revolution," (special section), July/August 1993.

What Causes Teen Pregnancy?

TEENAGE SEXUALITY

Chapter Preface

The most obvious answer to the question "What causes teen pregnancy?" is, of course, sexual intercourse. However, with today's birth control options, it is more appropriate to ask: "Why do teenagers have sex without preventing pregnancy?" Many experts have examined this question without reaching a unanimous conclusion.

In order to find answers to this question, social workers, public policy experts, teachers, and parents search for characteristics common among teenagers who have sex and get pregnant. One such characteristic is a poor educational history. Studies show that teenage girls who did poorly in school and felt that education offered few opportunities were more likely to become pregnant than girls who found education rewarding. According to a study published in the journal *Family Planning Perspectives*, "adolescents with high educational expectations are significantly less likely than others to become pregnant."

Another such characteristic is that nearly all teenagers share a sense of invulnerability. For them, pregnancy is more an abstraction than the logical outcome of sexual activity. Public affairs professor Douglas J. Besharov concurs. He writes, "Teenagers take risks. They experiment with alcohol. They drive fast. They feel indestructible." He quotes former Boston social worker Virginia Cartoof, who says, "Teenagers don't anticipate the next stage in life. They live for the moment."

Another characteristic is general ignorance about sex, despite the near universality of sex education programs. Dr. Doris Tirado, the medical director of Planned Parenthood in Baltimore, comments on adolescents' ignorance of sexuality: "Many of them believe you can't get pregnant the first time you have intercourse."

These and other reasons why sexually active teenagers get pregnant are discussed in the following chapter.

"In three generations, we've gone from attaching a stigma to illegitimate children to fostering a generation of children who have babies so that they can have somebody to love."

Family Breakdown Causes Teen Pregnancy

Suzanne Fields

In the first half of the twentieth century, society condemned unmarried pregnant teenagers. In the second half of the century that condemnation has given way to acceptance and even approbation, declares Suzanne Fields in the following viewpoint. She argues that the breakdown of the traditional nuclear family has created a generation of amoral adolescents who lack parental guidance. These adolescents, Fields maintains, get pregnant and bear illegitimate children who grow up poor and abused, and then perpetuate the cycle of teenage childbearing. Field is a nationally syndicated columnist.

As you read, consider the following questions:

1. According to the author, what are some of the reasons teenagers have for getting pregnant?
2. According to Fields, what attitude toward parenthood do many teenage boys have?
3. What course of action was available to pregnant teenagers in the 1950s, according to the author? How is the situation different today, in her view?

"Teenage Girls Tragically Think Babies Will Ease Their Plight" by Suzanne Fields, *Insight*, June 15, 1992. Copyright 1992, Los Angeles Times Syndicate. Reprinted with permission.

When something goes wrong, we have to blame somebody. That's human nature. That's why the 1992 Los Angeles riots created open season on scapegoats. Among them are Lyndon Johnson and the Great Society, juvenile delinquents, high school dropouts, drugs, crime, inner-city decay and racism.

They all count, but the gravest cause is the wreckage of the family. We can't expect young people to grow up with hope if there's nobody at home to nurture their best instincts. We can't expect children to grow up with a sense of responsibility when Mom is a child herself.

Someone to Love

In three generations, we've gone from attaching a stigma to illegitimate children to fostering a generation of children who have babies so that they can have somebody to love.

Abraham Lincoln High School in Denver provides a sad, but typical, everygirl story for today. Instead of letter sweaters, so typical of the 1950s, maternity clothes are in fashion. Boys and girls who carry books are taunted as nerds and dorks, but girls with swollen bellies are envied and celebrated. Of 1,400 students, 26 girls are already mothers and 53 more are pregnant.

There's considerably more cachet to getting knocked up than getting into the honor society. "I wanted somebody to live for, something that would make me respect myself," a high school senior tells Denver's *Rocky Mountain News*. "I just wanted something to be mine, to take care of, someone to be there for me."

A teenager in the 1950s who got pregnant usually got married (whether her boyfriend liked it or not) and pursued the rest of her education as best she could. Teachers encourage teenage mothers to stay in class today, to get their high school diplomas, but it isn't easy and day-care facilities in a high school are at best a distraction for the mom trying to learn.

Getting Pregnant Intentionally

Teachers and health counselors are particularly alarmed to find that increasing numbers of young girls see motherhood as a way out of their struggles at school and at home rather than an unfortunate and costly mistake. Sexually active teenage girls who used to go to "health clinics" to get birth control devices now tell nurses that they want to get pregnant. At one clinic in Denver, 15 percent of the teenagers were pregnant and another 40 percent said they "wouldn't mind" if they got pregnant.

A researcher at Denver General Hospital found that 71 girls whose pregnancy tests were negative were back within 18 months, testing positive. No one can doubt that these girls, with sufficient medical information conveniently at hand, know exactly how and why they are "with child."

Boys who enjoy the public persona of "stud" usually have no intention of becoming real fathers to their children or of marrying their teenage girlfriends. Thus the vicious cycle begins.

Children of children are less healthy and more abused than children of older parents. They're more likely to drop out of-school, become drug addicts and move into a life of crime. Two-thirds of teenage mothers aren't married. Most gang members are the children of single mothers.

Changing Social Mores

The proportion of births outside marriage has been rising in America for all age groups since the mid-1970s, suggesting a major social movement in this direction. One out of every four women who had a child in 1990 was not married. Overall, the nation's out-of-wedlock birthrate jumped from 5 percent of all births in 1960 to 27 percent in 1990.

National surveys indicate there is less stigma attached to having children outside of marriage than one or two generations ago. A national survey of 18-to-22-year-olds conducted in 1987 by Child Trends found that only 23 percent of the sample believed single women should never have children.

This acceptance has been reflected in myriad, generally positive news stories about movie-star couples who had children before they married, among them Warren Beatty and Annette Benning and Eddie Murphy and Nicole Mitchell. (Both couples eventually married.) In a recent *Vanity Fair* cover story celebrating Jack Nicholson's fatherhood, the actor says, "I don't discuss marriage much with Rebecca [Broussard]. Those discussions are the very thing I'm trying to avoid. I'm after the immediate real thing."

Such positive spins on portraits of unwed parents trouble scholars like Barbara Dafoe Whitehead, a research associate at New York's Institute for American Values. She believes that single parenthood puts mothers at risk of poverty while making children vulnerable to psychological problems. "As [the *Vanity Fair*] story shows," Whitehead wrote, "unwed parenthood is thought of not only as a way to find happiness but also as a way to exhibit such virtues as honesty and courage."

Clearly, many teens now find unwed parenthood acceptable. In one national survey of high school students, about half the black female sophomores and one-fourth of the whites said they would consider having a child out of wedlock. Compared with white teenagers, black teens are more likely to favor having their first child before age 20, yet they report an ideal age for their first marriage that is older than the age they consider ideal for a first birth.

Sarah Glazer, *CQ Researcher*, May 14, 1993.

In a recent survey of more than 1,300 juniors and seniors in public and private high schools throughout the country, teenagers complained that their parents didn't help them with homework. The sad fact for the children who have children is that they never learned their own lessons. Worse than that, they don't know how to become attentive parents, because they never had one.

"The large majority of all 'teenage' pregnancy is caused by adults. "

Adults Are Responsible for Teen Pregnancy

Mike Males

In the following viewpoint, Mike Males asserts that adults are primarily responsible for teenage girls' getting pregnant. Males contends that most reports dealing with the problem of teenage pregnancy blame the young women for their condition. He argues instead that men over eighteen—adult men—are responsible for most of the pregnancies of teenage girls. Adult men are also responsible for the majority of the sexually transmitted diseases and rapes teenagers suffer, he charges. Males is a freelance journalist living in Los Angeles, California.

As you read, consider the following questions:

1. Why have living conditions for teenagers declined so dramatically since the early 1960s, in the author's opinion?
2. According to the author, how can the incidence of teenage pregnancy be reduced?

"Infantile Arguments" by Mike Males, *In These Times*, August 9, 1993. Reprinted by permission of the author.

During the last two decades, American youth experienced the most rapid deterioration in economic and social conditions since the Depression. Youth poverty has jumped 51 percent since 1973. Violence, early pregnancy, crime, school dropout rates and other social ills predicted by poverty reversed previous declines and rose rapidly during the late '80s, according to government statistics.

"In the past 20 years or so, the social metric in America has shifted from child well-being to adult well-being," University of Texas sociologist Norval Glenn points out. No other industrial society devotes more resources to adults and fewer to youth than the United States.

America's Children Are Neglected

Today's American adults over age 40 are our richest generation in history. Yet one in five American youths now live under poverty guidelines—four times the rate in Norway, Sweden, Switzerland and Germany, double the rate in Britain, 60 percent higher than in Canada, according to a 1988 Urban Institute study.

Washington's response: blame the victim. The Reagan and Bush administrations ignored the economic and social conditions behind these youth problems. Instead—with the support of media and the private sector—policy-makers emphasized "prevention" measures aimed at the young people themselves. According to federal figures, violent-crime arrests of those under 18 years of age have risen 50 percent since 1983; drug arrests among young people have doubled since the early '80s; forced drug and mental-health treatment of young people has quadrupled since 1975. Behavior-education programs—such as those stressing drug and sex abstinence—are now government-mandated or recommended in 47 states.

But as these "prevention" measures have proliferated, the problems they were supposed to ameliorate have grown. Since the early '80s, violent crime and drug deaths among youths have doubled and childbirth rates have risen 20 percent. All those rates had previously been declining.

The "Teen" Pregnancy Mythology

Of many examples of failed youth policy that could be cited, the worst is "teenage" pregnancy—an issue so misrepresented by all interests involved that institutionalized mythology has replaced reasoned analysis.

The "teen pregnancy" issue plays itself out in the American Zeitgeist according to a standard ritual. Agencies survey, panels assemble, conferees meet. An avalanche of dire reports condemning the "$16 billion annual social costs" of "epidemic teenage pregnancy" follow.

Then comes the media hype. Commentators blame pregnancy rates on promiscuous "kids," declining moral values, Hollywood's influence and "peer pressure." Experts may disagree on the solutions—those on the left advocate more sex education and better access to birth control, while those on the right push abstinence and legal punishments aimed at teen mothers—but few authorities of any stripe question the premises of the debate.

Not Old Enough

Maggie is happy. She's pregnant. She's 12.

She has decided to keep her child.

It was not an easy decision, she tells a counselor at the clinic, because sometimes she feels like a child herself.

So she asked her girlfriends what to do. "Have the baby," they urged.

She asked her boyfriend's advice. "Have the baby," he commanded.

She asked her mother, knowing what she would say—and she did: "If you are old enough to mess around, you are old enough to have the baby. Go live with him and have his child."

The girl's mother "essentially gave this child to the 24-year-old gangbanger who got her pregnant," says Gayle Wilson Nathanson, founder and director of the Youth and Family Center in Inglewood, California, where Maggie goes for care.

Maggie wants a good life for her child, Nathanson says. But she has no money, no support system. She can't begin to understand what's ahead for her, and all the counseling in the world won't help her to be a mature parent because she simply is not old enough to comprehend.

Bettijane Levine, *Los Angeles Times*, September 9, 1992.

And those premises distort the troubling realities of what we call "teen" pregnancy. Thus, the solutions based on those assumptions are unworkable nonsense, often embodying serious sexist and racist implications. Consider some crucial, rarely mentioned facts:

• *The large majority of all "teenage" pregnancy is caused by adults.* Health agencies and programs funded by Congress' Adolescent Family Life Act condemn "peer pressure" to have sex (particularly among junior-high students). Nonetheless, "teenage" pregnancy, childbearing and sexually transmitted disease are predominantly *adult-teen* events.

National vital statistics reports show that 70 percent of all births among teenage women are fathered by adult men over age 20; one in six by men over age 25. Detailed figures, from the California Vital Statistics section's tabulation of 60,000 births among teenage mothers in 1990, are more shocking.

Of some 5,000 births among California junior-high girls, ages 11-15, only 7 percent were fathered by junior-high boys. Four in 10 were fathered by high-school-age boys, ages 16-18, and more than half by post-high-school adult men ages 19 and older.

Among high-school mothers, male partners averaged nearly four years older. The younger the mother, the wider the age gap. Male partners to mothers age 12 and younger averaged 22 years of age. Of 889 married California junior-high girls who gave birth in 1990, two-thirds of their husbands were past high-school age.

In addition, adult men fathered 2,000 children among California unwed junior-high girls in 1990, seven times more than were fathered by junior-high boys. And adult women over age 20 have some 3,000 babies fathered by high-school-age boys every year in California.

Adult-teen sex is also widespread among homosexuals. A 1978 survey of 500 male homosexuals found one-fourth admitted that, when over age 21, they had sex with boys age 16 and younger.

Adults, Teenagers, STDs, and Rape

Unsettling as these facts are, they get worse.

• *The large majority of the 2 million-plus "teen" sexually transmitted diseases (STDs) and sexually transmitted AIDS cases in the United States are also caused by adults.* Reliable gonorrhea and syphilis figures have existed for 35 years from the Centers for Disease Control; AIDS tabulations since 1988. They all point to an ugly pattern.

Among adults, STD rates among men are double those among women. But STD and AIDS rates among females under age 20 are double those among boys under age 20.

How are all these girls getting infected? Not only from voluntary relationships with adult men (who are many times more likely to carry STDs and AIDS than are teenage boys), but also from rape.

• *A federally funded 1992 study of 4,000 women indicates that some 1 million children are raped every year.* More than 60 percent of all rapes in the nation involve victims younger than 18, according to the study by the National Victims' Center, an advocacy group.

For one-third of all U.S. girls and one-fifth of all boys, rape and sexual abuse are their introductions to sex. A 1985 *Los Angeles Times* survey found rapists of children average 30 and victims 10 years of age. More than half of the rapists were "someone in authority."

Some 50,000 teen pregnancies every year are caused by rape. But the psychological devastation of rape has an even wider impact on the teen pregnancy rate. A 1992 study of hundreds of teen mothers by Washington researchers Debra Boyer and David Fine found that two-thirds have histories of rape and sexual abuse by offenders averaging 27 years of age. Abused girls report their first sexual experience two years younger than non-abused girls, and with a partner averaging five to six years older.

• *Poverty and "teen" pregnancy are so strongly correlated that for any state or locality, the annual "teen" birth rate can be accurately predicted from the youth poverty rate.*

Mississippi (1990 per-capita income $12,735) has a youth poverty rate—and also a youth childbearing rate—three times higher than Connecticut ($25,358). Los Angeles' poorest neighborhoods have teen pregnancy rates 20 times higher than its richest neighborhoods.

Three in 10 teenage girls in California's poorest county (Tulare, home to thousands of impoverished migrant workers) live in poverty and 5 percent give birth every year—rates six times higher than in California's richest county (Marin), where only one in 20 young people lives in poverty and the annual teen birth rate is below 1 percent.

Teenagers Get Blamed

The poor got poorer in the Reagan-Bush years. Yet it was far more convenient for Washington policy-makers to blame young women for the teen pregnancy rate than to blame themselves. Teenage girls make perfect scapegoats. For one thing, they have no political clout. And attacks on "teen mothers" perpetuate racist and sexist stereotypes that would otherwise be impolitic to promote.

Does the Clinton administration promise more enlightened, compassionate, reality-driven policy than the current moralistic blindness? . . .

Clinton's wife, Hillary, and his chief health official, Secretary of Health and Human Services Donna Shalala, are affiliated with the Children's Defense Fund (CDF), a program whose technical research papers are among the best in connecting poverty and adult-teen sex to early pregnancy.

Yet the CDF's public stance has been one of the worst in terms of advancing derogatory myths about teen sex. The CDF's popular poster campaign promotes '50s stereotypes of the stupid, "bad" high-school mother ("It's like being grounded for 18 years") and her selfish, dumb athlete-boyfriend ("Wait'll you see how fast he can run when you tell him you're pregnant").

In fact, high-school couples account for only one in seven "teen" pregnancies and fewer than 2 percent of all pregnancies in the United States, according to government figures. Nonetheless, CDF Director Marian Wright Edelman continues to blame teen sex on MTV video images and "spiritual poverty" among the young—downplaying true causes: economic poverty, rape, adult-youth sex. . . .

Adult Men Are Responsible

Sooner or later, escapism must he abandoned and facts faced: "teen" pregnancy is not simply the result of dumb, immoral, ignorant or careless kids. Rather, early parenthood is an index of the levels of poverty, abuse and bleak opportunities afforded young women. It is also a measure of their efforts to escape their harsh conditions by alliance with older partners—a survival strategy that research is finding as psychologically healthy, given the limited opportunities the American poor increasingly face. "Teen" pregnancy will decrease when poverty, abuse and unhealthy conditions forced on the young improve, when men are held responsible for their roles in teenage childbearing, and when politicians and interest groups no longer indulge in expedient myths.

"School failure is a crucial factor along the pathway that results in early childbearing."

Teenage Girls' Low Educational Expectations Pose Pregnancy Risks

Claire Brindis

Claire Brindis is an assistant adjunct professor in the Department of Pediatrics, Division of Adolescent Medicine at the University of California at San Francisco. She is also co-director of the university's Center for Reproductive Health Policy Research. In the following viewpoint, she argues that young women who have very low expectations of their education are more likely to become pregnant than teenagers who believe that completing high school and college will benefit them. Brindis contends that if young women feel discouraged about completing their education and see few prospects for successful employment, they have fewer reasons to avoid pregnancy.

As you read, consider the following questions:

1. According to Brindis, what effect does early childbearing have on the mother's education?
2. Why are girls more likely than boys to have poor educational expectations, according to the author?
3. What are some of Brindis's suggestions to reduce the incidence of teenage pregnancy?

From "Antecedents and Consequences: The Need for Diverse Strategies in Adolescent Pregnancy Prevention" by Claire Brindis. In *The Politics of Pregnancy*, Annette Lawson and Deborah L. Rhode, eds. New Haven: Yale University Press, 1993. Copyright © 1993 by Yale University. Reprinted with permission of the publisher.

There has been a surge of creative effort and constructive re-thinking around the issues surrounding adolescent pregnancy in the United States. Researchers, [social service] providers, and advocates are recognizing the interrelationships between the incidence of adolescent pregnancy and the prevalence of school failure, unemployment, poverty, and the clustering of adolescent risk-taking behaviors. These complex interrelationships require multipronged interventions that extend beyond more traditional approaches, which consist primarily of providing sex education and access to family planning services. Although progress has been made in improving even these basic approaches, there remain tremendous inconsistencies and a qualitative unevenness. Further, many adolescents continue to face intimidating psychological, physical, and social barriers that interfere with responsible contraceptive behavior.

It is also increasingly apparent that adolescent pregnancy may have as much to do with such factors as dropping out of school, isolation, poverty, unemployment, low self-esteem, and lack of hope for the future as it does with adolescent sexuality. Ironically, many of these factors have long been perceived as only the *consequences* of early childbearing. New evidence demonstrates, however, that they may in fact be the *antecedents* of pregnancy, which then intensifies their long-term impact. Based on the results of long-term tracking of pregnant adolescents into adulthood, as well as comparisons to other family members, a number of researchers have begun to argue that teenage pregnancy may not in itself have long-term adverse consequences. Rather than focusing on pregnancy, these researchers argue that attention needs to be paid to women's social *circumstances*, and to the poverty that is in fact the major predictor of adverse life outcomes. Simply stated, their conclusion is that adolescent pregnancy and childbearing alone may not be the negative experiences most previous research has purported them to be. Yet whether adolescent pregnancy or poverty is the crucial factor, it is vital that policymakers recognize that many of the problem areas associated with adolescent pregnancy are intimately interrelated, and that their negative and compounding impacts most certainly shape the overall issue of adolescent pregnancy, as well as any effort to develop and implement viable solutions to the problem.

Academic Failure and Adolescent Pregnancy

School failure is a crucial factor along the pathway that results in early childbearing. Although it has long been thought that girls drop out of school because they are pregnant, recent studies show that many girls who become mothers drop out *before* pregnancy. Data from the national High School and Beyond Study showed that, of all those who both dropped out of school and gave birth to a child, 28 percent had left school before conception. A survey of never-married women in their twenties showed that among those who both became pregnant and dropped out of school, 61 percent of pregnancies occurred *after* they had left school; a survey of very young welfare mothers showed that 20 percent were already out of school before conception.

Educational Aspirations

Adolescents with high educational expectations are significantly less likely than others to become pregnant, and those who become pregnant are significantly more likely than teenagers with low educational aspirations to have an abortion or to marry before the baby's birth.

Family Planning Perspectives, vol. 25, no. 4, July/August 1993.

Level of education is a more significant predictor of future prospects than either ethnic or class background, and to a great extent determines whether that future will be one of jobs or unemployment, welfare or independence, early or planned parenthood, and lawful or unlawful behavior. In a study comparing the impact of childbearing on school continuation, researchers examined school graduation rates of teenagers who gave birth while still enrolled in school and graduation rates for those who gave birth after dropping out of school. The research demonstrated that early childbearing significantly reduces the school completion rates of young women who had already dropped out of school before pregnancy or childbirth. In contrast, among adolescents still in school at the time of childbirth, the study found that childbearing appeared to have little direct impact on the chance of completing school. The strongest determinant of a teenage mother's eventual educational attainment was found to be whether she was in school at the time that she gave birth, rather than her age at the time of the birth.

Delays in School Completion

It is important to note, however, that young women who remain in school while they are pregnant (especially those who stay in school throughout the pregnancy and birth) are a self-selected and motivated group. Although the researchers examined eventual educational attainment (high school diploma or GED [general equivalency diploma]), they did not examine the timeliness of high school completion. It is likely that childbearing, while not preventing the woman from completing high school, did cause delays in school completion and most likely changed the nature and variety of available life choices, including the option to continue with postsecondary education.

A principal reason given by both sexes for dropping out of school is school itself: its perceived irrelevance to their needs, and their own poor academic achievement. School-related reasons were primary for 29 percent of blacks, 21 percent of Hispanics, and 36 percent of whites. Two national surveys have also produced substantial evidence about the association between school achievement and childbearing. The High School and Beyond Study, looking at each ethnic group separately, found that white, black, and Hispanic sophomores with low academic ability (the lowest third of their class) were twice as likely to become unwed parents by their senior year as those students with greater academic ability. The National Longitudinal Survey of Youth found that females in the bottom 20 percent of basic reading and math skills were five times more likely to become mothers over a two-year period than those in the top 20 percent.

Faults in the Educational System

Several researchers suggest that the poor academic achievement of many girls and their sense that school is irrelevant to their needs are, at least partially, attributable to the treatment they receive in the educational system. Recent studies show that both male and female teachers have different expectations of their students according to sex. Teachers are likely to give girls less attention than boys; to direct rote memorization questions at girls but to encourage independent thinking in boys by asking them complex, open-ended questions; to reprimand girls for speaking out of turn but to tolerate this behavior in boys; and to offer girls less substantive evaluation of their work than is offered to boys (for example, neatness of handwriting versus quality of content). In addition, educational materials such as books, films, and displays continue to emphasize male achievement throughout history and ignore the accomplishments of women. Many materials reinforce traditional gender-role stereotypes of women as homemakers and men as professionals, giving girls the impression that they have fewer opportunities than their male peers. When such experiences are combined with poverty, racial discrimination, and low parental education level, many young women may be inclined to see parenthood as one of the few meaningful or attractive future options available to them.

The High School and Beyond Study documents the relationships among dropping out of school, adolescent pregnancy, and lack of economic opportunity in a national study that followed young people during and after their high school years. Among the study's findings are that the nongraduate females, married or not, are six times as likely as graduate females to have children; nongraduate females are nine times as likely as high school graduate females to receive welfare assistance; and nongraduates are at least four times as likely as graduates to engage in unlawful behavior.

A Diploma Is Necessary

A major implication of this study is that the lack of at least a high school diploma is frequently associated with severely negative impacts, including incidence of early childbearing, welfare dependence, and unemployment. However, it is important to note that the sample in this cross-sectional study was limited only to those students who had been enrolled in high school for some time and does not provide any data about results on those students who had already dropped out of school even before entering high school. In addition, the study did not include information on variables of interest apart from school completion that may also have differentiated graduates from nongraduates, and that may have played a role in the outcomes measured. Nevertheless, the data in the study suggest that education, in conjunction with other factors (like poverty status), may be a key to explaining negative outcomes associated with early childbearing.

Few School or Employment Opportunities

Recently, several researchers have argued that the negative impact of adolescent childbearing on educational outcomes and subsequent employment may not be as serious as previously thought. Arline T. Geronimus and Sanders Korenman's research compares pairs of sisters who came from comparable backgrounds and began childbearing at different stages. Based on results that documented only negligible differences in the sisters' education and family income level, these researchers argue that delaying pregnancy will not help poor women escape poverty. A parallel study argues that circumstances associated with poverty, including poor education and an increased likelihood of secondary sector employment, contribute to an increased likelihood of adolescent childbearing, particularly among black teenagers. Regardless of their age when they first give birth, black women experience fewer employment opportunities. The anticipated payoffs of education are thought by these women to be so limited that early motherhood appears a viable alternative. However, such arguments fail to address the issue of long-term and costly impacts upon the life of the mother, her infant, family, and society in general. Whether or not a young woman bears a child early in life, society remains responsible to provide its youth—particularly its most vulnerable youth—with the educational and life opportunities that would make early childbearing a genuine option.

Such research suggests that teenage efforts to prevent pregnancy may have limited value; unless there are additional and effective educational or employment interventions, adolescents will continue to exhibit limited motivation to avoid early childbearing. Without these additional supports it becomes highly unlikely that a young woman, whether in her adolescent years or in her early adult years, will experience positive educational, health, and employment outcomes.

"Girls out here get pregnant because they want to have babies."

Cultural Influences Contribute to Teen Pregnancy

Leon Dash

Leon Dash, a *Washington Post* reporter and author of *When Children Want Children: The Urban Crisis in Teenage Childbearing*, reports in the following viewpoint on his study of the roots of adolescent pregnancy in a poor area of Washington, D.C. While living in Washington Highlands, Dash says, he found that the strong link between poverty and teenage pregnancy is amplified by cultural factors, especially among the black urban population. He suggests that patterns of teenage childbearing that were necessary for survival in earlier times continue to be passed down through the generations, even though they are now unhealthy. Among the patterns he examines are the cultural acceptance of unmarried adolescent parenthood and having a child as a rite of passage into adulthood.

As you read, consider the following questions:

1. What are some of the reasons that teenage girls give for getting pregnant, according to Dash?
2. What cultural attitudes toward teenage childbearing does Dash discuss?
3. According to the author, why do cultural attitudes like those in the viewpoint persist, even when they have become destructive?

"When Children Want Children" by Leon Dash, *Society*, July/August 1990. Reprinted by permission of Transaction Publishers, New Brunswick, New Jersey.

In early 1984, at the beginning of a project on adolescent child-bearing, I met Tauscha Vaughn for the very first time. We talked for several hours in her family's living room. She impressed me as a tough, extroverted, self-assured girl who knew where she was going and what she wanted out of life. She was clear that she did not want any children until well after she had finished her education and was married. In three days, she would be starting her junior year at Washington DC's Ballou High School.

Wanting Babies

An hour into our conversation, Tauscha grew weary of my questions relating to what teenagers in her community, the community of Washington Highlands, understood, did not understand, or misunderstood about contraceptives. She leaned forward across the coffee table and looked at me as if I was a naive child. "Mr. Dash, would you stop asking me about birth control?" Tauscha said in her husky voice. "Girls out here know all about birth control. There are too many birth control pills out here. All of them know about it. Even when they are 12, they know what birth control is. Girls out here get pregnant because they want to have babies."

Although I did not know it at the time, Tauscha Vaughn was doing so poorly at Ballou High School that she was on the edge of dropping out of school, and she did so at the end of 1984.

"What do you mean?" I asked.

"None of that is an accident!" she replied. "When girls get pregnant, it's either because they want something to hold onto that they can call their own, or because of the circumstances inside their home. Their mother does not pamper them the way they want to be pampered, or they really don't have anyone to go to or talk to or call their own. And some of them do it because they resent their parents."

Missing from Tauscha's assessment was the fact that most of the girls and boys she knew who were parents were also doing very poorly in school.

Pregnancy and Poverty Are Linked

I moved into Washington Highlands to do a study on adolescent childbearing for the *Washington Post* at the end of July 1984. Before choosing Washington Highlands, I collected city-wide data in Washington on household income levels, rates of births to teenage girls, and welfare recipient statistics from Washington's Department of Human Services.

Among Washington's eight political wards, Wards 7 and 8 east of the Anacostia River had the highest annual rates for teenage childbearing and the largest numbers of families living on welfare. In 1984, Ward 8 had the highest rates of births to teenage girls of any ward in Washington: 72 babies born to every 1,000 adolescent girls. It also had the highest number of people living in poverty, 26 percent, and the lowest median household income, $12,747.

Drug trafficking is a ready source of income and is the community's major plague. The illicit but popular drugs of use in order of preference in 1984 were phencyclidine, known more commonly as PCP, followed by cocaine, marijuana, and heroin. The order of drug preference [more recently] is the cocaine-derivative crack followed by PCP, then marijuana and finally heroin.

Studying Teen Pregnancy

After I moved into a one-bedroom basement apartment in Washington Highlands, my neighbors responded to my efforts to introduce myself and draw them into conversation with undisguised looks of suspicion or uncommunicative grunts. No one accepted that I was who I said I was, a *Washington Post* reporter interested in meeting and talking to teenage parents. At this early stage, I often felt the deep sense of isolation.

Before moving into Washington Highlands, I had reminisced about my own juvenile years growing up in New York City's Harlem and the Bronx. I understood the antagonism I initially met as a community's unfriendliness when approached by an unvouched stranger. One neighbor, Charles A. (Willie) Hood, even threatened me. Willie, like most of the people that I first approached, could not believe that I was genuinely interested in teenage pregnancy.

Pregnant teenage girls and adolescent mothers are an unremarkable sight in Washington Highlands. Willie thought in reality I was an undercover policeman trying to get information on the community's pervasive drug traffic. Willie himself was a part-time drug dealer.

But Willie eventually came to believe that I was a reporter interested in teenage childbearing. During the waning days of the summer of 1984, Willie and I spent days together walking around Washington Highlands. He began to open up about himself to me. Willie had married at age 19, had a child soon after, and another was due in a few weeks.

Feeling Like a Man

Older than most of his classmates, he vividly recalled how he felt when his 15-year-old girlfriend, an eighth-grader, told him that she was pregnant. "I almost dropped to my knees," Willie said. "I grabbed her and I hugged her. I was happy." But his reaction startled his girlfriend. She wanted an abortion.

Now, Willie said, he became angry. He threatened to beat her.

"Don't you ever let anything happen to that baby," he told her. She pretended to agree, but she secretly went ahead and had the abortion. After a brief breakup because of the abortion, Willie began to see her again. By this time, the girl was using birth control pills. That changed their relationship, Willie said. Because the girl would almost certainly not get pregnant, Willie told me, "I couldn't feel like a man." And that was the first clue for me to what I found is not an uncommon attitude among the youths of Washington Highlands. One becomes a man or one becomes a woman by having a child.

Wanting Babies

Kathryn Hall, whose Birthing Project in Sacramento, California, mainly serves African-American women, says the public assumes that older teens get pregnant by accident. "The literature shows that's not true. A recent research project asked that question directly. Most said it was not an accident, that they did not use birth control, that they wanted to have a baby—someone to love who'll love them back."

Hall says that more information on birth control or a return to family values—"whatever that means"—will not solve the teen pregnancy problem. "They will continue to get pregnant," she says, because "they see a baby as the solution to their problems."

Bettijane Levine, *Los Angeles Times*, September 9, 1993.

I met two girls who sought to become pregnant because they were afraid that they could not have children. Another teenager and junior high school dropout said she became pregnant because relatives and peers said that she was barren because she had not had any children by the age of 16. She became pregnant with the first of her two children to prove that she was fertile.

Debilitating Consequences

I did not conduct a survey during my investigation, but I did discover that the youths and adults that I became intimately involved with in six families did not become teenage parents because of the aimlessness and ignorance I had mistakenly presumed accounted for so much of the high rates of teen childbearing. But that did not make them any less vulnerable to the debilitating consequences of early childbearing and becoming a parent without a spouse.

The consequences become frightening when you look at the impact of teenage childbearing on the infants of adolescents. The children of unmarried teenage mothers are generally in poor physical health. There is a consistent tendency for the children of teenage mothers to have slightly lower IQ scores than children of older mothers when the children are measured at several years of age up to the age of 7.

The children of girls 17 years old and younger are less likely to adapt to the disciplines of school. The children of adolescent mothers are at higher risk to be born at low birth weight, and therefore at higher risk to suffer life-long learning disabilities. Children born when their parents were under 18 had lower cognitive scores than children born when their parents were ages 18 and 19. Children of adolescent mothers experience a greater probability of living in a non-intact home while in high school, have lower academic aptitude as teenagers, and are at higher risk of repeating their parents' pattern of early parenthood.

To many of these girls warnings from school teachers and counselors did not have the intended impact. Having a child was a tangible achievement, especially for those teenagers who understood implicitly or had been told explicitly that they were not likely to finish school. For junior high school and high school students who were several grades behind where they should have been in school, having a child gave them an elevated status among their peers. For many of them it was a rite of passage from adolescence to adulthood. While there was a fear of birth control there was little fear of pregnancy among the sexually active teenagers I interviewed.

Patterns Set by Forebears

The forebears of Washington Highlands resident Lillian Williams were poor, outcast black sharecroppers in North Carolina's Lenoir County. In her North Carolina childhood, Lillian Williams recalled that girls were not expected to do too much schooling. They were expected to have children at an early age. Children were put to work on the landowner's farm by the age of six. Life's priorities were the farm chores, learning how to cook, how to sew, and bearing children.

Survival came first. The inferior segregated education then locally available could be indulged when and if there was no other work to be done on the farm. After I began interviewing Lillian Williams, it was clear that her early childhood in the North Carolina sharecropping culture of Lenoir County bore directly on the urban turmoil of her adolescence and her adult life.

One legacy that Lillian brought with her to Washington was an established pattern of early childbearing in her family going back at least three generations to the early 1900s. Lillian observed the practice of early childbearing when she was growing up in her grandparents' home. Adolescent childbearing was an accepted practice and caused little comment from her grandparents, as she recalled.

Eventually, Lillian consciously duplicated the behavior she had seen, and her children subsequently imitated her behavior. Early childbearing had provided the basis for survival for her family in the tobacco-growing farmland of Lenoir County. Children's labor was an explicit part of the sharecropping culture. A landless black couple who were also childless could not get a sharecropping contract with the landowner.

The persistence of the custom in the city, however, had disastrous consequences for Lillian and her children. She tearfully acknowledged that she had imparted the pattern to her 11 children by her example. At least five of her seven oldest children were teenage parents by early 1987.

Lillian Williams handed on the legacy of her own impoverished life to her 11 children. She was not prepared, she said, to be a knowing, loving, and nurturing mother. She could not tutor her children in their school work. She was mean-spirited and would bite her children when they angered her. She would tell her children, "You'll never be nothing."

All of Lillian Williams' children, ranging in age from 22 to 9 years old, lived with her when I met her in 1984. The first seven of Lillian Williams' children were school dropouts. The eighth child, Janice, who was 19 in 1990, was a senior at Ballou High School. In 1987, her three youngest boys were either two or three grades behind where they should have been in school. At the same time three of Mrs. Williams' four daughters were unmarried mothers with six children between them. Her three oldest sons were unmarried, often unemployed, adolescent fathers.

Remedies

There are no simple remedies to this situation. I do believe that something can be done along two avenues that could begin to turn this situation around. Education is the key component: intensive academic work at the elementary school level with poor youths attending deficient schools in run-down urban areas beginning in the first grade, before the results of a head start program are allowed to fade.

A second approach can be made in terms of full employment for the young men and young women of communities like Washington Highlands. Over the course of my investigation, I was able to tell just by facial expression and body language who among the members of the six families was unemployed, had been unable to find work, or was recently laid off. A lot of the negative behavior I witnessed, I ascribed to the inability of many of the people in Washington Highlands to affirm themselves in stable, steady employment. Some of that behavior was directed at producing babies. A lot of the behavior was directed at criminal activity.

The stories of people like Willie, Mrs. Williams, and her children illustrate some of the reasons why poor, urban black teenagers in America today choose to become parents and drop out of school. The problems of many other American teenagers, such as poor white adolescent parents living in the rural poverty of Appalachia and the Upper Peninsula of Michigan, are still a major unexplored area for those of us who are concerned about this crisis.

"No single factor can explain teen pregnancy. "

A Variety of Factors Cause Teen Pregnancy

LaWanda Ravoira and Andrew L. Cherry Jr.

Although much information has been gathered about what causes teenage girls to become pregnant, the authors of the following viewpoint, LaWanda Ravoira and Andrew L. Cherry Jr., argue that no single factor causes teen pregnancy. In fact, they contend that many variables combine to create situations in which girls become pregnant. Ravoira is the state operations director for PACE Center for Girls. Cherry is a professor of social work at Barry University in Miami, Florida.

As you read, consider the following questions:

1. What five causes of teen pregnancy do the authors list?
2. According to Ravoira and Cherry, what effect does poverty have on teenagers?
3. How do relationships between parents and children affect the incidence of teen pregnancy?

Excerpted from *Social Bonds and Teen Pregnancy* by LaWanda Ravoira and Andrew L. Cherry Jr. (Praeger Publishers, an imprint of Greenwood Publishing Group, Inc., Westport, CT, 1992), pages 49-52, 59. Copyright © 1992 by LaWanda Ravoira and Andrew Lawrence Cherry Jr. Reprinted with permission of the publisher.

The most accepted antecedents associated with the phenomenon of teenage sexual activity and adolescent pregnancy include (1) school problems; (2) race and socioeconomic status; (3) age at which sex is initiated; (4) peer pressure; and (5) influence of parents and family relationships.

Many Factors

This range of variables suggests that no single factor can explain teen pregnancy. Indeed, a number of factors correlated with teenage pregnancy and early childbearing must be considered when seeking explanations or developing interventions.

The correlation of early sexual experimentation and pregnancy with poor school performance is one of the most often mentioned antecedents. K. Pittman argues that academic failure reduces a girl's desire to avoid pregnancy. Pittman identifies poor grades, poor motivation, and poor long-term goals as risk factors associated with teenage pregnancy. Other researchers also found that girls who become pregnant at an early age often had substantial school problems prior to becoming pregnant.

Similar findings are reported in a study conducted by M. Alvarez, R. Burrows, A. Zvaighat, and S. Muzzo. These researchers compared the sociocultural characteristics of pregnant adolescents of low socioeconomic status with a group of non-pregnant girls from the same area of Santiago, Chile. They reported low levels of schooling and significantly lower IQ scores of pregnant adolescents as compared with non-pregnant youth.

A second factor associated with early sexual activity and adolescent pregnancy involves race and socioeconomic status. During the 1980s, the poverty rate of one group, black children, was particularly troublesome—48 percent of these children lived in poverty. Poverty among black children contributes to the ongoing debilitating cycle of adolescent childbearing.

Pregnant and parenting teens are far too often the offspring of educationally and financially disadvantaged single teenaged mothers. For example, in the state of South Carolina in 1984, there were 1,964 babies born to black teens between the ages of 14 and 17, as compared to 465 infants born to white adolescents. Many of these youth came from educationally and financially disadvantaged homes. They were the offspring of parents who themselves conceived during their teenage years.

The Influence of Ethnicity

An ethnographic study conducted by D. Hogan and E. Kitagawa, using data from a random sample of more than 1,000 black females between the ages of 13 and 19 from Chicago in 1979, confirmed that a relatively large percentage of black teenagers from all types of socioeconomic and family backgrounds become pregnant before reaching age 20. Even so, this research suggests that black teenagers from a high risk social environment have an even greater chance of becoming pregnant.

A high risk social environment includes factors such as residing in a ghetto neighborhood and being from a lower class and non-intact family. The rates of pregnancy for black teenagers living in high risk areas were 8.3 times higher than the rates of pregnancy for girls from low risk areas. Over the life span, cumulatively, these rates remain significant,with only 9 percent of the low risk teenagers experiencing a pregnancy before age 18 compared with 57 percent of the high risk youth.

The age at which sex is initiated is a third critical antecedent associated with teenage pregnancy. The earlier the initiation, the longer the period of exposure to the risk of pregnancy.

A national survey of 15- to 19-year-old females conducted by L. Zabin, J. Kantner, and L. Zelnik found that teenagers who had intercourse at age 15 or younger were nearly two times more likely to get pregnant in the first six months of sexual activity than those who refrained from having intercourse until they were 18 years old or older. Those who first have intercourse at early ages are less likely to use contraceptives, thus increasing the risk of pregnancy. Two-fifths of the girls who became sexually active at age 15 or younger never used contraceptives; one-quarter of the girls who had intercourse at age 18 or 19 did use contraceptives.

Peer pressure, "the most blamed" factor, also contributes to increased teen sexual activity. B. Herjanic states that young adolescents below the age of 15 were probably the most vulnerable to pressures to engage in sex, as well as to the consequences of pregnancy. In a survey of 625 teens . . ., 43 percent of boys aged 15-18, 65 percent of girls aged 15-16, and 48 percent of girls aged 17-18 answered affirmatively to the question, "Have there been times when you have been on a date, when you had sexual contact even though you really did not feel like it?" J. Billy and J. Udry's research showed that best male friends influence females' sexual activity, but they could not determine if the best friend was a sexual partner of the girls questioned. Despite the assumption that females become sexually active because they cannot say no to their boyfriends, research by G. Cvetkovich and B. Grote suggests that neither can some boys say no to their girlfriends.

Parent and Family Relationships

The last issue in regard to adolescent sexuality and teenage pregnancy concerns the influence of parents and family relationships. Hogan and Kitagawa found that parental supervision of early dating was an extremely important predictor of teenage pregnancy. Furthermore, they found that rates of teenage pregnancy declined when parents supervised the adolescent's dating habits.

The attitudes and values of parents and adolescents also relate to teenage childbearing. Parents who are concerned about the educational achievements and activities of their children (e.g., monitoring homework and whereabouts) have a positive influence, thus reducing the incidence of adolescent pregnancy. Girls with similar backgrounds whose parents expressed minimum or little concern and showed low expectations regarding their daughters' educational achievement had a higher incidence of pregnancy than girls whose parents showed higher levels of concern and had high educational expectations.

Marrying Later . . . Experimenting Earlier

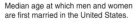

Median age at which men and women are first married in the United States.

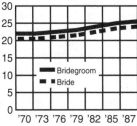

'70 '73 '76 '79 '82 '85 '87

Ages by which women first had sexual intercourse.

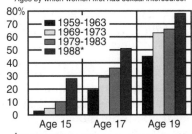

* Participants in the 1988 survey were 1/2 year older than earlier surveys.

Source: National Center for Health Statistics.

The makeup of the youth's household also has a significant influence on sexual activity and premarital intercourse. Adolescent girls reared without fathers are more likely to engage in sexual activity. Similarly, girls whose family changed from a two-parent family to a single-mother household are significantly more likely to become sexually active than girls from an intact family made up of natural parents.

In a study by M. Gispert, P. Brinich, K. Wheeler, and L. Krieger addressing the issue of the risk of repeated pregnancies, findings revealed that a positive relationship between the adolescent and her mother had a significant impact on whether or not the daughter would experience a second pregnancy. The quality of the relationship between the mother and daughter was assessed on the basis of interview responses to a selected number of questions. The relationship was rated as poor or good depending on the answers to the following questions: (1) Was your mother the first person you told of the pregnancy? (2) Was your mother aware of the sexual relationship between you and your boyfriend? (3) Was there agreement between mother and daughter regarding the outcome of the pregnancy, educational goals, rules about dating, and the use of contraception? This study also indicated that the absence of a father was associated with higher repeat pregnancies.

Data from the random sample of black teenagers in Chicago mentioned previously showed that teens from non-intact families had one-third higher rates of initial sexual intercourse than those from intact families. Having numerous siblings and a sister who became a teenage mother also raised the rate of sexual intercourse by female siblings by one-fifth. This research found that sexual activity among girls who date is 76 percent higher with lax parents than with parents who strictly supervise early dating.

Strained parent-child relationships and communication and the lack of parental supervision also contribute to greater risks of teenage pregnancy and childbearing. On the other hand, parents who have good relationships and communication with their children may experience more influence over their children's lives and their sexual experimentation. . . .

Understanding Why Teens Become Pregnant

The range of antecedents associated with teenage pregnancy indicates that no single factor can explain the issue. By reviewing the antecedents correlated with teenage sexual behaviors and adolescent pregnancy, we can begin to understand why many teenage girls become pregnant and become mothers. Appropriate prevention and intervention strategies are critical for teenagers and society as a whole because of the dire consequences associated with adolescent childbearing.

Periodical Bibliography

The following articles have been selected to supplement the diverse views presented in this chapter.

Amy Cunningham	"Sex in High School: What's Love Got to Do with It?" *Glamour*, September 1993.
Lloyd Eby and Charles A. Donovan	"Single Parents and Damaged Children: The Fruits of the Sexual Revolution," *The World & I*, July 1993.
Mary Rogers Gillmore et al.	"Substance Abuse and Other Factors Associated with Risky Sexual Behavior Among Pregnant Adolescents," *Family Planning Perspectives*, November/December 1992. Available from The Alan Guttmacher Institute, 111 Fifth Ave., New York, NY 10003.
Jessica Gress-Wright	"The Contraception Paradox," *The Public Interest*, Fall 1993. Available from 1112 16th St. NW, Suite 530, Washington, DC 20036.
D. Hollander	"Family Instability, Stress Heighten Adolescents' Risk of Premarital Birth," *Family Planning Perspectives*, November/December 1993.
Ann Hulbert	"Poor Conceptions," *The New Republic*, November 12, 1990.
Kristin Luker	"Dubious Conceptions: The Controversy over Teen Pregnancy," *The American Prospect*, Spring 1991. Available from PO Box 7645, Princeton, NJ 08543.
Moody	"Magic Morals," March 1992. Available from the Moody Bible Institute, 820 N. LaSalle Blvd., Chicago, IL 60610.
David Muram et al.	"Race and Personality Traits Affect High School Senior Girls' Sexual Reports," *Journal of Sex Education and Therapy*, vol. 17, no. 4, 1991. Available from Guilford Publications, Dept. 4K, 72 Spring St., New York, NY 10012.
David Muram et al.	"Teenage Pregnancy: Dating and Sexual Attitudes," *Journal of Sex Education and Therapy*, vol. 18, no. 4, 1992.

How Can Teen Pregnancy Be Reduced?

TEENAGE SEXUALITY

Chapter Preface

Teen pregnancy was rarely a problem in the United States until late in the twentieth century. Teenage girls who got pregnant were either already married or immediately married the father. Married teenagers still routinely bear children without public concern. What concerns public policy experts, social workers, teachers, and parents today are unwed pregnant teens. According to William A. Donohoe, professor of sociology at LaRoche College in Pittsburgh, Pennsylvania, "In the 1950s, it was not uncommon for teens to marry and have children. In the 1980s, teens engaged in more sex, but were less inclined to marry, due largely to the legality and easy availability of abortion, and the declining stigma attached to unwed motherhood." The trend toward unwed teen pregnancy has continued in the 1990s.

Many experts search for causes of teen pregnancy in order to find ways to prevent it. Some charge that the welfare system in the United States contributes to teen pregnancy by providing the financial wherewithal needed to raise a child. Robert Rector of the Heritage Foundation argues, "The data I have very strongly suggest that the welfare system overwhelmingly contributes to out-of-wedlock births, with a high percent being to young women." Sharply reducing such benefits would, according to this line of reasoning, lead to a reduction in teen pregnancy. Others, however, disagree. They point to statistics showing a decline since the 1970s in the cash value of Aid to Families with Dependent Children (AFDC). Kristin Moore, executive director of the Washington-based research organization Child Trends, Inc., insists, "I don't think welfare has anything to do with sexual activity. It's not what's in their head when they're having sex." Obviously, for experts such as Moore, reducing welfare benefits would not solve the problem of teen pregnancy.

Others blame sex education courses for the rise in teen pregnancy. Reporter Bob Olmstead contends that too much sex education "mostly whets young sexual appetites, causing still more pregnancies while sex-ed classes and condom-dispensing clinics proliferate." Critics advocate abolishing sex education programs to reduce teen pregnancy. American Enterprise Institute scholar Douglas J. Besharov, on the other hand, argues that too little sex education leads to teen pregnancy. He asserts, "If we are to make real progress against teen pregnancy, the long national silence about contraception and sexuality must end."

Thus what one expert sees as a solution to the teen pregnancy problem is often seen by another as a cause of that same problem. These contradictions reveal the complexity of this issue. The viewpoints in this chapter discuss some possible solutions.

"We need an aggressive social bias in favor of the use of the contraceptive Norplant for sexually active girls."

Norplant Will Reduce Teen Pregnancy

Catherine O'Neill

Catherine O'Neill is the cofounder of the Women's Commission for Refugee Women and Children in Los Angeles, California. In the following viewpoint, O'Neill argues that offering the contraceptive Norplant to sexually active teenage girls can help reduce the number of teenage pregnancies. Because Norplant is surgically implanted and is effective for five years, it will help teenage girls reach maturity without the risk of pregnancy, O'Neill maintains.

As you read, consider the following questions:

1. Why does O'Neill oppose teenagers' bearing children?
2. Some people believe that teenagers should not use Norplant because, unlike condoms, it offers no protection against sexually transmitted diseases. How does O'Neill respond to this objection?
3. Why does the author object to programs designed to help teenagers who have children?

"Teen Sex: The Case for Norplant" by Catherine O'Neill, *Los Angeles Times*, May 5, 1993. Reprinted by permission of the author.

In many ways, the feminists have missed the boat on one of the most critical issues affecting young women, children and communities across this land. By emphasizing abortion to the exclusion of other issues, too many women's organizations have neglected an equally important goal: working with young, sexually active women so that they do not get pregnant in the first place.

Prevent Teen Pregnancies

More and more babies are being born to mothers who are too young to drive, to vote or to drink alcoholic beverages. Yet we send these teen-agers home from hospitals with babies in their arms, and deem them "responsible" to raise those children. For many, we soon start sending welfare checks to support their babies. And now, we are recognizing that we need a new array of social services: parenting classes, nurseries in public high schools and on and on.

That has to change. Babies are entitled to be born to adults, and I have begun to question whether—even if her body function can make it happen—a young girl in our society should have the right to choose to become a mother at 14.

What can we do about it? I believe we need an aggressive social bias in favor of the use of the contraceptive Norplant for sexually active girls. With Norplant inserted under their skin in a simple procedure, those 13-year-olds will have five more years to become young women with a sense of the possibilities the world might have in store for them before confronting the responsibilities of motherhood.

There are those who might say that in selecting this option, we are encouraging promiscuity, that there might be negative side effects and that if a young woman uses Norplant, she might be less likely to insist on her partner's use of a condom and therefore be at higher risk for AIDS.

Reducing Teen Sexual Activity

First, on promiscuity. I come from the "virgin bride" tradition of courtship, where fear of pregnancy often set the parameters of sexual conduct. But I recognize that we cannot put the genie back in the bottle. Young teen-agers are having both sex and babies. We may not be able to stop them from having sex, but we can do a lot more to stop them from having babies resulting from those casual sexual contacts.

I believe we should also try to inculcate in young people a respect for themselves and their bodies, so that sexual contact is associated with deeply held feelings and promiscuity is reduced. But we cannot hold society hostage to that goal.

As for the second objection: Surely there are side effects in a 14-year-old's having an abortion, becoming a mother or giving a child up for adoption. Norplant is reversible. Parenthood is not. I have talked with many women involved in public health and they believe that of the choices available now, Norplant is the most appropriate for sexually active young women.

Teenagers and Norplant

[In a 1991 study of Norplant in Texas,] a large proportion of [the women in the] sample was younger than 21, and many were younger than 18. This fact leads us to speculate on the potential impact the implant may have on unplanned pregnancies among teenagers and among other women who do not always use methods correctly or consistently. Unlike the pill and barrier methods, the implant's effectiveness is not dependent on correct and consistent use. Therefore, pregnancies that result from incorrect use should not occur among implant users.

Margaret L. Frank et al., *Family Planning Perspectives*, September/October 1992.

As for AIDS, it would be tragic indeed if babies across America were born because girls were denied Norplant with the hope that fear of pregnancy might encourage greater use of condoms. Girls whose low self-esteem often contributes to casual sexual contact should not be put at risk of motherhood with the hope that their insistence on condoms will carry the day. Too many of them are not strong, and they will not insist. We need to expand AIDS education and the practice of "safe sex" and condom use. But that should be separate from a serious attempt to avert teen-age pregnancy. Each is a terrible problem with a different solution.

At a meeting on women's issues at the University of Southern California, I raised the question of whether we were ignoring the pervasive reality of teen-age motherhood. Cmdr. Helena Ashby of the Los Angeles Sheriff's Department replied that she had volunteered at a community clinic and found that some of the babies who were being born to teen-age mothers had great-grandmothers in their late 40s. Clearly, some dramatic and aggressive social intervention is required.

Thus far, society seems to favor making it possible for young mothers to go on living "normal" lives. Last year, I visited a child-care center at Santa Monica High School, where the babies of 15-year-old mothers are cared for while their mothers work to get their high school diplomas. Laudable, I thought at the time. Now, I'm not sure that it is not being presented as too "normal." Yes, I want these young mothers to have a chance to make it as responsible members of society, but I want them to be "rare birds." I don't want teen-agers to have babies. I want them to have the chance to go to high school, college or trade school, without society's taking full responsibility and doing contortions to accommodate the consequences of their actions.

And I want the babies they will have someday to have intact, responsible, two-parent families, in which the parents feel a sense of their own possibilities and commit to having families as a choice, not an accident.

I was lucky. My two sons were born by choice to young, college-educated parents who felt the great weight of parenthood and the sacrifices and trade-offs it called for. My daughter, born later in my life, was received by loving parents who immediately began sacrificing to put money away for her college education, which would come at a time when they were close to collecting Social Security.

In the best of circumstances, parenting is hard and childhood is complicated. And society should use all its social, moral and scientific weight to prevent teen-age girls from getting pregnant. . . . We shouldn't rely on government-funded abortions. We want government to work aggressively to avert those pregnancies.

"[Teenagers are] reluctant to use Norplant because it is more complicated to reverse than other contraceptives and because it is visible under the skin."

Norplant Will Not Reduce Teen Pregnancy

Tom Bethell

The Laurence G. Paquin High School for Expectant Teenage Mothers in Baltimore, Maryland, was the first school in the United States to offer its students the contraceptive Norplant to avoid pregnancy. However, Tom Bethell argues, many teenagers—especially those in the inner cities—bear children because they choose to, not out of ignorance about how to avoid pregnancy. Therefore, Bethell contends, the availability of Norplant will have little effect on teen pregnancy rates. Bethell is the Washington correspondent for the *American Spectator*, a conservative monthly journal of opinion.

As you read, consider the following questions:

1. According to the author, why do teenage girls choose to have children?
2. Federally funded Norplant implants are available through Medicaid in every state. Why does Bethell find this troubling?
3. What reasons does Bethell give for his skepticism about the efficacy of Norplant in reducing teenage pregnancies?

From "A Girls' School in Baltimore" by Tom Bethell, *The American Spectator*, February 1993. Copyright 1993, *The American Spectator*. Reprinted by permission of *The American Spectator*.

The Laurence G. Paquin High School for Expectant Teenage Mothers is a bleak brick fortress in a desolate section of east Baltimore; a squiggle-painted, cinder-block, boarded-up-row-house, upside-down-sofas-on-the-sidewalk kind of a neighborhood, with drug lookouts wearing woolsox headgear posted at nearby corners. Paquin's student body is composed entirely of expectant mothers or teenagers who already have given birth, some of them twice. Almost all are black. Paquin has been in the news because Norplant [is] dispensed free at the school's clinic. This is a new form of contraception, consisting of six capsules that are inserted under the skin on the underside of the upper arm. They release a hormone called progestin which blocks ovulation for up to five years. With the implant, a teenager doesn't have to worry about forgetting to take the pill.

The Paquin School

The Paquin School is ghetto-proofed, a sign outside proclaiming it to be a Drug-Free School Zone. There are no windows at all on the ground floor, mere slits upstairs, and stadium lights suspended from the four corners of the building's roof. A phone outside the front and only entrance allows visitors to identify themselves and to be buzzed in if considered friendly. Inside, there were bright lights and Christmas tree decorations, wall slogans ("At the End of Broken Dreams You Need Someone, Us—the Paquin Family"), plaques, and a display case showing a satin-finished christening set for twins, made in the school's garment-making shop. There were framed letters from George and Barbara Bush and other dignitaries. "The play outfits for the grands [grandchildren] are just perfect," Mrs. Bush wrote, "and they will love them. ShonTae Farrare has done a wonderful job personalizing them." Girls in the inner city, and their offspring, have names like that now: ShonTae, Taniqua, Shaquira, Tamika, Tallisha, Tayesha.

Babies were crying softly in the background and young women wearing slacks and loose outfits were walking in the hall. Two or three were carrying plastic bassinets with babies. They have a whole Toddler Center, with cots and cribs and baby rattles and multicolored wall alphabets—Paquin University, it is called, with "an infant stimulation/learning program designed to promote an adaptive cognitive style." It can handle up to thirty infants and children, aged six weeks to six years. They were just finishing lunch, which the students and their babies have together in the cafeteria. The sign on the cafeteria wall read: "You Are the Apple of Our Eye. . . . So Hang On . . . Don't Drop Out." About 300 girls attend the school each semester, but I gather that few stay for more than a year.

As I waited to talk to the principal, Dr. Rosetta Stith, I copied down a cheerless message framed on the office wall: "Our school must be dedicated to being a change agent through activities that offer young school-age mothers a measure of stability, hope, and a sense of reality to deal with a world that is constantly torn between uncertainty, unrest, and violence."

Asay, by permission of the *Colorado Springs Gazette Telegraph*.

The principal, Dr. Stith, fortyish with upswept silvery hair, was happy to talk and she mentioned all the media attention—AP, UPI, *Newsweek*, Bettina Gregory of ABC News. Norplant is "just another form of birth control, like having another car to drive," Stith told me. She wanted me to know right off that the students are well warned that the implant does not protect against venereal and viral disease. But this they already know. When Karen de Witt of the *New York Times* visited a classroom of thirty pregnant girls at the school, and Stith asked them what did give protection, they chanted in unison: "Condom, condom, condom." A note of mockery here? They have been told over and over about birth control and condoms, they're all pregnant anyway, and now a new item has been added to the contraceptive menu.

The assumption underlying this latest weapon in the arsenal of the therapeutic state is that conception among inner-city blacks is largely accidental. *Washington Post* reporter Leon Dash questioned this in his 1989 book *When Children Want Children*, based on months of research in the Washington ghetto. One 16-year-old, Tauscha Vaughn, said to him: "Mr. Dash, will you please stop asking me about birth control? Girls out here know all about birth control. There's too many birth control pills out here. All of them know about it. Even when they twelve, they know what it is. Girls out here get pregnant because they want to have babies."

Later in the book Dash claimed that the four pregnant teen-agers in one family he interviewed "wanted children for a variety of reasons—to achieve something tangible, to prove something to their peers, to be considered an adult, to get their mother's attention, and to keep up with an older brother or sister." Another 16-year-old girl he met baited her virginal 18-year-old cousin as "barren" because she had not yet had a child.

Deliberate Teen Pregnancy

Stith would have none of this wanted-child argument. She took at face value what the girls tell her in school—"You don't think it's going to happen to you, then one day you find you're pregnant," and so on. "It's not deliberate," Stith reassured me. She did express some exasperation, though. "You have to have a driver's permit to drive, a voter's card to vote, but you don't have to have anything to be a parent." How about a marriage license, or an end to welfare? She does not accept that teenagers make cost/welfare-benefit analyses of childbearing, because the babies keep coming while the "public assistance grants have been decreasing." (Yet, according to the *New York Times*, she does believe that the welfare state fosters dependency, and that as a result young women in her school do not have to think about the consequences of pregnancy.) . . .

Like that of Washington, D.C., the population of Baltimore (735,000) has declined 25 percent from its 1950 peak. The city is now about 60 percent black. One in ten Baltimore girls aged 15 to 17 gave birth in 1990, and teenagers accounted for 23 percent of the city's births in 1991. Teenagers can become eligible for Aid to Families with Dependent Children when they have children themselves. About 112,000 mothers in Baltimore received AFDC in September 1992—86 percent of them black. The great majority also receive food stamps, and of course Medicaid.

It is probably true that in deciding whether to have further children, the young women do not make marginal calculations about AFDC payments. This merely means that incremental change in the welfare system—which is all that we are going to see in the current political climate—will make no difference. The liberal assumption that government aid "helps" people in proportion to the amount given is still largely intact. If this view prevails in policy debates, life in the inner city will deteriorate further.

The great problem at present is that unwed mothers on welfare, and the young men who impregnate them, are indirectly told that they do not have to be responsible for their behavior. Mothers on AFDC are called the "underclass" but they also constitute a privileged class—unloved but still privileged. The overall effect of the welfare state is less devastating to them than to the fathers. True, there are not enough weddings and too many funerals, and the mothers live in chaotic extended families, but there are babies and in-laws, showers and christening parties, and the material essentials are provided for them. The young men are "deprived" at a more fundamental level, however. Their provider role is usurped by the state. Embittered, many take to a life of crime on the streets.

The Norplant Controversy

Here and there, liberals are showing signs of recognizing that all is not well in the cities, and Norplant is apparently their latest riposte. Unless I am mistaken, it is not going to make much of a dent. There is also a considerable irony here. Shortly after Norplant was approved by the FDA [Food and Drug Administration], in December 1990, the *Philadelphia Inquirer* stirred up controversy by publishing an editorial—"Poverty and Norplant: Can Contraception Reduce the Underclass?"—which suggested that welfare mothers should be offered incentives to use the device. This was immediately denounced as racist by both black and white members of the paper's news staff. In a letter to the editor, the president of the Philadelphia Association of Black Journalists attacked the editorial as a "tacit endorsement of slow genocide." A second, apologetic editorial followed, and the editorial page editor, David Boldt, said he "deeply regretted" the way the earlier editorial had linked race, poverty, and birth control. (He also complained to the *New York Times* about the "summonses from the thought police for violating the no-right-turn rule.")

Since then, however, the offensive editorial's recommendation has been quietly implemented. The implant is now covered by Medicaid in all fifty states. "In what some see as a troubling paradox," a writer noted in an unbylined *New York Times* news story, "truly poor women can get Norplant more easily than those who have modest incomes." This in turn "is stirring profound and troubling questions about personal rights and public policy." The paper, doubly troubled, failed to note what was so "troubling." No doubt it was that inner-city women on Medicaid—black women, overwhelmingly—now really do have an incentive to use Norplant, whereas the working poor do not. A Norplant kit costs $365, and a private doctor may charge $500 to insert it. This is a lot more than the zero cost encountered by those on Medicaid.

"The thinking has changed," the author of the *Inquirer* editorial told me, referring to the new acceptability of Norplant incentives. The potential for controversy "depends on who says it, and who does it."

Norplant Is Not Working

Early indications are that the inner cities are not about to be depopulated soon. About 500,000 women now use Norplant (up from 100,000 in 1992), but 61 percent of sales are to doctors in private practice. Foundations are also making them available to women not covered by Medicaid. According to the *Washington Post*, Planned Parenthood of Metropolitan Washington has found teenagers in the capital "reluctant to use Norplant because it is more complicated to reverse than other contraceptives and because it is visible under the skin." "I've heard it can give you cancer," Paquin student Quadrine Kelly, six months pregnant, told Karen de Witt.

"It's downright criminal that [bureaucrats] provided this wrong-headed incentive leading vulnerable teenage girls down a primrose path that produced millions of babies."

Welfare Reform Could Reduce Teen Pregnancy

Phyllis Schlafly

In the following viewpoint, Phyllis Schlafly argues that liberal social policies begun in the 1960s have contributed to the crisis of teenage pregnancy and childbearing in the United States. According to Schlafly, the easy availability of generous welfare benefits encourages unmarried teenagers to have children. Schlafly argues that reforming the welfare system to exclude unmarried parents under age eighteen will discourage teenagers from getting pregnant. Schlafly is the well-known founder and president of the Eagle Forum, an organization dedicated to opposing communism, supporting free-market economic policies, and especially supporting social policies that strengthen the family.

As you read, consider the following questions:

1. According to the author, how and why has the social spending begun in the 1960s affected teenage childbearing?
2. What specific proposals does Schlafly support to reform the welfare system?

"Welfare Reform Should Cost Less, Not More" by Phyllis Schlafly; a position paper dated July 15, 1993. Reprinted by permission of the author.

Representative Jan Meyers (R-Kan) has come up with the best idea for real welfare reform that anybody has had since welfare became an entitlement in the 1960s. Unlike most "reforms," it will cost the taxpayers less, not more.

Human Nature and Government Spending

Her bill is based on an understanding of human nature as well as of the slippery slope of bureaucratic spending programs. It's so straightforward and full of common sense that it makes us wonder, "why didn't somebody think of this before now?"

Rep. Meyers's bill does three things: (1) it freezes AFDC [Aid to Families with Dependent Children] at current levels and returns funds to the states in the form of block grants, (2) it provides that no AFDC benefits can be given at all unless paternity is established, and (3) it provides that no AFDC benefits can be given unless both the mother and father are at least 18 years of age.

Freezing the ceiling is the only way to stop the out-of-control spiral of spending that began in the 1960s. Letting the states handle AFDC through block grants will allow them flexibility to adopt innovative welfare solutions appropriate to local conditions.

Prohibiting AFDC benefits until paternity is established will make it clear, Rep. Meyers believes, that the responsibility of having a child rests with the father and mother, not with the taxpayers. The father can no longer walk away from his responsibilities and say to the mother, "You don't need me; you have welfare."

The third requirement is the most innovative part of Rep. Meyers's bill, and it shows a good understanding of the human element. Rep. Meyers obviously understands teenagers and incentives and the role both play in our mushrooming welfare costs.

Welfare and Teen Pregnancy

For the last couple of decades, welfare "reformers" have suggested various "incentives" to get recipients off welfare, into a job, into training, or, in regard to teenagers, to stay in school. None of these incentives has worked very well, and the bottom line is, they always cost more money.

There are, indeed, incentives in the welfare system that do work, but they are the wrong kind of incentives.

In 1990, 68 percent of all teenage births were to unwed mothers under the age of 19. The record shows that more than half of them immediately go on AFDC and then stay on welfare until they are over 30 years old.

The public is led to believe that these girls just "find themselves pregnant" because they haven't had explicit sex education. However, most surveys show that the girls knew plenty about sex and contraceptives; they wanted to have the babies—for various reasons such as wanting someone to love, or for self-esteem, or to acquiesce to boyfriend or peer pressure.

So, along comes Big Brother Federal Government and offers her an irresistible deal—to pay her as much as $500 a month of AFDC cash plus $300 in food stamps, pay all her medical bills, and find her a new place to live. She doesn't have to work, but if she wants more schooling or job training, the government will pay for it and even pay for a baby sitter while she attends.

What does this teenage girl have to do to receive these goodies paid for by the U.S. taxpayers? She just has to have two illegitimate babies, that's all.

Teenagers know in advance that they can be "sexually active" and Big Brother government will pay the costs of whatever happens. As Rep. Meyers says, "Is it any wonder we have more juvenile delinquency, violent gangs, drug abuse, high-school dropouts, and teenage out-of-wedlock pregnancies?"

Welfare Reform Needed

It was once called "bastardy." Then "illegitimacy." Then "out-of-wedlock birth." And now, frequently, wholly sanitized, "non-marital birth."

Whatever it's called, it is at the root of our social problems. . . .

It is the growth in out-of-wedlock birth that is pushing up the welfare numbers. The Congressional Research Service reports that 71 percent of the new cases in the Aid to Families with Dependent Children program, from 1987 to 1991, were headed by a never-married mother. (In earlier years welfare was generated by divorce, widowhood or marital separation.) . . .

More voluntary out-of-wedlock birth yields more dependency, more welfare, less parental control, which yields more crime, drugs, unemployment and poor education, which yields more voluntary out-of-wedlock birth, more dependency, and so on, cyclically, without end.

Circles, vicious or otherwise, can only be continued or cut. The way to cut this circle is to send a message that we will stop subsidizing voluntary illegitimacy.

Ben Wattenberg, *The San Diego Union-Tribune*, July 18, 1993.

Wake up, Americans. The bureaucrats haven't used your tax dollars to do good, but to do bad. It is bad enough that they wasted billions of our hard-earned money on a program that has failed miserably for 20 years, but it's downright criminal that they provided this wrong-headed incentive leading vulnerable teenage girls down a primrose path that produced millions of babies who are growing up without a father.

Rep. Meyers's proposal to deny AFDC payments to children under 18 means that the teenagers will know in advance that they won't be rewarded for their irresponsible behavior with separate spending money, and that they will still be dependent on their own parents. The parents of teenagers will be put on notice that they are responsible for the behavior and whereabouts of their teenage children.

Wrong Incentives

Of course, this plan won't stop all out-of-wedlock births, but it will remove the wrong incentives that encourage teenagers to make bad choices that lock them into welfare dependency. More AFDC payments are not the solution; they are the problem.

Rep. Meyers's Welfare and Teenage Pregnancy Reduction Act is strong medicine for a very sick patient, the welfare system, but it's essential. It would be a great boon to the taxpayers to freeze spending increases, but it would be even greater for our society to freeze the increase in fatherless children.

"I do not believe that the schools should in effect approve illegitimacy by allocating funds and personnel to the care of infants."

Eliminating Government Programs Could Reduce Teen Pregnancy

Howard Hurwitz

Since the 1970s many states have started programs designed to help keep pregnant teenagers and those who already have children from dropping out of school. These government programs have increased society's acceptance of teenage childbearing, Howard Hurwitz contends. Hurwitz, a contributor to *Human Events*, a conservative daily newspaper in Washington, D.C., argues that eliminating such programs, especially those in schools, will send a clear signal that bearing illegitimate children is unacceptable.

As you read, consider the following questions:

1. Why does Hurwitz contend that school programs for teenage girls with babies are unnecessary?
2. What effect have these programs had on keeping teenagers with children in school, according to the author?
3. What does Hurwitz mean by "rewarding immorality"?

"Should We Reward Teen Pregnancy?" by Howard Hurwitz, *Human Events*, February 10, 1990. Reprinted by permission of Human Events Publishing, 422 First St. SE, Washington, DC 20003.

It was about two decades ago that I interviewed a girl who had been out of school for a month. In response to my question about the reason for her long absence, she replied, "I had a baby."

This did not knock me out of my chair. What did give me pause was the tone of voice and manner of the fifteen-year-old. I have received more passionate responses when I have inquired about the time of the day.

I returned the girl to class and gave the information to the girl's guidance counselor. I did not seek post-natal care for the girl's infant, nor did I do anything other than to see to it that she resumed her program in the school, since that was the reason for her return.

Government-Funded Programs

We have, however, come a long way, baby. Fourteen states now provide money for child care for teenage girls who attend school. We have about a half-million adolescent mothers a year in the United States and about seven in ten are unmarried.

Many high schools provide child care while the teenage mother goes to class. In some cities, there are special schools for expectant teenage mothers where in addition to the regular curriculum the girls are instructed in the care of infants.

Jordan High School, in Los Angeles, has an Infant Center that cares for 20 babies up to the age of two. It is financed by the State of California. So popular is the center that two of the girls have two infants each being taken care of while they go to class. There is a waiting list, but the administrator is not worried. She knows that the dropout rate will be so high that girls on the waiting list will be accommodated.

The Jordan Infant Center has been operating since 1983. About 40 per cent of the girls enrolled in the school have children. The administrator told a reporter, ". . . having a baby is the least of their problems." Even at this late date, such a remark gives me pause; nor do I become more relaxed when it is explained to me that "a lot of the girls come from dysfunctional households. . . . There may be substance abuse in the home; a lot of their own mothers are young; they are living in the housing projects."

A social worker added, "In some of these families, a girl reaches thirteen or fourteen and never receives recognition for doing anything good until she has a baby. In some communities it's like a rite of passage." It is in this spirit that the girls show off their babies, passing them around among friends.

No Special Assistance Needed

I remember one teenager who was being graduated from a high school I headed. She brought a well-dressed little boy to my office. I thought he was her brother. She told me that he was her son and that he was four years old.

No Special Help

Again, the girl had been given no special assistance from the school, other than a safe environment in which she could learn to the best of her abilities. Whatever help she may have been given was extended by her family and institutions other than the school.

New Thinking Is Needed

Optimistic assessments of teenage pregnancy patterns in the United States often point to two putatively favorable trends: reductions in the total number of births to teens, and a decrease in the pregnancy rate among teens who can be considered to be "sexually active." For example, from 1970 to 1987 the total number of births to U.S. women under the age of 20 declined from 656,000 to 472,623, a reduction of some 28 percent.

But during those same years, the number of female adolescents aged 15-19 declined by nearly 400,000, and the number of abortions performed annually on adolescents rose by at least 250,000. Moreover, in 1970 the vast majority of births to teenagers were in wedlock—some 459,000, or fully 70 percent. Today the numbers are nearly reversed: some 64 percent of all births to teenagers are nonmarital. In 1987, 302,500 children were born out-of-wedlock to women aged 15-19, an increase of 53.5 percent despite the declining number of teens in this age bracket. . . .

Patterns of teenage pregnancy, abortion, and out-of-wedlock childbearing, though stabilizing somewhat in the 1980s, continue to worsen. After a trial of two decades, national pregnancy prevention policies have failed to reduce pregnancy rates, have succeeded in lowering birth rates only through a sharp concomitant rise in abortions among adolescents, and have coincided with an unprecedented increase in teenage sexual activity. For the sake of the next generation of American children, it is time for a generous dose of domestic "new thinking" about one of the nation's most intractable social problems.

Charles A. Donovan, *Family Policy*, November/December 1989.

The spate of special aid now being given to girls who have babies and wish to attend school is justified on the ground that they would otherwise be unable to complete their high school education. The fact is that few of them do. On the other side of the coin, we have imprinted society's approval of the immoral conduct that has led to the institutionalization of illegitimacy.

Unmarried mothers, or married ones for that matter, have the right to attend school. There was a time when this might be an embarrassment; that time is long since past in many communities. I do not, however, believe that the schools should in effect approve illegitimacy by allocating funds and personnel to the care of infants.

Teenagers Must Be Responsible

Families sustained by our pervasive provisions for aid to dependent children and institutions other than the schools should bear the day-care burden. If much of it should fall on the teenage mother, I see that as all to the good.

No, I am not calling for the return of the Scarlet Letter, but I do not see rewarding immorality as a value that should be cultivated in our crumbling schools.

"Social attitudes, pressures and sanctions once served to promote long-lasting marriages and to discourage destructive sexual behavior. They can again, if Americans want them to."

Society's Condemnation of Illegitimacy Can Reduce Teen Pregnancy

Stephen Chapman

Stephen Chapman is a nationally syndicated columnist. In the following viewpoint, Chapman asserts that abandoning both the explicit sex education classes in schools and the easy acceptance of teen sexuality and childbearing will help society send the message that teen sex and pregnancy are wrong. He maintains that, if society adopts a strict attitude of disapproval toward teenagers' having sex, they will stop and the teen pregnancy rate will decline.

As you read, consider the following questions:

1. Why are teen pregnancy and childbearing harmful for those who are unmarried, according to Chapman?
2. How do teenagers in the 1990s differ from those in the 1950s, according to the author?
3. What parallel does Chapman draw between smoking and teenage sex and pregnancy?

"Real and False Solutions for Teen Pregnancy" by Stephen Chapman, *Conservative Chronicle*, October 2, 1991. Reprinted by permission of Stephen Chapman and Creators Syndicate.

American teen-agers, who have proven heroically resistant to learning algebra and grammar, are quick studies when it comes to a more basic subject, human reproduction. They're good at it and getting better, which is bad news for them, their children and the nation.

The Illinois Department of Public Health reported that the number of births to teen-age mothers in the state rose by a brisk 7.6 percent in 1989, the third consecutive yearly increase, mirroring national trends. There is no particular hope in sight, according to state health director John Lumpkin. Severe as the problem is now, he says, "we can expect that the teen birth numbers in the future will get worse."

Palliatives or Resignation

Everyone agrees this is a terrible development, and no one proposes to do anything serious to change it. The usual responses are glib palliatives or expressions of resignation. Neither the optimism nor the despair is warranted. The situation isn't beyond correction, but radical ills require radical remedies.

Actually, the problem has been misstated. Teen-agers having babies is nothing new: Their fertility rate in the 1950s was nearly double what it is today. The difference is that in the 1950s, the kids having babies were married. What we have among adolescents today is not an epidemic of pregnancy but an epidemic of irresponsibility. Teen-agers, like adults, are abandoning the only sound structure for raising children, which is stable marriage.

Today, in Illinois, about 80 percent of babies born to teen-age mothers are illegitimate. Among blacks, the figure is 97 percent. Nationally, the illegitimacy rate among girls between the ages of 15 and 19 more than doubled between 1957 and 1987. It's growing worse among grown-ups as well. In 1960, only one of every twenty births was to an unmarried mother. Today, it's one of every four.

This is bad for several reasons. The most important is that it exposes the babies to all sorts of unnecessary risks. Bryce Christensen, director of the Center on the Family in America at the Rockford Institute, in Rockford, Ill., has found that children born into single-parent homes are more likely than other children to die in infancy, to be poor, to drop out of high school, to have children themselves as teenagers, to smoke, to suffer unemployment and to be on welfare.

It's also dangerous for the mothers, who are five times more likely to be poor than married mothers. And it's no blessing to taxpayers, who often get to support the mothers and their children for years, assuming a role that the fathers routinely spurn.

The facile answer for this problem, pushed by Planned Parenthood and others, is to educate kids about sex and assure them access to contraception—even if it means handing out condoms and birth control pills in public schools. This is like saying the way to prevent teen-agers from driving drunk is to let them have all the booze they want at home.

The Problems of Illegitimacy

There are several reasons why illegitimate births are undesirable. The one reason with the widest appeal is that illegitimate children tend to grow up in poverty. A child raised in a single-parent environment is 500 percent likelier to be poor than his neighbor with two parents. And a child growing up in poverty is in turn likelier to turn to criminal pursuits.

Another reason? Well, they come in at you from all sides. We worry about the population explosion. And the place to begin, on that score, is to curb accidental babies.

Still another reason? Illegitimate babies suggest loose sexual habits and these in turn imply an increase in venereal disease, in the spread of AIDS, and in children born diseased.

More? One reason almost to whisper the point in our blase age. Loose sex is wrong. It is anti-moral. It is forbidden by most religions, with special emphasis on adulterous sex. . . .

It is hard to remind ourselves of it, but most human beings do nor do not do things because it is right or not right to do such things. To corrupt the moral architecture that proscribes sexual wantonness is to turn one's back not only on moral dicta, but also on empirical superstructures, that poverty, disease, criminality we have concrete reasons for bemoaning.

William F. Buckley Jr., *Conservative Chronicle*, December 18, 1991.

The teen-agers of the 1950s, despite having little in the way of sex education and less in the way of contraception, managed to postpone childbearing until after marriage. What is missing today is not the knowledge or the means to prevent pregnancy, but the will. There are ways to strengthen teen-agers' self-control, but for public schools to become accomplices in premarital sex is not one of them.

Ultimately the surest solution is sexual restraint. To advocate that adolescents (or adults) curb their appetites is to invite being called a prude, something many Americans fear far worse than they fear teen-age pregnancies. And even those who would like to see an end to sexual license have abandoned hope that anything can be done about it.

They make the same mistake as the Americans of a generation ago—assuming that what is always will be. There was nothing in the order of nature preventing large numbers of unmarried teen-agers from having babies 30 years ago, and there is nothing in the order of nature compelling them to have babies today. Social attitudes, pressures and sanctions once served to promote long-lasting marriages and to discourage destructive sexual behavior. They can again, if Americans want them to.

Does this sound like the height of absurdity? Thirty years ago, it was absurd to think that Americans would soon abandon cigarettes in droves—much less that they would begin stigmatizing and restricting those smokers who wouldn't quit. Yet it happened. Why? Because people came to understand that the damage from smoking far outweighed its pleasures.

Society Should Oppose Teen Pregnancy

The same is true of sex and childbirth among unwed teen-agers, of divorce and of much of the sex that takes place outside of marriage. Most Americans, however, seem resigned to living with the problem and all the damage it causes. A society can do that about as well as an individual can live with emphysema.

"If we are to make real progress against teen pregnancy, the long national silence about contraception and sexuality must end."

Improved Education Could Reduce Teen Pregnancy

Douglas J. Besharov

In the early 1990s, the federal government did little to reduce teen sex or teen pregnancy, according to Douglas J. Besharov. Besharov, a resident scholar at the American Enterprise Institute, a think tank in Washington, D.C., and a visiting professor at the University of Maryland School of Public Affairs, argues that this inattention appears to be changing, and he recommends a policy to the Clinton administration. He contends that abstinence should be taught, not preached, to those who have yet to become sexuality active. To those who are already active, Besharov recommends providing accurate and explicit information about reproduction, sex, contraception, and sexually transmitted diseases. Dealing with these issues in a straightforward manner, Besharov believes, will make teen pregnancy less likely.

As you read, consider the following questions:

1. Why are teenagers more likely to become pregnant than older women, according to the author?
2. What are some of the specific ideas Besharov has for reducing the incidence of teen pregnancy?
3. According to Besharov, how should parents deal with the subjects of teen sex and pregnancy?

Excerpted from "Teen Sex: Risks and Realism" by Douglas J. Besharov, *The American Enterprise*, March/April 1993. Copyright © 1993, *The American Enterprise*. Distributed by The New York Times/Special Features.

Despite its avowed commitment to traditional family values, the Bush administration never mounted a serious effort to reduce teen sex or teen pregnancy. This is likely to change. . . . When introduced by Bill Clinton in December 1992, [Surgeon General nominee Joycelyn] Elders made a point of telling the nation that she would be responsible for federal efforts to combat teen pregnancy. She said that her goal was "for every child to be a planned, wanted child."

Such attention to our 30-year rise in teenage pregnancies—and associated high rates of abortion, sexually transmitted diseases, and out-of-wedlock births—is long overdue. Unfortunately, there is a real danger that a revived federal effort, like programs in so many local communities, will become embroiled in controversies over condom distribution in the schools, alternative lifestyles, and the rights of parents to have a say in what their children are taught when the real solutions lie elsewhere.

Most sexually active teenagers engage in careful contraceptive practices most of the time, but large subgroups do not. To understand why they don't, we need to explore the interrelated problems of risky behavior, contraceptive failure, and intendedness.

Risky Behavior

Teenagers take risks. They experiment with alcohol. They drive fast. They feel indestructible. "Teenagers don't anticipate the next stage in life. They live for the moment," says Virginia Cartoof, a former social worker in inner-city Boston. Unprotected sex is just one of a host of dangerous behaviors in which they engage. . . .

Moreover, the more risky the teenager's overall behavior, the greater the likelihood of risky sex. Donald Orr and his colleagues at the University of Indiana studied condom use among inner-city female teenagers in Indianapolis and found that only about 50 percent of them reported that their partners had ever used condoms. Significantly, the figure fell to a frightening 29 percent among "risk-takers," defined as drug or alcohol users, school dropouts, and those who commit minor delinquencies.

Inner-city teens and young teens are not the only risk-takers, however. A study conducted by the University of Maryland found that 50 percent of females who sought a pregnancy test at the school's health center had not used a contraceptive. Reasons cited by these college students were: "I knew it was risky, but I took a chance" (62 percent); "I didn't think I'd have sex at the time" (56 percent); and "I'm not really very sexually active" (46 percent).

The etiquette of dating is another reason why so many teens (as well as older singles) do not use contraceptives. Call it the vestiges of Victorian morality or simply good manners, but many Americans do not think it is "right" to be prepared for casual sex. "It has to do with a puritanical society. For women especially, planning sex is not OK," explains Susan Davis, a contraception counselor at a Washington, D.C.-area Planned Parenthood office.

As a result, males and females of all ages are often caught without a contraceptive at the time of intercourse and end up having unprotected sex. This is a particular problem for teenagers, whose sexual experiences are rarely planned and often sporadic. Many girls do not want to admit, even to themselves, that they are sexually active. Says Ellen Godwin, a Planned Parenthood abortion counselor, "Getting the pill just establishes that in a very real way."

Fear is another reason why teenagers do not use the pill. They are afraid of the pill's possible side effects, particularly cancer, according to Dr. Doris Tirado, medical director of Planned Parenthood of Baltimore. Older women have the same fear. A 1985 Gallup poll found that 75 percent of American women surveyed believed that the pill caused "serious health problems." One-third thought the pill caused cancer, while an additional 30 percent thought it was linked to heart attacks and strokes. Actually, studies show that women who have used the pill will have fewer endometrial and ovarian cancers than those who have not.

Davis agrees that her clients have an inordinate fear of birth control pills. She says of cancer, "It's the fear of our times. Of course, [teenagers] don't think of pregnancy as carrying any risk. They have no understanding of the trade-off. There is so much fear associated with using the pill. We are constantly, constantly fighting the very negative feelings about the pill. Many women, of all ages, are convinced that they can get cancer, not heart disease. Always, it's that the pill causes cancer."

There is also a certain amount of selective cognition here. One young mother said, "I can't use the pill because it makes me sleepy," a side effect not discovered in over 30 years of use. Teens also dislike the pill because of possible weight gain, never thinking that pregnancy too can add pounds.

Contraceptive Failure

When social conservatives say that the only sure form of contraception is abstinence, they have a point. While some forms of contraception fail when they are used less often than others, they all fail sometimes. The recent use of the term "safer sex" rather than "safe sex" is a welcome recognition of the inevitable risks involved.

Contraceptive failure rates are often presented in two ways: the failure rates in clinical trials (usually involving married couples) and the failure rates of the "typical user" (based on surveys of the general population). Based on various studies, James

Trussell of Princeton University estimates that the clinical failure rate was 0.1 percent for the pill, 2 percent for the condom, and 6 percent for the diaphragm. However, the typical user failure rates were substantially higher: 3 percent for the pill, 12 percent for the condom, and 18 percent for the diaphragm.

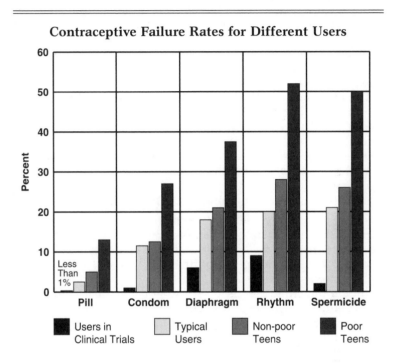

Contraceptive Failure Rates for Different Users

Sources: J. Trussell, R. Hatcher, W. Cates Jr., F.H. Stewart, and K. Kost, "Contraceptive Failure in the United States: An Update," *Studies in Family Planning*, vol. 21, no. 1, Jan/Feb 1990; and E. Jones and J.D. Forrest, "Contraceptive Failure Rates Based on the 1988 National Survey of Family Growth," *Family Planning Perspectives*, vol. 24, no. 1, Jan/Feb 1992.

Not surprisingly, teenagers have higher failure rates than do "typical users," with economically disadvantaged teenagers having even higher rates. Elise Jones and Jacqueline Dorroch Forrest, both of the Alan Guttmacher Institute (AGI), found that for never-married teenagers whose family incomes were under 200 percent of the poverty line, the reported failure rate for the pill was 13 percent, compared to 6 percent for their more affluent counterparts. Condom failure rates were also twice as high: 28 percent versus 13 percent. Failure rates for less effective methods are even higher: 52 percent to 27 percent for the rhythm method, and 50 percent to 26 percent for spermicides.

By now, the many ways that condoms can fail should be well known, but many people may not understand how so many teenagers who claim to be on the pill become pregnant. The modern pill contains much lower dosages of estrogen than the pill used in the 1960s and 1970s. While these newer pills cause significantly fewer side effects than the earlier ones, they also require more precise use. Missing just one pill puts a woman at risk of pregnancy. Missing more is an invitation to pregnancy, as Patty Aleman, a nurse-practitioner at the Capital Women's Center relates. "One college freshman came in for an abortion and said she was taking the pill. When I pressed her about it, she said, 'Well, I did miss three days.'"

The lifestyles of many teens are not consistent with maintaining this kind of daily routine. Virginia Cartoof found that many of her clients lived in crowded households where pills got lost. Often, there was no money to replace them immediately. Other teens did not always spend every night in the same place and would forget to take their pills along.

The Intendedness Question

Some contraceptive failures are the product of just plain ignorance. One teen client of a Planned Parenthood clinic told her counselor that she could not believe she was pregnant because she used her diaphragm every time she had sex. When the diaphragm was examined, it had a hole in the middle. The diaphragm the clinic had used for fitting clients had a hole in it, so according to the teen, "When I got home and noticed there was no hole in mine, I punched one in."

Nevertheless, the association between poverty and self-reported contraceptive failure rates raises the tricky question of intendedness. Some young people may consciously or unconsciously desire to become parents. As Cartoof explains: "For teenagers especially, motherhood is a way to achieve status. Not using birth control, in other words, may be a subconscious way of becoming a mother. So while many teenagers may say, 'I sure didn't want this to happen to me,' the fact of the matter is, there are significant benefits. They automatically become adults overnight. It gets them out of school." In studying residents of public housing in Atlanta, Robert Durante, associate professor of pediatrics at the Medical College of Georgia, and his colleagues found that in communities where the rates of adolescent pregnancy are high, adolescents do not believe that pregnancy would be a negative event in their lives. Consequently, they are less likely to try to prevent pregnancy.

Some inner-city males manipulate these feelings not only to obtain sex but also to quite deliberately get their girlfriends pregnant. University of Pennsylvania sociologist Elijah Anderson describes a sexual game where young girls are lured into having sex by the promises from older boys of love and marriage. Because the inner city has a dearth of good jobs, he argues, peer groups emphasize sexual prowess as evidence of manhood, with babies serving as proof.

Anderson quotes one woman who became pregnant at the age of 17 as remembering how the boys will "take you out. Walk you down to Center City, movies, window shop. They point in the window, 'Yeah, I'm gonna get this. Wouldn't you like this? Look at that nice livin' room set.' Then they want to take you to his house, go to his room: 'Let's go over to my house, watch some TV.' Next thing you know your clothes is off and you in bed havin' sex, you know."

What Can Be Done?

Improve sex education in the schools. Well-taught sex education courses increase knowledge, at least in the short run. But there are bad sex education courses as well as good ones. Some curricula are better than others, some teachers are more effective than others, and some students are better learners than others.

The lack of knowledge among teenagers about sexual matters is striking. Dr. Tirado bemoans the incredible ignorance of many adolescents about reproduction. "Many of them believe you can't get pregnant the first time you have intercourse."

The vast majority of people, including most parents, see sex education as the answer to this lack of knowledge. A 1985 Gallup poll, for example, found that a whopping 84 percent of parents agreed that "public high schools should include sex education in instructional programs."

The problem is that there is already a great deal of sex education going on. Almost all school districts offer some sort of sex education. A 1988 national survey by the Alan Guttmacher Institute found that 40 states and the District of Columbia either required or encouraged sex education, and a later AGI study found that 93 percent of teachers worked in schools that provided sex education.

The unavoidable conclusion is that many young people who have had sex education still seem abysmally ignorant about their own bodies and the reproductive process. Susan Davis gives educational talks to junior high students. She has found that although most of the girls have had some form of sex education, they do not understand their own reproductive cycles, and they do not know how to tell when they are ovulating and what time of the month sex is safest.

More disappointing, sex education programs appear to have little impact on young people's behavior. Reviewing research on sex education for *Pediatrics*, James Stout and Frederick Rivara of the University of Washington concluded, "The available evidence indicates that traditional sex education programs in junior and senior high schools have little or no effect either positively or negatively on altering the age of onset or frequency of adolescent sexual activity, on increasing contraceptive use, or on preventing unplanned teenage pregnancy."

We live in a time when two-thirds of all 17-year-olds cannot identify the Reformation or the Magna Carta and cannot place the Civil War in the correct half-century. Just as we need to improve the way we teach academic subjects like math, English, and history, so too must we improve sex education courses. There should be a sharper focus on the mechanical details of reproduction, contraception, and personal hygiene.

Being more explicit about sexually transmitted diseases might also help. Each year, about one in six sexually active teenagers contract a sexually transmitted disease, making disease a greater risk than pregnancy. To discourage smoking, some school health classes pass around pictures of smokers' lungs to show the negative consequences of smoking. The same could be done with pictures that show the effects of sexually transmitted diseases.

Earlier Sex Ed Will Help

For many young people, sex education comes too late. Between 30 percent and 50 percent of all teenagers receive their first real sex education course after the tenth grade, according to a 1988 AGI study. Yet we know that an increasing number of younger teens are sexually active. Analyzing data from the 1988 National Survey of Adolescent Males, Freya Sonenstein and her colleagues at the Urban Institute found that while 92 percent of 15- to 19-year-old males reported being taught about the biological aspects of sex, 34 percent had already had their first intercourse. Similarly, while 79 percent reported being taught about contraceptive methods, 39 percent had already had sex when they received the instruction; 73 percent were taught about AIDS, but 55 percent had already had sex; and 58 percent were taught about how to say no to sex, but 39 percent were already sexually active.

For most communities, then, local mores suggest that substantial sex education should start at least by the time that young people enter high school. Especially in earlier grades, the contents of the instruction should be sensitive to the developmental status of the children and the values of the community. We do not need more attempts, like that in New York City, to teach first graders a story about two lesbians who go to a "special doctor" to get artificially inseminated. The issue is not just homosexuality. Try to explain artificial insemination to a six-year-old. On second thought, don't.

Support abstinence. Adults tend to blame today's movies, TV, and music for teen sexuality, probably because these media are their main windows into the lives of the young. But peer pressure is at least an equal and certainly more proximate cause.

Many young girls—and boys—do not want to start having sex, but they feel forced to do so by peer pressure. The image most older people have about the initiation of teen sex is that of a young male, his hormones at full throttle, importuning the girl who is holding back. While this is no doubt still the predominant scenario, the modern world is more complicated. One 13-year-old boy described how he felt forced to have sex with his 14-year-old girlfriend after she repeatedly challenged him to prove his manhood, recounts Patricia Rodriguez, a graduate student at the University of Maryland.

"There is also pressure from one girl to another. I was talking with one 16-year-old girl who went out and had sex because her best friend did," notes Jane Pratt, the editor-in-chief of *Sassy*, a magazine for teenagers. "As it turned out, the friend was lying because she did not want to admit that she was a virgin."

Marion Howard, a professor of obstetrics and gynecology at Emory University, surveyed 1,000 teenage girls in Atlanta. When asked what subject they most wanted to learn about in sex education, 82 percent of the girls answered, "How to say no without hurting the other person's feelings."

Abstinence Education

Due in part to pressure from parents' groups, an increasing number of sex education courses mention abstinence. AGI reports that 40 states and the District of Columbia either require or encourage abstinence education.

Carefully controlled research has found that adding a message about abstinence to sex education efforts can reduce teen sexual activity, at least temporarily. Summarizing the literature on the subject, Brent Miller, a professor of Family and Human Development at Utah State University, writes, "Several programs that recently have shown positive effects on pregnancy-related behaviors include messages both to delay sexual involvement and to use contraception once sexual activity begins."

But in the real world, it is not clear how well the abstinence message is delivered. "They tell you that you shouldn't feel forced to have sex, that you should have sex only when you want to—when you are ready for it," recalls one 15-year-old. This same message is delivered to 13-year-olds and 17-year-olds alike, with no mention of how to decide when one is "ready." Echoing what many young people are taught about abstinence, the same 15-year-old says, "Oh, they never talk about that. It's up to you."

This kind of frank discussion is a well-intentioned—and necessary—effort to reduce the mystery and stigma associated with sex, but it leaves out an important concept: Sometimes, it can simply be too early to have sex. The signal that teens get suggests that when it comes to sex, even very young teenagers have the same rights as adults. Perhaps, but they do not have equal judgment. Younger teens especially should be unambiguously told to at least delay sexual activity. Schools have no compunctions about actively discouraging other unhealthy behaviors like smoking and drinking. They should be as aggressive about discouraging too-early sex.

Increase parental responsibility. Parents can also help, although many now feel powerless in the face of the rising tide of teen sexuality. A 1985 Harris poll, for example, found that only 4 percent of parents nationwide believed they had a "great deal of control over their teenagers' sexual activity," 37 percent thought they had "some control," but 40 percent said they had "not too much control," and 18 percent said that they had "no control at all."

They are wrong. Lines of communication and trust between parents and children can help instill wiser behavior. Thus, a key feature of many abstinence programs is parental involvement. For example, Reducing the Risk, an abstinence program in 13 California high schools, includes a class assignment that involves talking with parents about abstinence and contraception. . . .

Condoms and Teen Sex

Many professionals who study behaviors related to contraception advocate condom distribution in schools not so much to expand access to them, but as a way to erase Victorian notions about morality and sexuality (which would do more to encourage their use). And that's just why social conservatives and many parents oppose distribution so strenuously. They think that it will make sex among teenagers seem commonplace, thereby encouraging even more of it.

This is a tough trade-off to make, especially since there are so many other reasons for nonuse. . . .

More effective public and private responses to teen sexuality require that we come to grips with the realities of the behaviors involved. There needs to be sustained, public dialogue about young people's sexuality and how we can help them deal with it. The discussion must respect the sensibilities of all sides, but it must also be frank. This will not be easy, because of the discomfort that many of us, even those who think of themselves as social liberals, feel about public discussions of sexuality. But if we are to make real progress against teen pregnancy, the long national silence about contraception and sexuality must end. Good luck, Dr. Elders.

"We cannot respond effectively to teenage motherhood without responding also to the broader range of social problems that make motherhood seem to be a teenager's best option."

Improving Teenagers' Quality of Life Could Reduce Teen Pregnancy

Deborah L. Rhode

Many teenagers who get pregnant come from poor, inner-city neighborhoods, have little interest in education, have difficult family lives, and have little hope that the future will be better. In the following viewpoint, Deborah L. Rhode argues that in such circumstances, many teenage girls feel that having a child will improve their lives; they see little reason to try to avoid pregnancy. Rhode argues that society must take responsibility to help young women at risk of becoming pregnant overcome the racial, economic, and educational obstacles they face. Only then, she argues, will these teenagers feel that avoiding pregnancy is worthwhile. Rhode is a professor of law at Stanford University.

As you read, consider the following questions:

1. According to the author, why have both liberal and conservative attempts at reducing teen pregnancy fallen short?
2. How do the policy suggestions the author presents differ from others she describes as having been unsuccessful?

From "Adolescent Pregnancy and Public Policy" by Deborah L. Rhode. In *The Politics of Pregnancy*, Annette Lawson and Deborah L. Rhode, eds. New Haven: Yale University Press, 1993. Copyright © 1993 by Yale University. Reprinted with permission of the publisher.

During the past quarter-century, although fewer teens were having children, more were having sex, more were becoming pregnant, and more were becoming single mothers. By the late 1980s, the United States had the highest teen pregnancy rate in the developed world. Approximately 45 percent of adolescent females were sexually active before marriage, an increase of over 15 percent since 1971, and substantial numbers used contraceptives intermittently or ineffectively. The result was a million teen pregnancies each year, and about four-fifths of these were unintentional. An estimated four out of every ten American women were becoming pregnant at least once before age 20, a rate that has doubled since 1950. About half of that group were carrying their pregnancy to term (20 percent of all adolescents), and half of those who did so were unmarried. By the late 1980s, estimates indicated that less than 5 percent of all unmarried teens and less than 1 percent of blacks were placing their children for adoption, a dramatic shift from earlier eras. The rate of teenage childbirth among blacks has become almost two and one-half times greater than among whites; among Hispanics, the rates have become almost twice as great. Over a quarter of single black women have had at least one child by the age of 18. Although teens under age 15 have accounted for only 2 percent of all adolescent mothers, their rate of pregnancy has been increasing.

No Consensus

Although such patterns are widely assumed to constitute a social problem, there is no consensus on its cause or cure. At the risk of some oversimplification, it makes sense to distinguish two dominant positions in public debate. Most liberals "begin with the premise that teenagers should not have babies [while most] conservatives begin with the premise that single teenagers should not have sex." For conservatives, the problem involves primarily moral and fiscal concerns: premarital sexuality is not only objectionable in itself, it promotes other objectionable practices, such as abortion and the destruction of fetal "life," or nonmarital childbearing and the erosion of traditional values and financial self-sufficiency. For liberals, the problem involves primarily health and socioeconomic status: single parenthood is linked with disrupted education, reduced employment opportunities, and an increased likelihood of poverty for mothers, as well as heightened medical risks and developmental difficulties for their children.

Each of these definitions of the problem is itself problematic on both descriptive and prescriptive levels. Most conservative and liberal accounts distort the dynamic they seek to counteract. Both constituencies have overstated the adverse consequences of adolescent pregnancy and understated the barriers to addressing it. Such distortions are in some sense endemic to the American political process. The most effective way of getting an issue onto the policy agenda is usually to paint it as a crisis that can be addressed without major political conflict or financial expenditure. Yet the construction of the issue best suited to attracting public notice and building coalitions for reform is often ill-suited to generating adequate policy responses. This is clearly the case with adolescent pregnancy. Conflicting definitions of the problem have resulted in political compromises that are inadequate to serve societal needs.

Symptoms of Social Decay

From conservatives' perspective, recent increases in teenage sexuality, pregnancy, and nonmarital childbirth are both a cause and consequence of deeper social difficulties. As growing numbers of adolescents reject conventional family patterns, more adults have viewed the situation with subdued "moral panic." In their view, the problem is immorality, not poverty, and stems from cultural permissiveness, a decline in parental authority, and a weakening of community sanctions against illegitimacy. . . .

From conservatives' perspective, however, [many] policies are still too permissive. Public subsidies for birth-control programs are held accountable for legitimating conduct they should seek to prevent. According to New Right legislators such as former Senator Jeremiah Denton, author of the federal Adolescent and Family Life Act, "the most effective oral contraceptive yet devised is the word 'no.'" Under conservatives' analyses, any outreach program designed to prevent pregnancy rather than sex appears counterproductive; it encourages the activity that creates the problem.

Most available research, however, fails to support such claims. Studies of contraceptive and abortion services generally find no evidence that their availability has increased sexual activity. The vast majority of adolescents seek assistance only after they have engaged in sexual intercourse. Comparative data underscore the point. Many European countries have rates of adolescent sexual activity equivalent to those in the United States, but substantially higher rates of contraceptive use and lower rates of adolescent pregnancy and abortion.

Liberal Assumptions

Although liberals tend to be more permissive toward teenage sexual activity, they are typically no less judgmental than conservatives about teenage childbirth. Both groups share assumptions about the experience of adolescent pregnancy that rest on dubious factual premises. Most public debate conflates unintended with unwanted pregnancy and ignores data indicating that adolescent attitudes fall across a spectrum. The frequent caricature of children having children is highly distorted: two-thirds of all births to teenagers are to 18- and 19-year-olds, and only a tiny percentage are to mothers under 16. The equally common assumption that early pregnancy constitutes a direct path to poverty is equally exaggerated. The leading longitudinal study by Frank Furstenberg, Jeanne Brooks-Gunn, and S.P. Morgan, involving predominantly black adolescent mothers in Baltimore, found that the majority were eventually able to obtain a high school education, secure full-time employment, and avoid welfare dependency. About two-thirds of the children have completed or are close to completing comparable levels of schooling and only a quarter have become teenage parents themselves.

So, too, many factors commonly assumed to be consequences of early pregnancy—educational difficulties, low self-esteem, poverty, and unemployment—appear to be partial causes as well. For example, although adolescent mothers are more likely to drop out of school than peers of similar socioeconomic backgrounds, it is unclear how much of this difference is due to childbearing and how much to lower academic commitment and competence. Recent studies suggest that most young mothers leave school before becoming pregnant rather than the converse and that mothers who give birth while in school are as likely to graduate as their peers. If such findings are confirmed, then labeling early parenthood the paramount problem will misrepresent the appropriate solution.

Expanding Teenagers' Horizons

Teen pregnancy is less about young women and their sex lives than it is about restricted horizons and the boundaries of hope. It is about race and class and how those realities limit opportunities for young people. Most centrally, however, it is typically about being young, female, poor, and non-white and about how having a child seems to be one of the few avenues of satisfaction, fulfillment, and self-esteem. It would be a tragedy to stop worrying about these young women—and their partners—because their behavior is the measure rather than the cause of their blighted hopes.

Kristin Luker, *The American Prospect*, Spring 1991.

A growing number of scholars have also suggested that early pregnancies are more adaptive for economically and racially subordinate groups than is commonly acknowledged. According to researchers such as Arline Geronimus, Mary Edwards, and Mark

Testa, teenagers who are no longer in school may find advantages to having their most intensive parenting demands during a period when they have fewest employment opportunities and greatest access to free childcare assistance from their relatives. Since young black mothers are likely to live in an extended family, they often have better access to networks of kin support and childcare than older mothers. From a physiological standpoint, early motherhood is far less problematic than conventional accounts imply. Most health risks currently associated with teenage childbirth are attributable to socioeconomic status and the failure to obtain adequate prenatal care. If such care were available, some analysts believe that childbearing by poor women between ages 16 and 19 would pose fewer risks to mothers or newborns than later childbearing because many medical problems associated with poverty increase with age.

Disputed Conclusions

Such claims have become matters of considerable dispute. Some commentators challenge the conclusions regarding health difficulties and claim that if risks to infants after the first few months of birth are considered, early childrearing carries significant disadvantages. Recent research also suggests that a substantial number of young mothers remain outside of support networks and find family childcare inadequate. Even if, as the Baltimore study suggests, most adolescent mothers are eventually able to achieve financial independence, a significant number experience enduring poverty and many face prolonged periods of severe hardships. So, too, children of teenage mothers have disproportionate difficulties, such as high rates of delinquency and low rates of educational attainment. Although it is unclear how much of their problem is attributable to socioeconomic variables and how much to parental age and capacity, at least some evidence suggests that young adolescents are less well equipped for certain childbearing demands. In any event, the existence of such controversies points up the need for qualifications largely missing in current policy debates.

Similar qualifications are necessary to assess conventional solutions for the adolescent pregnancy "problem." Recent data call into question the widespread assumption that economically and racially subordinate groups gain significant benefits from deferring parenthood until marriage or the completion of education. Divorce rates for such young couples are substantial, and various factors, including relatively high rates of unemployment, violence, suicide, and substance abuse, have reduced the pool of eligible male partners. Although the extent to which such factors explain current racial differences in family formation remains subject to debate, it is clear that marriage is not an adequate solution for many pregnant adolescents.

Moreover, because women of color remain concentrated in occupations that offer low pay and little return for completing secondary education, they often have relatively little to lose from early childbearing. Thus, some longitudinal studies have found little difference in the labor market position of black women who gave birth in their teens and those who did not. Similar findings have emerged from research comparing adolescents who became mothers with their sisters who delayed childbearing: deferral of parenthood and additional schooling did not significantly increase income or reduce welfare dependency. By contrast, a recent study of largely black Baltimore teenagers found that those who obtained abortions did better economically and educationally than adolescents who gave birth, even after controlling for various demographic and motivational factors.

Although such conflicting data underscore the need for further research, one general point attracts widespread consensus. Childbirth patterns are responsive to socioeconomic and cultural forces that vary considerably across class, race, and ethnicity. As research . . . makes clear, expectations about future opportunities play an important role in shaping collective norms and individual choices at both conscious and preconscious levels.

The point of this discussion is not, as Arline Geronimus emphasizes, that "in the best of all possible worlds, teen childbearing would be personally or socially optimal." It is, however, to suggest that "we are very far from the best of all possible worlds, and that there are serious flaws in the logic of current policy approaches intended to get us there.". . .

Public Policy Solutions

In formulating more effective public policies, a critical first step is to convince decision makers and their constituents to rethink the problem that teenage pregnancy presents. No significant progress can occur as long as Americans view the issue in terms of individual rather than societal responsibilities and insist on policies that reflect traditional family values rather than contemporary adolescent needs. The alternative framework proposed here begins from different premises and demands different resource priorities. Its objectives are to enhance adolescents' capacity for informed and uncoerced choices and to expand the choices available. These objectives in turn require policy initiatives that not only increase birth-control information and assistance, but also respond more effectively to education, employment, health, and welfare needs.

A more promising policy approach will depend on more systematic research. Despite the recent attention to the adolescent pregnancy "crisis," we know surprisingly little about certain key issues. What factors predict effective use of contraceptives among sexually active teens? What strategies are most successful in promoting responsible sexual behavior and how do they differ across gender, class, age, race, and ethnicity? How much of the disadvantage for young mothers and their children is attributable to age and how much to other demographic and socioeconomic factors? What individual coping strategies and social programs are most effective in reducing that disadvantage?

Yet despite these gaps in current understanding, we know more than enough about the inadequacies of current frameworks to identify more promising alternatives. The most obvious inadequacy involves birth-control information and assistance. Widespread ignorance among teenagers concerning the substantial risks of unprotected sexual activity and the relatively low risks of contraceptive use demonstrates the need for fuller information. Increasing rates of AIDS among adolescents further underscore the urgency of that need. Yet since existing educational programs have had little measurable impact on contraceptive behavior, more innovative campaigns are necessary from multiple sources, including schools, community organizations, and the media.

"Voluntary Motherhood"

Such campaigns should include greater attention to decision-making skills for both sexes. Encouraging men to exercise greater responsibility in sexual relationships from an early age is a crucial part of reproductive freedom for women. More emphasis should also center on empowering female adolescents to resist pressures for unwanted sexual intercourse or parenthood. Many teenage women report engaging in sexual activity that they do not find pleasurable, and deciding to have a baby more because of peer and family influence than because of affirmative desires to rear a child. All too often, single motherhood becomes an ill-considered means to other ends: a way to assert independence, to punish parents, to gain prestige, or to win approval from their child's father. Better education, mentoring, peer counseling, and community outreach strategies should be available to help young women assess and assert their own best interests. Especially for young teenagers, abstinence can be a feminist strategy, but not on the terms conservatives usually offer. Rather, the objective should be a revived but reformulated understanding of what the nineteenth-century women's movement labeled "voluntary motherhood."

To make reproductive choices truly voluntary will also require more accessible birth control. A majority of sexually active teens lack adequate reproductive health services, and many are deterred by the cost, distance, nonconfidentiality, and stigma associated with existing clinics. To reduce unplanned pregnancies, we need to reduce the barriers to reproductive planning, such as parental notification and consent requirements, harassment of clinic users, and shortages of free or low-cost services. Comprehensive health programs located in or near schools are among the most promising outreach strategies, for they can avoid singling out participants who request contraceptive assistance and can offer accessible follow-up services. Development and distribution of alternative birth-control technologies, such as RU 486, should become higher public priorities.

Yet if we are serious about not just removing the obstacles to choice but expanding the choices available, further initiatives are necessary. First and most fundamental, we must find ways to improve school programs and reduce dropout rates. Particularly in low-income communities, the current educational structure seems irrelevant to immediate needs and promises little economic security. Female adolescents who lack confidence in their own abilities and future prospects often see little to lose from early pregnancy and childbearing. Low expectations about educational and vocational opportunities readily become self-fulfilling prophecies. Young women who leave school are disproportionately likely to become pregnant, to have multiple pregnancies, and to experience poverty and welfare dependency.

Breaking this cycle will require changing adolescents' aspirations and experience. More programs are needed to expand life-planning options, build self-confidence, improve school performance, increase literacy, and strengthen vocational skills. Additional support is necessary for scholarships and bilingual assistance. These initiatives must be coordinated with other opportunities for vocational training, job placement, and higher education, so that participants can see ways to achieve status and self-worth apart from early parenthood. We cannot respond effectively to teenage motherhood without responding also to the broader range of social problems that make motherhood seem to be a teenager's best option. Nor can we address the inadequacy of paternal support without also addressing the inadequacy of unemployment, education, and drug treatment opportunities.

Welfare Reform

The importance of some of these initiatives has attracted growing attention. Recent changes in federal welfare regulations require adolescent AFDC [Aid to Families with Dependent Children] recipients to obtain job training and skills instruction if childcare is available, and to participate in continuing education if they lack a high school degree. Although the effectiveness of these requirements has yet to be assessed, past experience with similar vocational programs suggests grounds for caution. Participants typically register minor income gains in comparison with program cost. So, too, recent efforts to increase paternal child support for AFDC families are likely to be of limited effectiveness, given most fathers' inadequate financial resources. Significant progress for adolescent parents is likely to require broader macroeconomic interventions and antipoverty initiatives, such as increases in minimum wage, job-creation strategies, and expanded health, housing, childcare, family counseling, and income-transfer policies.

More emphasis must also center on expanding prenatal services and coordinating responses to various risk-taking behaviors, including drug and alcohol abuse, as well as unprotected sexual activity. The necessity of such initiatives is underscored by the increasing number of infants who are deformed or disabled as a result of maternal addictions. Recent efforts to prosecute addicted mothers rather than provide adequate treatment programs again points up the risks in placing blame at the individual rather than societal level. It is neither just nor effective to condemn teenage mothers who make tragic choices while ignoring the constraints on choices that are available.

All these policy initiatives must be formulated with greater community involvement and more responsiveness to variations within and among ethnic groups. Third-generation Puerto Rican women have different concerns from those of recent emigrees from Mexico, and blacks from urban ghettos face different constraints from those of teenagers from middle-class suburbs or impoverished rural communities. Public policies need to take fuller account of culturally specific attitudes and kinship support structures affecting early childbirth. No single set of interventions will be equally effective with all subgroups; rather, we need multiple strategies that directly enlist families at risk.

The policy alternatives identified here do not constitute a modest agenda. But neither can we expect major progress until we translate our rhetorical concerns into resource commitments. Coherent policies on teenage pregnancy require a redirection of adult priorities.

Periodical Bibliography

The following articles have been selected to supplement the diverse views presented in this chapter.

Nan Marie Astone	"Thinking About Teenage Childbearing," *Report from the Institute for Philosophy and Public Policy*, Summer 1993. Available from University of Maryland, College Park, MD 20742.
Douglas J. Besharov	"A Moral Choice," *National Review*, August 9, 1993.
Lawrence Criner	"The Condom Brigade," *The Wall Street Journal*, July 23, 1993.
Edwin J. Delattre	"Condoms and Coercion," *Vital Speeches of the Day*, April 15, 1992.
Linda Ellerbee	"Remembering Immortality," *Liberal Opinion Week*, June 21, 1993. Available from 108 E. Fifth St., Vinton, IA 52349.
Sarah Glazer	"Preventing Teen Pregnancy," *The CQ Researcher*, May 14, 1993. Available from 1414 22nd St. NW, Washington, DC 20037.
Gayle Hanson	"Norplant Joins War on Teen Pregnancy," *Insight*, March 8, 1993.
Barbara Kantrowitz	"A 'Silver Bullet' Against Teen Pregnancies?" *Newsweek*, December 14, 1992.
Mary McGrory	"Surgeon General Nominee Dares to Face Teen Pregnancy," *Liberal Opinion Week*, July 26, 1993.
Nancy Meanix	"Molly Kelly the Chastity Lady," *St. Anthony Messenger*, November 1992. Available from 1615 Republic St., Cincinnati, OH 45210.
Richard John Neuhaus	"A Better Choice," *National Review*, August 9, 1993.
Richard John Neuhaus	"The Wrong Way to Go," *National Review*, February 1, 1993.
Susan Tifft	"Better Safe Than Sorry?" *Time*, January 21, 1991.
Louise Warrick et al.	"Educational Outcomes in Teenage Pregnancy and Parenting Programs: Results from a Demonstration," *Family Planning Perspectives*, July/August 1993. Available from The Alan Guttmacher Institute, 111 Fifth Ave., New York, NY 10003.
Mike Yorkey	"Charting a Different Course," *Focus on the Family*, November 1992. Available from PO Box 35500, Colorado Springs, CO 80935-3550.

Is Sex Education Necessary?

TEENAGE
SEXUALITY

Chapter Preface

The subject of sex education ignites arguments that, in their volume and passion, almost match those on the related subject of abortion. But unlike the abortion debate, which tends to have just a few clear-cut issues, there is a wide spectrum of opinion on whether sex education belongs in schools and, if it does, what kind of education it should be.

Thus on the broad battlefield of sex education are scattered skirmishes among disparate groups. In one corner are parents fighting for their right to present sexuality to their children in their own way—or not at all—versus those who see sex education in public schools as a vital need in today's world or a moral obligation of society to its youth. On another side of the field are those who believe education should stress abstinence (allied occasionally with those who believe it should teach conservative moral or religious values) in grim battle with those who insist sex should be presented as a positive, enjoyable, and guilt-free activity (perhaps seconded by those who believe society must encourage acceptance of all sexual lifestyles).

In a central spot on the battlefield yet another group is making a stand. It insists that teens will engage in sex no matter what, so they must be told how to avoid pregnancy. This group's foes include, among others, those who believe sex should only be used for procreation; those who believe teaching about birth control condones and encourages sexual activity; and those who want society to insist on celibacy for all except those in a mutually faithful monogamous marriage. Right next to this skirmish, a contingent that a decade ago worried about the contagion of herpes—a painful sexually transmitted disease (STD) that has no cure—has been joined by legions of those who are terrified by the spread of AIDS. Some of them advocate strong programs emphasizing ways to minimize the dangers of contracting AIDS and other STDs. They are assailed by those who insist that "the only safe sex is no sex."

The issues are heartfelt. And the consequences of each choice are critical. The authors of the following viewpoints tread a minefield as they attempt to define paths toward the various goals they see as paramount.

"We owe it to our children and their children to provide them with the [sexual] information they need."

Sex Education Is Necessary

Sol Gordon

Sex education in public schools has remained a controversial issue for over two decades. Critics of sex education argue that teaching students about sex causes them to experiment, while supporters counter that information about reproduction is necessary to combat unwanted pregnancy and sexually transmitted diseases. The following viewpoint is written by psychologist Sol Gordon, professor emeritus at Syracuse University and a well-known expert on sex education. In it, he argues that quality sex education is necessary to help teenagers deal with their sexuality.

As you read, consider the following questions:

1. According to Gordon, why does the United States have a high rate of teenage pregnancy?
2. Why does the author write that parents and the media are ineffective sex educators?
3. What types of questions does Gordon think sex education should address?

"What Kids Need to Know" by Sol Gordon, *Psychology Today*, October 1986. Reprinted with permission from *Psychology Today* magazine. Copyright © 1986 American Psychological Association.

If you tell kids about sex, they'll do it. If you tell them about VD [venereal disease], they'll go out and get it. Incredible as it may seem, most opposition to sex education in this country is based on the assumption that knowledge is harmful. But research in this area reveals that ignorance and unresolved curiosity, not knowledge, are harmful.

Our failure to tell children what they want and need to know is one reason we have the highest rates of out-of-wedlock teen pregnancy and abortion of any highly developed country in the world. And we pay a big price monetarily and otherwise in dealing with the more than one million teenage pregnancies every year, as well as several million new cases of sexually transmitted diseases.

Poor education, of course, is only one cause of teenage pregnancy. Such factors as poverty, racism and sexism are even more crucial. But there is ample evidence to show that relevant sex education is part of the solution to teenage pregnancy.

At the Institute for Family Research and Education at Syracuse University, we have been studying questions related to sex education for more than 15 years. Some people still seem to think they can and should be the only sex educators of their children. My response is, "How can that be? You'll have to wrap your children in cotton and not allow them to leave their bedrooms, watch TV or read newspapers or current magazines. You certainly can't allow them to have any friends or go to any public school bathroom."

The idea that kids get information about sex from their parents is completely erroneous. Even the college-educated parents of my Syracuse University students offer very little. In survey after survey in a period of 12 years involving more than 8,000 students, fewer than 15 percent reported that they received a meaningful sex education from their parents. Usually girls were told about menstruation. The rest of the teaching could be summed up in one word: DON'T. The boys were on their own except for an occasional single prepuberty talk with Dad, who made vague analogies involving the birds and bees and ended the talk with "if worst comes to worst, be sure to use a rubber."

Poor Sex Education

One reason parents have for not educating their children is discomfort with their own sexual feelings and behavior. Part of this discomfort derives from the fact that they themselves received little or no sex education as children. Without one's parents to draw upon as a model, the cycle of noncommunication is repeated from generation to generation.

If parents don't do the job, do kids get their sex education through the media? Of course not. TV is full of antisexual messages of rape, violence and infidelity. This is especially true of the soaps, watched by an increasingly large number of teenagers via delayed video recordings. When was the last time you saw a really good sex-education program on TV or an article in your local newspaper? There are a few exceptions to this sex-education wasteland. Teenagers who read, particularly girls, do get some good information from Judy Blume and her novels, such as *Forever* and *Are You There God? It's Me, Margaret,* and magazines such as *Teen* and *Seventeen*.

LEARNING THE HARD WAY

© Rosen/Rothco. Reprinted with permission.

What about schools? Probably fewer than 10 percent of American schoolchildren are exposed to anything approaching a meaningful sex education. There are some good programs and some dedicated and well-trained teachers, but I doubt there are a dozen school districts that have a kindergarten through 12th-grade sex-education program that even approaches those available in Sweden. American teenagers typically score abysmally low on sex-knowledge questionnaires.

Sex education in the United States today, where it exists at all, is usually a course in plumbing—a relentless pursuit of the fallopian tubes. The lack of real education is obscured by the answers to surveys that ask students if they've had sex education in their schools. More than half respond, "Yes." What most surveys don't ask—or if they do, what doesn't get reported—are the really important questions such as:

(Q) How much sex education did you have?

(A) Two classes in menstruation for girls only in the sixth grade.

(Q) How effective was the education?

(A) I slept through it.

(Q) By whom was it taught?

(A) One gym teacher proclaimed to the boys, "Hey fellows, the thing between your legs is not a muscle—don't exercise it."

Useful sex education should tell children what they want and need to know. And we know what they want to know. At the Institute for Family Research and Education at Syracuse University, we have reviewed more than 50,000 questions teenagers from all over the country have submitted, anonymously, to us and to their teachers. Not one teenager has ever asked a question about fallopian tubes. Young people want to know about homosexuality, penis size, masturbation, female orgasm, and the answers to such questions as how can I tell if I'm really in love, what constitutes sexual desire, what is the best contraceptive, when are you most likely to get pregnant and various questions about oral and anal sex. Recently, the most frequent one seems to be why boys are only interested in girls for sex.

Proper Framework

Before I talk to teenagers about questions like these, I try to place the issue of sexuality in a proper framework. I tell kids that of the 10 most important aspects of a mature relationship, number one is love and commitment. Number two is a sense of humor. (I advise parents not to have teenagers unless they have a sense of humor.) Number three is meaningful communication. Sex is somewhere down on the list, just ahead of sharing household tasks together.

I also tell them that I, like most parents, don't think teenagers should engage in sexual intercourse. They are too young and too vulnerable. They aren't prepared to handle the fact that the first experiences of sex are usually grim. Almost no one will have an orgasm. The boy gets his three days later when he tells the guys about it.

Fewer than one in seven use a reliable form of contraception the first time they have sex. In contrast, the large majority of Swedish teenagers use contraception the very first time and consistently afterwards. But knowing that most teenagers will have sex before they finish high school, I say to them, if you are not going to listen to me (or your parents) about postponing sex, use contraception.

The simple message—No. Don't, Stop—doesn't work. The double message—No, But. . . .—is more effective. Look at how alcohol education is now being handled by many parents and school organizations. They say, "I don't think you should drink, but if you get carried away and you drink anyway, don't drive. Call me and we'll arrange alternate transportation." When it comes to premarital sex, a parent might start with "No" and try to convince the teenager to hold back but also provide the "But"—reliable contraceptive information. As the Talmud says, expect miracles but don't count on them. . . .

Other Questions

What else do we need to tell young people? Tell the boys not to worry about penis size. You can't tell the size of the penis by observing its detumescent state. (Freud got it wrong—men are the ones with penis envy.) Reassure girls about their vaginas— one size fits all.

A Right to Know

I believe that education about sexuality is information that students have a right and a need to know, just as they have a right and a need to know fractions or English grammar. If we approach sexuality education with this goal uppermost in mind (rather than viewing sexuality education as a political statement, as a way of solving the teenage pregnancy problem or as a way of gaining access to students for other services), we are forced to focus on creating programs that make it as easy as possible for teachers to present sensitive information accurately, and in a manner that enables students to learn, to retain knowledge and to apply what they've learned.

Lana D. Muraskin, *Family Planning Perspectives,* July/August 1986.

One or a few homosexual experiences or thoughts don't make a person homosexual. Homosexuals are people who in their adult lives are attracted to and have sexual relations with others of the same sex. The preference is not subject to conscious control. Sexual orientation is not a matter of choice. It's not OK to be antigay.

For teenagers, few questions are as urgent as: How can I tell if I'm really in love? I've probably listened to more nonsense in this area than any other. I've heard the same rubbish so many times that I've come up with some standard responses to the following:

Love is blind. I think love is blind for only 24 hours. Then you have to open your eyes and notice with whom you're in love.

Love at first sight. I advise people to take another look.

You can fall in love only once. This silly idea can have tragic results. How many young Romeos and Juliets have committed suicide after the breakup of a torrid love affair, thinking that life is over for them? No, I tell them, you can fall in love at least 18 times.

Will I know when I'm really in love? Certainly. If you feel you are in love, you are. (Parents should never trivialize a teenager's love affair. However brief, it's always serious.) But I tell teenagers there are two kinds of love—mature love and immature. Mature lovers are energized. They want to please each other. They are nice to parents who are nice to them. Immature love is exhausting. Immature lovers are too tired to do their schoolwork. They are not nice to those they should care about—parents, siblings, even their dogs and cats.

The Need for Sex Education

Sex-education courses that cover even a few of these real concerns are being taught almost nowhere in this country. It's up to parents to make a start, whether they are comfortable with the subject or not. You don't have to be comfortable to educate your children. I daresay most of us are uncomfortable about a lot of things these days, but we keep doing our jobs anyway. We should at least teach teachers, psychologists, clergy, social workers and others who work with youngsters how to respond to young people's questions.

We owe it to our children and their children to provide them with the information they need in a manner they will accept. I sometimes use humor. It helps reduce anxiety and puts teenagers in a receptive mood. An old Zen expression says, "When the mind is ready a teacher appears."

"The disparity between the sexual code propounded at school and that generally promoted at home has only grown greater."

Sex Education
Is Harmful

Dana Mack

Dana Mack is an affiliate scholar at the Institute for American Values in New York, an organization that researches issues relating to the American family. In the following viewpoint, Mack argues that the comprehensive sex education programs most teenagers receive in school are harmful and cannot succeed in preventing teenagers from having sex. Mack maintains that the programs undermine family values and actually encourage young people to have sex by presenting sexuality as a viable option for unmarried teenagers.

As you read, consider the following questions:

1. How does Mack describe the first sex education programs of the early 1970s? How do these programs compare with those of today?
2. What aspects of the current sex education programs does Mack believe are inappropriate or harmful?
3. According to the author, what conclusions should be drawn from the research done in Falmouth, Massachusetts?

From "What the Sex Educators Teach" by Dana Mack. Reprinted from *Commentary*, August 1993, by permission; all rights reserved.

When I was in elementary school, a quarter of a century ago, sex education was a matter of one or two delicate films on the physical signs of "growing up." At the age of ten or eleven, girls and boys were herded into separate rooms—usually in the company of a parent. There, in industrial-gray pictures and solemn monotones, they were introduced to the world of gametes, ovaries, and menstruation. Not exactly titillating material, this reproductive information. But those were the days when teenage boys and girls still glanced shyly at each other across dance floors—before carnal knowledge had become a *cause célèbre* of education.

Comprehensive Sexuality Education

Today, as everyone knows, sex education is a different story altogether. In a growing number of schools, children are no longer allowed to approach puberty wondering over the mysteries of love. The pleasures of sex are bared for them, and all the latest sexual paraphernalia explored. These are the days when kids pass condoms, "dental dams" (a kind of condom for oral sex), and "finger cots" (condoms that fit over the finger for heavy petting) around the classroom—the days of "comprehensive sexuality education," where all erotic possibilities are unveiled.

It was in the early 70's that the schools first determined to get involved in teaching children about sex. For many educators who came fresh from the university, the 60's doctrines of sexual "liberation" were calls to action. They assumed the task of disseminating these doctrines to a high-school youth still largely under the sway of parental influences they considered all too retrograde and all too chaste.

So successfully was this task performed that by the end of the 70's a government-sponsored national evaluation of the goals of sex-education programs in American high schools glowingly revealed that a catechism of liberation had already entrenched itself. According to this study, commissioned by the Department of Health, Education, and Welfare during the Carter administration, the most "exemplary" sex-education programs were on the way to fostering significant "changes in sexual attitudes and behaviors" by promoting "a reduction of sexual guilt" and "an acceptance of alternative life-styles."

It was, of course, noted that the anti-traditional "values" conveyed in sex-education classes were "not supported by all members of society"—that, indeed, they were "in conflict with the belief held by some [sic] people that sex should be enjoyed only within the context of marriage." But both educators and government officials either ignored such people or dismissed them out of hand.

In the years since this first comprehensive evaluation appeared, the disparity between the sexual code propounded at school and that generally promoted at home has only grown greater. Educators and liberal policy-makers, probably sensing the possibility of an AIDS-inspired resurgence of sexual austerity, have extended their imperial designs from the postpubescent to the prepubescent population. In many school districts, discussions of human sexuality have now entered the early elementary grades; and these discussions are broaching topics—from "self-pleasuring" to pedophilia—which even the most daring parents would be hard put to discuss comfortably with their young children.

Thus, *The National Guidelines For Comprehensive Sexuality Education*, published in 1991 by the Sex Information and Education Council of the U.S. (SIECUS), advises that children as young as five be told that "it feels good to touch parts of the body," that "some men and women are homosexual, which means that they will be attracted to . . . someone of the same gender," and that "adults kiss, hug, touch, and engage in other sexual behavior with one another to show caring and to share sexual pleasure."

Indeed, in those 70 or so school districts which have implemented the *Learning About Family Life* curriculum designed by Barbara Sprung and published by Rutgers University Press, there are no more secrets of connubial love, even for kindergartners. They know exactly what their parents are doing at night in bed, and what fun they are having doing it. The curriculum explains sexual relations to five-year-olds in the following way: ". . . The man puts his penis in the woman's vagina and that feels really good for both of them. . . ."

Innocence Lost

Even if they have not been thus instructed in kindergarten, children are likely to learn in the next few years about other varieties of sexual pleasure and sensual adventure. By fourth or fifth grade they know enough about conception and sexual disease to unroll condoms on bananas, and to discuss the merits of mutual masturbation as an alternative to "higher-risk" involvement. By seventh grade they are reviewing the pleasures and perils of oral and anal sex, using the street names for these acts (so as—in the words of one AIDS educator—to "get beyond the euphemism of sexual language"), and role-playing "limit-setting" situations in which such hygiene-conscious responses as "No glove, no love!" will become dating reflexes. And in high school—between trips to the nurse's office for condoms—they consider the manifold options of sexual pluralism: bisexuality, transvestism, sadomasochism, even bestiality.

It seems that no age is too young, no act too depraved to be excluded from the zealous reach of the "sexuality-education" experts. To these educators, the sooner and the more completely kids are divested of innocence in sexual matters, the less vulnerable they will be to repression, victimization, and disease. Thus, if the trend-setters of SIECUS have their way (and, increasingly, they are getting it), kindergartners across the country will become comfortable with their genitals by shouting "penis" and "vulva" in the classroom. And if Planned Parenthood has its way, our high-school students will, as a matter of course, debate the ecstasies versus the risks of brachiopractic penetration (better known as "fisting"—i.e., the practice among homosexuals of inserting an entire fist into the partner's anus).

A Perversion of Nature

Group sex education amounts to a perversion of nature. It makes public and open that which is naturally private and intimate. Any teaching about sex in a public setting violates privacy and intimacy. Sex education in the classroom is an insidious and unnatural invitation to sexual activity; it is erotic seduction; and it is even a form of child molestation, violating the natural latency and post-latency periods of child development, periods which are crucial for normal development of the whole person.

Randy Engel, interviewed in *The New American*, January 27, 1992.

It should be mentioned here that love and romance play no part in the brave new world of sexual instruction. When children become amorous, the sex-education experts contend, their rational judgment becomes impeded and contraception and disease-prevention are inhibited. Only by "breaking through fantasy and emotional barriers" and by indoctrinating students in a series of "rational . . . behavior sequences" involving "negotiating skills" and "explicit scripts," these experts say, can we bring our children into adulthood alive, sexually uninhibited, healthy, and childless.

Most evaluations, even the friendliest, of contemporary sex-education programs—whether of classroom health instruction, of condom-availability programs, or of school-based contraceptive clinics—reveal the startling ineffectuality of this cold and licentious approach to human sexuality. Yet, though evidence mounts to show that sex education is failing miserably in its self-proclaimed efforts to stem early childbearing and sexual disease, educators refuse to reconsider the wisdom of their approach.

To be sure, statistics on teenage pregnancy and venereal disease suggest that children in white middle-class areas are better able than their contemporaries in the urban ghettos to weather the implicit attacks on morality and family life waged by state-of-the-art sex-education programs. But my own research also suggests that our more socioeconomically fortunate children are by no means entirely immune.

This research was conducted in 1992 in Falmouth, Massachusetts, a small town nestled on the southwestern tip of Cape Cod. Falmouth is predominantly an adult community. It features pristine white colonial guest houses, up-scale boutiques, summer residences, a significant population of retirees, and a world-class institute of marine science. It does not feature a large number of children. Out of a total population of 27,000, Falmouth's public-school enrollment comes to fewer than 5,000.

One would think, considering its demographic makeup, that education in Falmouth would reflect the values of a staid and rather sleepy community. No such thing. Falmouth is near the cutting edge of sex education, boasting not only a sex-education curriculum well in the spirit of the SIECUS guidelines, but the most radical condom-availability program in the nation. It is the first (and up to now the only) program to encompass junior high as well as high school, the first and only to offer condoms to children as young as twelve without parental permission.

Two mandatory eighth- and ninth-grade sex-education classes in Falmouth have been in existence since the AIDS scare hit the media with force a decade ago. Like most such courses today, these are ostensibly directed toward abating "high-risk behavior" among teenagers. According to the school Health Coordinator, Helen Ladd, they stress "sexual decision-making skills" and "values clarification" rather than morality. That is, they disdain traditional rules of sexual conduct as quaint and judgmental, preferring to offer children "information" and the "choice" of being sexually active or not.

Sex-education instructors, however, make the "choice" of sexual activity look far more acceptable than that of celibacy. While students are told, in explicit detail and over a period of many weeks, how to stimulate their partner's erogenous zones, how to initiate casual sex, and how to keep it safe from pregnancy and disease, only 45 minutes each semester are devoted to sexual abstinence. The full range of intimate relationships is probed in the classroom, but embarrassment in sexual matters is hardly tolerated. Conception and childbearing are discussed, but marriage, says Ladd, is never mentioned as a prerequisite to parenthood. The gamut of sexual orientations (including bisexuality and transvestism) is introduced, without prejudice as to whether some might be more wholesome than others. As for family life, it is touched upon only in discussions of child/parent conflict, battering, and incest. . . .

Sex-Ed Ideology

Considering that they were subjected to a two-year propaganda campaign, it is not difficult to understand why many

137

Falmouth citizens—and many parents among them—came to regard condom availability in the schools as necessary public intervention. Nor, under these circumstances, is it surprising that Falmouth parents have paid little attention to the active competition the school is waging for the souls of their children, or of the battle it has pitched between the conflicting ideals of teenage sexual continence and libertinism, between a family-centered and a self-centered world view.

Nor, finally, is it a wonder that those who do challenge the sex-education program for its ideological slant find themselves labeled as troublemakers and religious fanatics. "We are pretty much treated like outcasts," laments James Remillard, the president of Concerned Citizens. Remillard blames this ill will more on ignorance than on spite or on fundamental differences in sexual morality. Parents, he says, respect the schools as public institutions, and want to trust educators. They are generally unaware of the more controversial elements of the sex-education program, because the school makes it a point to misrepresent the program as largely informational.

But if Remillard exonerates parents to some extent, he is becoming ever more suspicious that educators will stop at nothing to undermine parental authority in the interests of pushing their notions of teenage sexual liberation. . . .

Sex Is Commonplace for Teenagers

The school nurse at Falmouth High, Shirley Cullinane, estimates that about half of the students there are sexually active. While many of these boys and girls are promiscuous, and boastful about their promiscuity, some of the girls complain about feeling pressured to have sex. "Some of the [older] boys have four and five girls," she contends. Why do the girls stand for being treated as nothing better than concubines? Because, it seems, they (and especially the younger ones) like the attention and the social prestige of dating, even though it often presumes unwelcome sex.

Cullinane, the mother of seven, tries to talk to Falmouth High students about her own innocent high-school years, and about her celibate two-year courtship with her husband. "They think I'm lying . . . when I say I was a virgin when I got married," she says of their reaction. "The girls think there is no way you can go out with a man for two years and not have sex with him."

But Cullinane, like the Health Issues instructors, does not advocate abstinence. Rather, in the conviction that she cannot change student behavior, she tries to encourage students to protect themselves from pregnancy and sexual disease by using condoms.

This effort has not been crowned with success. Cullinane gave out approximately five condoms a week, when the condom-availability program was instituted. These, she says, went mostly to girls. But in the first two months of the 1992-93 school year, despite consistently offering them to youngsters she knew were sexually active, she was able to dispense only two condoms—both to the same freshman male.

Why do the students spurn condoms, even when the school nurse offers them free of charge? Some refuse on the basis that they dull sexual feeling. But most, Cullinane believes, refuse because they "trust" the people with whom they are having sexual relations to be free of sexual diseases. There is little fear of HIV infection among Falmouth's youth, probably because these children know—despite all the propaganda to the contrary—that it poses little danger to non-drug-using heterosexuals.

Yet where other sexually transmitted diseases (STD's) are concerned, Falmouth's teenagers are simply reckless. School health instructors issue warnings about the risks of diseases other than AIDS, but these go in one ear and out the other. Even the Falmouth Schools' Health Coordinator, Helen Ladd, laments that students do not care what they are told about VD "risks." "I would be hesitant to sell my prevention program on the basis of numbers," she says. And well she should be hesitant. According to Massachusetts Board of Health statistics, the incidence of chlamydia among 15- to 19-year-olds in Falmouth has increased 300 percent since 1989.

More of Everything

In the nine years since the Health Issues sex-education course was conceived at Falmouth High, so also have an impressive number of babies been conceived. Teenage pregnancy in town is in fact rising by 10 percent a year, and is cutting across all socioeconomic barriers.

While many of the babies conceived to teenagers are aborted, single motherhood is also on the rise. In 1992, 49 babies were born to teenage mothers in Falmouth (up from 38 in 1991). Forty-five of these mothers were single, their average age the youngest ever—17.9 years.

Faced with the clear failure of school policies and programs regarding pregnancy and venereal disease, what does the school health administration have to suggest? More of everything. For one, more condoms: Cullinane says that students do not really like the condoms the school offers, so it will be changing brands in the hope of finding a more comfortable fit and appealing look. For another, more information about the spread and symptoms of sexual disease. For still another, more suspension of moral judgment on sexual activity, so that children will feel "comfortable" about coming for advice and condoms. (Yet according to Cullinane herself, girls now "come in four or five at a time . . . and sit around my office talking about . . . oral sex.") And then, more warnings about risk-taking, and even more mandatory courses—presumably offering more discussion of "defensive strategies," more disparagement of "gender roles," and more "alternatives" in sexual behavior.

The "more of everything" theory is a promising one, no doubt, for those who make a living off adolescent anxiety and sex. But it is hardly the answer to the well-being of Falmouth's teenagers, who are already alienated by the profusion of hygienic "information" (and misinformation) in the classroom, who refuse the "support system" of sexual counseling, and who want nothing to do with sexual "alternatives."

And it is the "alternatives" which make them most uncomfortable. Indeed, while students display skepticism toward the school's crusade against AIDS, STD's, and date rape, they express outspoken ridicule toward its crusade for sexual diversity. In particular they remain relentlessly and vocally intolerant of homosexuality, openly joking about it in the classroom in obvious efforts to gall the instructors. . . .

"How would you react if a boy, here, at Falmouth High asked you out?" a teacher demands of the males during a classroom discussion of "homophobia." The answers she receives are so brutal as to prompt one to pray there are no budding homosexuals present in the classroom.

Instructors tend to blame student resistance to the portrayal of homosexuality as a viable and wholesome life-style on backward parents who instill "traditional" values at home. But there is little evidence that parents are forcing untoward prejudices on their young. Rather the opposite. Parents who support the condom-availability program note the innate conservatism of their children in the matter of homosexuality with some regret and dismay, many expressing the hope that they will eventually learn to "live and let live" without sitting so cruelly in judgment. Many other parents also acknowledge that classroom discussion of homosexuality taps into deep-seated adolescent fears—both of identification and confrontation with homosexuals.

But if these parents would only awaken from their school-day nap, they would find that the issue of homosexuality is not the only component of sex education which is shaking down their children's delicate and immature sexual constitutions. All the various components of programs like the one in Falmouth add up to a philosophy which, in extolling the validity and pleasure of the sexual experience without reference to love, intimacy, or long-term commitment, while simultaneously sending the message that males are rapacious predators and females helpless victims, has left children feeling resentful, angry, and confused—and even more vulnerable than ever to disease and early pregnancy.

"Young people should question, explore, and assess sexual attitudes and feelings to develop their own values."

Schools Should Provide Candid Education on Sexuality Topics

Debra W. Haffner

In the following viewpoint, Debra W. Haffner, executive director of Sex Information and Education Council of the United States (SIECUS), posits that teaching comprehensive and thorough sexuality education classes starting in the early years and continuing through high school is the best way to encourage healthy attitudes toward sex in adulthood. According to Haffner, young people must learn to develop values in order to make good decisions about their sexuality and this moral decision making is a fundamental component of successful sex education.

As you read, consider the following questions:

1. Haffner maintains that there are four primary objectives for a comprehensive sex education program. What are they and why are they important?
2. Why does the author believe the support of religious organizations is necessary to successful sex education?
3. What are sex education programs supposed to accomplish, according to Haffner?

From "Sexuality Education in Public Schools" by Debra W. Haffner, *Education Digest*, September 1992. Reprinted by permission of the author.

Sexuality education is the lifelong process of acquiring information and of forming attitudes, beliefs, and values about identity, relationships, and intimacy. School-based sexuality education is more than anatomy and physiology. It includes an understanding of sexuality in its broadest context—sexual development, reproductive health, interpersonal relationships, affection and intimacy, body image, and gender roles. "Sexuality education"—rather than "sex education"—conveys the holistic nature of the instruction.

Appropriate Sex Education

Most professional educators believe it is important for school systems to implement comprehensive K-12 programs in sexuality education, with subject matter and content appropriate to each age and grade/developmental level. In earlier grades, topics may be integrated into comprehensive health education programs and may help children learn about family relationships, growth and development, self-esteem, and good health habits. These topics may help children begin to identify peer pressure and develop decision-making skills. Programs will become more specific about human sexuality as children approach puberty.

A comprehensive school-based sexuality education program should have four primary objectives:

Information. Young people should have accurate information about human sexuality, including growth and development, human reproduction, anatomy, physiology, masturbation, family life, pregnancy, childbirth, parenthood, sexual response, sexual orientation, contraception, abortion, sexual abuse, AIDS, and other sexually transmitted diseases.

Attitudes, values, and insights. Young people should question, explore, and assess sexual attitudes and feelings to develop their own values, increase self-esteem, develop insights concerning relationships with members of both genders, and understand obligations and responsibilities to others.

Relationships and interpersonal skills. Young people should develop interpersonal skills, including communication, decision making, assertiveness, peer-refusal skills, and the ability to create satisfying relationships. Sexuality education programs should prepare students to understand their sexuality effectively and creatively in adult roles, e.g., as spouse, partner, parent, and community member. This includes helping them to develop their capacities for caring, supportive, noncoercive, and mutually pleasurable intimate and sexual relationships in adulthood.

Responsibility. Young people should exercise responsibility in sexual relationships by understanding abstinence and ways of resisting pressures to become prematurely involved in sexual intercourse, as well as by encouraging the use of contraception and other sexual health measures. Sexuality education should be a central component of programs designed to reduce the prevalence of sexually related health problems, including teen pregnancy, sexually transmitted diseases, and sexual abuse.

© Margulies/Rothco. Reprinted with permission.

HIV [Human Immunodeficiency Virus]/AIDS education should take place in the context of comprehensive health and sexuality education, not in an isolated program but rather integrated into an approach that includes the objectives listed above. The HIV/AIDS unit should include:

Reducing misinformation. Eliminate misinformation about HIV infection and transmission, and reduce associated panic.

Delaying premature sexual intercourse. Help young people delay premature sexual intercourse; this includes teaching them to recognize the implications of their actions and gain communication skills to confront peer pressure and negotiate resistance.

Supporting safer sex. Encourage teenagers who are sexually active to use condoms each time they have any kind of intercourse or practice only sexual behaviors that do not place one at risk of pregnancy, sexually transmitted diseases, or HIV infection.

Preventing drug abuse. Warn children about drug use and teach young people skills for confronting peer pressure and negotiating resistance.

Developing compassion for people with AIDS. Encourage compassion for people with AIDS or the HIV virus.

Few students have participated in K-12 sexuality education programs. Sexuality topics are most likely introduced in grade 9 or 10, as part of another subject such as health or physical education. A review of state-recommended or state-developed curricula illustrates the limitations of existing programs. HIV/AIDS curricula are even less likely to deal openly and honestly with sexual topics.

Sex Education Receives Wide Support

There is vast support for sexuality education. In 1986, a Louis Harris poll found that over 95 percent of adults want HIV/AIDS education taught to their children, and 77 percent think courses for 12-year-olds should include information about birth control. Almost two thirds say courses should include information about homosexuality, abortion, sexual intercourse, and premarital sex.

Many national professional organizations support sexuality education. In 1991, 51 of them came together as the National Coalition to Support Sexuality Education, supporting the national mission that all children and youth receive comprehensive sexuality education by the year 2000. Members, today numbering 59, include the American Medical Association, the National Education Association, the YWCA of the USA, the American Nurses Association, the Children's Defense Fund, the American School Health Association, and the National Urban League.

Churches, synagogues, and other religious institutions are also a major force in development of attitudes and values about sexuality and sexuality education. Many national religious organizations have openly supported school-based sexuality education for decades.

In June 1968, an "Interfaith Statement" adopted by the National Council of Churches, the Synagogue Council of America, and the U.S. Catholic Conference included among its guidelines for developing sexuality education programs this statement: "[We] must recognize that school sex education, insofar as it relates to moral and religious beliefs and values, complements the education conveyed through the family, the church, or the synagogue. Sex education in the schools must proceed constructively, with understanding, tolerance, and acceptance of difference."

Religions Support Value-Based Programs

Almost every major Protestant denomination endorses and/or supports sexuality education, including the Southern Baptist Convention, the United Church of Christ in the USA, the Episcopal Church, the Lutheran Church of America, the Lutheran

Church-Missouri Synod, the United Methodist Church, the Presbyterian Church, and the United Presbyterian Church. Vocal religious opposition most often emanates from smaller fundamentalist groups.

The following statements exemplify support for sexuality education by Protestant denominations: As far back as 1974, the Presbyterian Church, USA, released a study document that explained that the object of sexuality education in the schools has been "what the home cannot as readily provide: systematic and scientifically accurate information, developmentally geared to the age of the child, audiovisual aids, discussion with peers, and so on." The Evangelical Lutheran Church of America declared that "the church's entire educational program needs to incorporate the 'whole person' motif" and that "its curricula should recognize that all persons are sexual beings, whose words and deeds express their ideas of appropriate sexual behavior." In its 1980 *Book of Discipline*, the United Methodist Church recognized "the continuing need for full and frank sex education opportunities for children, youth, and adults."

As educator William Stackhouse notes, "Until recent years, the response of religion to human sexuality-related concerns through their service activities was limited and traditional in scope. Programs on marriage preparation and enrichment, family life, and orphaned and unwanted children have long been part of religious-based service. But recently—and, again, often developed in large part out of the need expressed as women have shared their experiences—the religious institutions and individuals have become involved in service programs that relate to a broader range of concerns, including family communication about sexuality, adolescent sexuality, reproduction, pregnancy termination, gay/lesbian concerns, sexual violence, and AIDS.". . .

Organized religion can and, as shown here, does play a major role in promoting an understanding of human sexuality as one of the most affirming expressions of equality, mutual respect, caring, and love among human beings.

Comprehensive sexuality education is an important part of the education program in every grade of every school. Classes conducted by specially trained teachers complement the sexuality education given children by their families and by religious and community groups. School-based education programs should be carefully developed to respect the diversity of values and beliefs represented in the community. Curricula and resources should be appropriate to the age and developmental level of the students. Religious groups and spiritual leaders have a special role to play in helping communities develop sensitive, responsive programs for young people.

"Sex should only be discussed in a moral and religious framework. In the public schools, there is no need to discuss sex."

Schools Should Not Provide Sexuality Education

Haven Bradford Gow

Haven Bradford Gow is contributing editor for the Catholic League for Religious and Civil Rights and a syndicated columnist. In the following viewpoint Gow criticizes sex education programs. He argues that both the information presented in these programs and the teaching methods used to present the information are "glaring failures" in preventing and reducing teen sexual activity. Gow contends that in fact these programs have actually encouraged teenagers to start having sex.

As you read, consider the following questions:

1. According to the author, why are parents questioning the need for any sex education programs in the schools?
2. Why does Gow contend that "value-free" programs are especially harmful?
3. What does the author suggest should replace sex education programs?

"Sex Education in School" by Haven Bradford Gow, *Conservative Review*, August 1991. Reprinted by permission of *Conservative Review*, McLean, Virginia.

Bishop William Newman of Baltimore told religious educators and publishers at a Washington, D.C., conference that a U.S. bishops' task force he directs is working on a revision of its 1981 sex education guidelines.

Bishop Newman said, "There's a lot more to sex education . . . than the sexual or biological facts. . . . We really have concentrated more on the theological base."

Parental Involvement

According to the U.S. bishops' 1981 guidelines, "Education in Human Sexuality for Christians," sex education programs "should not be imposed on families"; indeed, the report urged educators planning sex education programs to "begin with parents, include parents throughout the planning and execution of the programs, and have parents conclude or evaluate the programs."

The U.S. bishops' guidelines further pointed out that "the content of sex education embraces knowledge, values, science and religious belief"; the guidelines said sex education programs should cover "not only such aspects of sexuality as love, intercourse, family planning, responsibility, chastity, Christ, joy, and pro-creation, but also such subjects as homosexuality, abortion, divorce, rape, prostitution, venereal disease and pornography."

The U.S. bishops are proceeding on the controversial assumption that sex education belongs in the classroom; but increasing numbers of parents and scholars are not only beginning to question the efficacy of sex education in the schools but also are claiming that such programs really are usurping and denigrating parental rights, responsibility and authority in this delicate and sensitive area involving a child's emotional, psychological, physical, moral and spiritual development.

Sex Education Programs Are Counterproductive

For example, Thomas Walsh, a prominent Boston attorney and a member of the Board of Directors of Morality in Media of Massachusetts, points out that studies reveal that sex education programs in the schools are counterproductive; he also insists that such programs often violate the moral and religious beliefs of the parents and, moreover, transgress parental rights and authority.

Mrs. Rhea Chudy, a dedicated mother and parochial school teacher in Brandon, Manitoba, Canada, observes that "The schools have no business teaching anything about sex to our children. That privilege belongs to parents alone. I have five children (ages 18 to 24) and I have instructed them regarding sexual matters. The schools were dishing out all kinds of information, but I told the children to disregard it as it was given with no morality and no regards to the sacredness of the person." Dr. Dinah Richard, an abstinence education expert in San Antonio,

Texas, echoes Mrs. Rhea Chudy's trenchant observations.

Dr. Richard maintains that "value-free" or "morally neutral" sex education programs are glaring failures. She states: "You can take Planned Parenthood's own research and materials and show that sex education programs in the schools are failures." The Louis Harris poll it sponsored in 1986 found that among teens who had had sex education, their likelihood to engage in sex increased. So did the likelihood for teen pregnancies and sexually transmitted diseases. Another study, by W. Marsiglio and F.L. Mott, which appeared in *Family Planning Perspectives*, reinforced the notion that greater levels of sex education tend to increase sexual activity. And M. Zelnick and Y.J. Kim's 1982 study concluded that current sex education doesn't work. These are just a few of the many studies.

Asay, by permission of the *Colorado Springs Gazette Telegraph*.

Ken Chang, a devoted father and manager of the 7-Eleven store in Mt. Prospect, Illinois, says: "My wife and I are from South Korea, where it is considered disgraceful for children to be talking or even thinking about sex. In school, children already have many important subjects to study; they are in school to learn to read, write, do math and to be good human beings. Sex education does not belong in the schools. When I was growing up, my parents and I never even discussed sexual matters, we just learned about sex naturally."

Mrs. Jean DeCola, a member of St. Raymonds Church in Mt. Prospect, has this to say: "The schools have no business telling our children and grandchildren about sex; sexual matters are private, matters that should only be discussed in the home. We must teach our children to read the Bible and learn God's way regarding sex and marriage."

Joseph W. Gow, a dedicated father in Arlington Heights, Ill., provides this perspective. "Sex should only be discussed in a moral and religious framework. In the public schools, there is no need to discuss sex. Instead, schools should help parents and churches teach moral values like courtesy, kindness, honesty, moral courage, self-respect, respect for others and the Golden Rule of treating others the way we would be treated. If children know and practice such moral values, they will automatically know what is proper and improper sexual conduct."

Dr. Eugene Diamond, professor of pediatrics at Loyola University Medical School (Ill.) and the author of *The Positive Value of Chastity*, readily agrees with Joseph Gow's trenchant observations. Dr. Diamond declares:

> We must not assume that educators are any better at giving sex education than parents. . . . It has been known for years that parents ineffably impart to their children a sound understanding of sex as part of naturalness, respect, love, stability, procreation, a part of the moral dimension of human existence. From the earliest age, our children imbibe attitudes and values without their parents ever talking explicitly of sex.

Teenage Pregnancies Actually Increasing

Despite the fact that at least 70 percent of all high school seniors in institutions of learning throughout the United States have been exposed to sex education programs, the statistics demonstrate that teenage sexual activity, sexual diseases, pregnancies and abortions are on the increase. For example: Over 50 percent of America's young people have had sexual intercourse by age 17; more than one million unwed teenage girls become pregnant each year; of those who give birth, 50 percent are not yet 18.

Moreover, teen pregnancy rates are at or near an all-time high; over 4,000 teenage girls each year now have abortions. Unwed teenage births increased 200 percent between 1960 and 1980.

It is all too clear that the solution to the glaring problem of teen sex and pregnancies is not sex information programs that divorce sex from morality, and which scorn and ridicule any effort to uphold and affirm the sacredness of sex, marriage, and family.

"Teaching sexual abstinence as one 'option' among others offers little support to young people today who . . . 'desperately want support not *to have sex.'"*

Sex Education Programs Should Demand Abstinence

Nancy Pearcey

In the following viewpoint, Nancy Pearcey contends that parents should be wary of abstinence-based sex education programs. Pearcey argues that although many schools promote abstinence, many programs merely suggest that abstaining from sex is healthier for psychological and medical reasons. Pearcey contends that the abstinence programs must teach morality—engaging in sexual activity is morally wrong. Pearcey is a freelance writer on science and social issues.

As you read, consider the following questions:

1. What is the trend in teen sexuality and what impact has widespread sex education had, according to the author?
2. According to Pearcey, how have many programs incorporated the abstinence message?
3. What messages and what teaching method does the author advocate for reducing and preventing teen sexual activity?

"Teenage Sex: Why Saying 'No' Is Not Enough" by Nancy Pearcey. The complete article appeared in the February 1991 issue of and is reprinted with permission from *The World & I,* a publication of The Washington Times Corporation, © 1991.

When a recent study revealed that the rate of teen sexual activity rose during the 1980s, leaders of the family planning industry were quick to interpret it as a failure of the decade's social conservatism.

The study, released by the Alan Guttmacher Institute, showed that the proportion of high school girls (aged 15 to 17) who had experienced intercourse rose from 32 percent in 1982 to 38 percent in 1988. The increase continued a trend that began in the sixties and that some observers expected to reach a plateau in the eighties. It was, after all, in the eighties that the nation was forced to face the risks of sexually transmitted diseases (especially AIDS), inspiring, as the *Washington Post* put it, "an onslaught of public health messages urging [teens] to abstain from sex."

It was also in that decade that social conservatism gained greater political prominence, resulting in, as Jacqueline Darroch Forrest of the Guttmacher Institute said, "an administration where people were preaching about the importance of not having sex."

Teens Have Always Had Sex

Family planning representatives have long argued that trying to get young people to refrain from sexual relations is not a viable strategy for dealing with sexually transmitted diseases or adolescent pregnancy. Susan Newcomer, director of education for the Planned Parenthood Federation of America (PPFA), says it is "unrealistic" to expect teens to practice sexual abstinence. She argues that "teens are having intercourse, they have always done so, and no amount of exhortation will cause them to stop" (in "Is It O.K. for PPFA to Say 'No Way'?"). Adults who try to get teens to stop having sexual relations, Newcomer insists, succeed only in getting them to stop listening to adults. In a similar vein, Michael Hall, executive director of Planned Parenthood of Santa Cruz, says teens "will be totally turned off" if adults tell them that certain sexual behaviors are right or wrong.

So when Forrest suggests that "preaching" about abstinence has failed to stem the tide of teen sexual activity, the unspoken implication is that family planning representatives were right all along—that social conservatism is out of touch with the times, that the message of abstinence outside of marriage does not work, that kids will not listen.

Yet, ironically, the same Guttmacher study turned up other data that contradict such a conclusion. It found that over the same period the use of condoms by teens more than doubled. As Forrest comments, this finding suggests "that people are hearing the messages about sexually transmitted diseases and the importance of condoms." In other words, in the eighties young people were subjected to urgent admonitions to use condoms and they responded; they changed their behavior.

Apparently, when the message is about sexual restraint, the experts tell us young people do not listen to adults. On the other hand, when the message is about condom use, the data show that they are willing to accept guidance from adults and act on it. We might wonder whether American teens have fallen prey en masse to a habit of selective attention. In reality, young people *are* responsive to what they are taught—but we must understand *what* they have been taught. . . .

Efforts to Curb Teen Sexuality

Family planning advocates . . . now realize that as a society we must find a way to curb adolescent sexual activity. In fact, in the past few years, many family planning organizations have begun to write sex education curricula designed to discourage adolescent sexual relations, reflecting a growing consensus that young people need support for the decision to say no. Abstinence education has become a fast-growing movement in sex education today.

The movement has not been without controversy, however. While educators agree on the importance of teaching abstinence, they disagree on *how* to teach it. Some remain within the standard value-free approach to sexuality, incorporating abstinence as an "option" for teens while stressing that there are no universally right or wrong choices. Others take a value-based approach, advocating abstinence as the only appropriate course for unmarried teens and teaching that sexual intercourse is an expression of a lifelong commitment. The proliferation of abstinence programs makes it important for educators and parents to understand the different philosophies underlying these two approaches.

Abstinence Education

Abstinence became an issue in sex education after the passage of the Adolescent Family Life Act (AFLA) in 1981. Administered through Title XX, the AFLA has supported the development of several curricula that take a value-based approach to abstinence education.

The conviction expressed in the legislation that public education can and should support values in courses on sexuality has aroused considerable opposition. The AFLA promptly became the subject of a lawsuit by the American Civil Liberties Union, whose lawyers argued that the promotion of sexual abstinence is an unconstitutional state endorsement of religious values. In 1988, however, the Supreme Court ruled the act constitutional, arguing that coincidence with the teachings of some religions does not make the act itself inherently religious.

The challenge to the AFLA in the courts has gone hand in hand with several challenges in Congress. Yearly since 1985, bills have been introduced in the Senate to rewrite Title XX to eliminate several of its distinctive features. On the state level, local laws and educational policies modeled after the AFLA have frequently been attacked, and curricula written with Title XX funding have come under intense criticism.

The fact that the AFLA has generated such controversy is revealing: It shows how strongly opposed many are to a value-based approach to sex education in the public schools. Before passage of the AFLA, most federally funded sex education programs came under Title X [the Family Planning Services and Population Research Act of 1970] and were based on a nondirective decision-making methodology. Nondirective methods treat the teacher less as an instructor than as a facilitator who helps students to explore options and clarify their feelings. Children are presented with a moral dilemma and are then prodded to think up all possible alternatives (whether morally approved or not), to discuss them with their classmates, and finally to decide which to make their own "value." Teachers are urged not to indicate that any behavior is right or wrong. As long as the student has gone through the prescribed process, any choice he makes is valid, regardless of its content.

Value-Free Sex Education

It is easy to see why this approach to sex education is described as value-free. It's also easy to see that it is far removed from the way parents and teachers have traditionally taught children about powerful and potentially damaging things like premarital sexual activity. Parents typically let their children know in no uncertain terms what is expected of them. To be sure, an effective parent discusses why certain behaviors are approved and listens carefully to a child's feelings when teaching how to apply moral principles to specific situations. But the principles themselves are taught in a didactic, authoritative manner: This is right, that is wrong.

Which is to say, parents use a directive, as opposed to a nondirective, method. Title XX programs are likewise directive: They take an unapologetic stand against adolescent sexual activity; they give students practice in using refusal skills; and they offer students a rationale for abstinence, teaching that sexuality is a powerful means of affectional bonding to be reserved for building strong marriages and warning that indulgence during adolescence is fraught with hazards such as sexually transmitted diseases, out-of-wedlock pregnancy, disruption of family relationships, and psychological distress. . . .

Stung by the popularity of abstinence-based programs, however, many groups went beyond criticism of the AFLA and by the end of the 1980s began developing their own materials to meet the demand for abstinence-based curricula. A recent catalog of materials distributed by ETR Associates (a Planned Parenthood educational offshoot) describes various curricula with phrases such as "help[s] make sexual abstinence a positive, viable alternative for young people"; "promotes abstinence as the positive choice for young people"; "guide for helping teenagers postpone early sexual involvement"; "subjects covered include abstinence as the only completely safe sexual behavior"; "includes sections on saying no." The Center for Health Training in Seattle distributes a guide entitled "Helping Teens Wait," which lists a wide variety of programs promoting abstinence.

Abstinence Is Foolproof

Today's reliance on contraception as a panacea is really tragic because, even prescinding from the admittedly enormous problem of persuading many people to contracept at all, no form of contraception is foolproof, as the current statistics testify all too eloquently. Only abstinence is totally foolproof.

K.D. Whitehead, *Fidelity*, November 1991.

Despite the common theme of abstinence, most of these curricula differ sharply from AFLA programs. They avoid the directive method (characterizing it as "preaching" and "moralizing") and seek instead to graft an abstinence message onto the standard nondirective decision-making approach. Susan Wilson, executive coordinator of the New Jersey Network for Family Life Education, explains that the problem with directive programs is that they "dictate 'correct' choices and condemn alternatives." A good program, she says in *Siecus Report*, is one that "support[s] the decision to say 'yes' as well as 'no'" to sexual involvement.

Supporters of the AFLA contend that the decision to say yes *has* been supported in standard value-free curricula, to the extent that the risks of adolescent sexual involvement have been vastly understated. This point is tacitly acknowledged in many of the abstinence-oriented programs developed by family planning groups, in that they now incorporate information on the negative consequences of premature sexual activity. Many also teach refusal skills to help students withstand peer pressure and offer reasons for postponing sexual relations, such as family values, religious conviction, avoidance of pregnancy and disease, and the opportunity to build cross-sex friendships free from sexual pressure. It looks as though the authors have been reading the [value-based abstinence] materials put out by Sex Respect and Teen Aid.

Yet, no matter how persuasively the case is built for abstinence, students are quickly reassured that whatever they choose
to do sexually is immune from criticism. As sex educator Mary
Lee Tatum explains in *Family Life Educator*, the goal must not be
to "simply 'tell' young people what behavior is acceptable" but to
foster "independence" by helping them make their own decisions. The way to do this, she says, is to "encourage abstinence,
but not to the exclusion of other decisions people might make."

As an example of this approach, *Choosing Abstinence*, published
by ETR Associates, recommends teaching youth that "at this
time in their lives it would be a wise choice to say no to sex."
But it goes on to caution teachers not to give the slightest hint of
a "negative reproach to students who are or who have been sexually active." The implication is that abstinence is simply a pragmatic choice for certain age groups and that adults must be ever
so careful not to suggest that alternative choices are wrong.

Individual Differences

Somehow, sexuality has become an area of life in which choices
are reduced to individual differences, devoid of ethical content.
For example, Planned Parenthood's pamphlet "Teen Sex? It's
Okay to Say No Way" tells young people that, in regard to sexual
behavior, "People aren't better or worse, just different." It goes
on: "Your friends have different looks and personalities. Their
needs and values may also vary." The message is that selecting
sexual values is akin to selecting a hairstyle—something that depends solely on an individual's personality.

The odd thing about all this is that teachers have no trouble at
all telling children that there are moral rights and wrongs in a
whole host of other areas. Every day teachers tell adolescents to
be honest on tests, to play fair on the playground, to stay away
from illegal drugs—and no one seems to find this sort of moral
training of children an unacceptable infringement on their freedom. Yet many sex educators feel that to tell adolescents to abstain from sexual relations outside of marriage is, in Wilson's
words, to "leave teens no choice and rob them of decision-
making and responsibility."

As parents see it, telling kids what's right and wrong is precisely
what provides the parameters within which the notion of moral
choice makes sense at all. How can children choose to do right if
adults refuse to give them any idea what *is* right? Yet nondirective
abstinence curricula consistently retreat from anything that re-
sembles moral training. The authors of *Teen Sexual Behavior*, published by the American Alliance for Health, Physical Education,
Recreation, and Dance, go so far as to recommend telling children, "Although we adults feel it's in your best interest to delay
intimate sexual behaviors, you and only you will decide when you

will become sexually involved."

This is practically an invitation to young people not to listen to adults. The conviction among sex educators that kids won't listen anyway has so shaped such curricula that it may well become a self-fulfilling prophecy.

Not-So-Hidden Values

Abstinence education with a nondirective methodology ends up being little different from the standard value-free approach. Teaching sexual abstinence as one "option" among others offers little support to young people today who, as the authors of *Choosing Abstinence* put it, "desperately want support *not* to have sex." For instance, *Teen Sexual Behavior* engages students in an activity designed to help them "decide when sex is right in a relationship." The lesson concludes that "the best rule of thumb is, if you feel uncomfortable about the behavior you're considering, give the relationship more time before you act." This is a curriculum that claims it is "not value free," yet it does not offer any clearer guideline to sexual behavior than a subjective feeling of comfort.

One should not conclude, however, that nondirective programs endorse no values. The hidden value in many such programs is the right to contraception and abortion. In a typical curriculum, nonjudgmental consideration is given to a wide range of options: abstinence, masturbation, premarital relations, contraception, homosexuality, abortion, whatever. The only option *not* regarded with equanimity is "unprotected" sex—that is, without contraception. Here sex educators shed their inhibitions against "preaching" and "moralism" and adopt a very directive approach. Using contraceptives is presented as a social and ethical responsibility.

For instance, in *Teen Sexual Behavior*, the authors tell teachers that abstinence is "the best sexual practice for teenagers" and "should be encouraged over any other sexual behavior for the age group." But when the text goes on to discuss teens who are sexually active already, the language becomes markedly stronger: "Teens who become sexually active are ethically entitled to knowledge" of birth control, and "Teens experiencing a crisis resulting from sexual behaviors are ethically entitled to compassionate and bias-free assistance" (free, that is, from any philosophical bias against abortion, as the context makes clear). Notice that abstinence is described in pragmatic terms as a prudent practice, but access to birth control and abortion is described in stringent ethical terms. The clue to educators' real values is the point at which they switch from a nondirective teaching style to a directive one.

As long as abstinence is presented as a pragmatic option while contraception is treated as an ethical requirement, we are likely to continue to see the trends revealed in the Guttmacher study. On the one hand, the rate of sexual activity will increase despite hand-wringing about its consequences, because significant adults are telling young people that there is no right or wrong in this area—that each person must decide for himself what feels "right for you." Needless to say, a teenager's feelings are not much counterweight to our increasingly sex-saturated culture. On the other hand, the use of contraceptives will likewise increase, because in this area the same significant adults are making highly directive statements, telling the young in no uncertain terms that to use contraceptives is a social responsibility.

All of which gives the lie to the pessimistic notion underlying so much sex education that teens do not listen to adults. Teens *do* listen, and their behavior is perfectly consistent with the message they are getting—even, sadly, from many of the new programs touted as abstinence-based.

"The abstinence-only curricula are problematic because of their reliance on instilling fear and shame in adolescents in order to discourage premarital sexual behavior."

Many Abstinence-Based Programs Are Harmful

Leslie M. Kantor

Encouraging teenagers to wait to become sexually active until they are adults is a worthwhile goal, argues author Leslie M. Kantor in the following viewpoint. According to Kantor, however, many new sex education programs may be harmful. These programs, Kantor criticizes, rely on frightening teenagers with the consequences of early sex—pregnancy, a host of sexually transmitted diseases (STDs), and long-term negative psychological effects. These programs also contain medical misinformation about STDs and HIV/AIDS and the effectiveness of condoms, reinforce race and gender stereotypes, and fail to teach decision-making skills, Kantor contends. Kantor is the director of the SIECUS Community Advocacy Project. The Sex Information and Education Council of the United States (SIECUS) is the best-known sex education organization in the United States.

As you read, consider the following questions:

1. What are some of the objections the author raises to the sex education programs she discusses?
2. According to Kantor, what negative effects might teenagers experience when they participate in one of the abstinence-only programs?

From "Scared Chaste? Fear-Based Educational Curricula" by Leslie M. Kantor, *SIECUS Report*, December 1992/January 1993. Copyright by the Sex Information and Education Council of the United States. Reprinted by permission.

There has been a recent proliferation of sexuality education curricula that rely upon fear and shame to discourage students from engaging in sexual behavior. Referred to as abstinence-only curricula, these programs typically omit critical information, contain medical misinformation, include sexist and anti-choice bias and often have a foundation in fundamentalist religious beliefs. These programs are in direct opposition to the goals of comprehensive sexuality education curricula, which seek to assist young people in developing a healthy understanding about their sexuality so that they can make responsible decisions throughout their lives. A number of the curricula have been developed by Far Right organizations including Respect, Inc., Teen Aid, The Committee on the Status of Women in Illinois, and Concerned Women for America. The curricula are widely promoted by well-known, Far Right organizations including Focus on the Family and Citizens for Excellence in Education, the action group for the National Association of Christian Educators. SIECUS has documented close to 100 communities which have faced organized opposition to family life and sexuality education programs or communities which have been thwarted in their attempts to implement programs by Far Right efforts within their areas. . . .

Fear and Shame

The focus on abstinence is not the issue; rather, the abstinence-only curricula are problematic because of their reliance on instilling fear and shame in adolescents in order to discourage premarital sexual behavior. A number of abstinence-based programs exist which provide support for postponing sexual behavior without utilizing scare tactics to achieve that end. Fear-based programs exaggerate the negative consequences of premarital sexuality and portray sexual behavior as universally dangerous and harmful. SIECUS believes that abstinence is a healthy choice for adolescents and that premature involvement in sexual behaviors poses risks. The SIECUS position statement on adolescent sexuality states: "Education about abstinence, alternatives to genital intercourse, sexual limit-setting, and resisting peer pressure should support adolescents in delaying sexual intercourse until they are ready for mature sexual relationships." Those adolescents who choose to postpone intercourse until after marriage also benefit from learning sexual health information during the teen years. . . .

SIECUS has reviewed eleven fear-based curricula using the *Guidelines for Comprehensive Sexuality Education, Kindergarten Through Twelfth Grade* as criteria. Following are brief reviews of these fear-based sexuality education programs. . . .

Characteristics of Fear-Based Curricula   The SIECUS content analysis of fear-based curricula identified a number of commonalities among the programs, including: gaps in information, medical inaccuracies, an exclusive focus on abstinence as the only appropriate choice for adolescents and sexist, homophobic and anti-choice biases.

Problems with Abstinence Programs

The following strategies are common to all eleven curricula reviewed:

• Scare tactics are used as the major strategy for encouraging premarital abstinence from sexual behavior.

• Information about contraceptive methods is omitted. If the availability of contraception is mentioned, failure rates are emphasized and often overstated.

• Students are required to look exclusively at the negative consequences of sexual behavior. Opportunities are not provided for students to explore their own values about premarital sexual behavior.

• Medical misinformation about abortion, STDs, HIV/AIDS and sexual response is prevalent.

• Sexual orientation is not discussed or homosexuality is described as an unhealthy "choice."

• Sexist bias is evident in descriptions of anatomy/physiology, sexual response, and sexual behavior. Stories, role plays and other exercises illustrate stereotypical gender roles.

• People with disabilities are entirely omitted or are illustrated as non-sexual.

• Racist and classist comments exist within the texts and stereotypes about various communities are underscored.

• Religious bias influences the curricula and only one viewpoint on sexual behavior is discussed.

• A limited number of family structures are included and nontraditional families are depicted as troubled.

The following sections discuss these common strategies of fear-based curricula in greater detail.

Scare Tactics

Fear and Shame The curricula promote fear about sexuality through a series of scare tactics. A number provide overwhelming lists of the negative outcomes of premarital sexual behavior ranging from selfishness to loss of communication skills to death.

Students are told over and over again that even if certain consequences of sexual behavior such as pregnancy and STDs may be prevented through the use of condoms and other contraceptive methods, a host of disastrous psychological, social and spiritual outcomes inevitably result from premarital sexual behavior: "Premarital sexual activity does not become a healthy choice or a moral choice simply because contraceptive technology is employed. Young persons will suffer and may even die if they choose it" (*Facing Reality*).

FACTS lists the consequences of premarital sexual behavior as: "pregnancy, financial aspect of fatherhood, abortion, guilt associated with abortion, AIDS, STDs, guilt, rejection, loss of reputation, inability to bond in the future, challenge not to compare sexual partners, alienation from friends and family, poverty, and inability to complete school" (junior high manual). *Families, Decision-Making and Human Development* posits that: "Sexual irresponsibility always produces negative consequences for relationships." "Irresponsible" sexuality is defined as sexual behavior outside of marriage. Each of the curricula link sexuality to poverty, emotional trauma, and long-term difficulty in achieving satisfying relationships.

Teen Aid lists the following as consequences of premarital sexual activity "beyond pregnancy or STDs":

• "loss of reputation; limitations in dating/marriage choices; negative effects on sexual adjustment-premarital sex, especially with more than one person, has been linked to the development of difficulty in sexual adjustment (Guilt has been a pervasive problem in this regard.);

• negative effects on happiness—premarital sex, especially with more than one person, has been linked to the development of emotional illness; loss of self-esteem—this can be particularly important in girls;

• preoccupation with sexual matters—may result in neglecting other important life endeavors (e.g., athletic activities/achievements, homework/grades, family relationships);

• family conflict—parental disapproval of sexual activity and possible premature separation from the family; confusion regarding personal value (e.g., 'Am I loved because I am me, because of my personality and looks, or because I am a sex object?');

• loss of goals—early marriage or pregnancy may limit career choices and educational opportunities" (*Sexuality, Commitment and Family*).

The sheer volume of supposed problems resulting from premarital sexuality is designed to scare students out of exploring sexual behavior of any kind. . . .

No Sexual Behavior Tolerated

A number of other curricula also outline the dangers of non-coital sexual behavior. In an *RSVP* exercise on sexual response, students are told that teens develop a sort of "tolerance" to sexual activity and that it takes increasing amounts of stimulation to achieve the same arousal over time. Sexual activity, in the exercise entitled "The Woo Scale" is likened to the analogy of a frog which is boiled to death without knowing it when the heat is turned up gradually. Another idea promoted by this concept is that any sexual activity will eventually progress to intercourse. Worse, students may feel pressured to follow this model of sexuality since it is promoted as normal: "If they [students] cross the underwear limit, it will be very difficult to stop anywhere before reaching sexual intercourse because of the level of stimulation" (*RSVP*). The message that sexual activity always gets beyond the control of the people involved is used to frighten students. . . .

Reprinted with special permission of King Features Syndicate.

Statistically, most people in the United States do engage in premarital intercourse and many people certainly go on to lead enjoyable, accomplished lives. However, teens may not understand this reality and again, may abstain out of fear and shame rather than out of understanding their personal values and the real benefits of abstinence.

Topics Omitted   Fear-based curricula typically fail to discuss subjects dealing with sexual activity, sexual decision-making and skill building.

A number of topics are completely omitted by the fear-based curricula including discussions about sexuality throughout the life cycle, masturbation, fantasy, sexual dysfunction, contraception, reproductive health, gender roles, and sexuality and the arts. Even topics which are discussed within the curricula, like abstinence, are superficially taught without opportunities for students to develop decision-making, refusal and negotiation skills.

For example, one important abstinence message which is consistently overlooked by the fear-based programs is: "People need to respect the sexual limits set by their partners" (*Guidelines for Comprehensive Sexuality Education,* SIECUS). The fear-based programs illustrate sexual behavior as something that quickly gets beyond the control of the participants, and describe young men, in particular, as unable to stop past a certain point. Students are not taught to listen to the boundaries communicated by their dating partners. Also, alternatives to sexual intercourse are not discussed by the curricula except in descriptions related to the dangers of petting.

Frightening Teens About STDs

Medical Misinformation   Fear-based curricula fail to provide students with critical, up-to-date information about STD transmission, prevalence and treatment. Rather than serving to enlighten students about their real STD risks, the STD and HIV/AIDS information is used as yet another scare tactic to frighten students about sexual behavior.

A strategy used throughout the curricula to instill fear about sexuality in students is including outdated or false medical information. The majority of factual errors deal with STDs (inaccurate data on STD rates, omission of human papilloma virus/condyloma information, inaccuracies about physiological consequences of infections) and HIV/AIDS information (failure to identify high risk behaviors, inaccurate medical descriptions, judgmental language about routes of transmission). . . .

Accurate Information Is Necessary

STDs and HIV/AIDS   Adolescents have a need for accurate, comprehensive information about STDs and HIV/AIDS. The fear-based programs omit most of the information which is crucial to STD prevention for sexually active teens and much of the information which is included is inaccurate.

Withholding critical information includes omission of the most common viral STD in the United States, human papilloma virus/condyloma from many of the curricula including *Free Teens* and *Sex Respect.* The Teen Aid curricula do list HPV (the virus which leads to condyloma) but list HPV as a separate disorder from condyloma without explaining the connection. Cervical cancer is also listed separately from condyloma in the Teen Aid curricula although there is a clear association between condyloma and cervical dysplasia (*Me, My World, My Future*). . . .

The fear-based programs blame people with HIV/AIDS for having the disease. The Teen Aid curricula both include separate chapters on HIV/AIDS which embrace the concept of high risk populations and list only "male homosexuals, IV [intravenous] drug abusers and female prostitutes" as members of high risk groups. The adolescents addressed by this curriculum may distance themselves from these groups and fail to realize that their behavior is what can put them at risk for HIV infection. In another curriculum, the authors go so far as to break transmission into two categories: "voluntary" and "involuntary." Voluntary transmission is defined as transmission from IV drug use and sexual intercourse while involuntary transmission is defined as transmission through blood transfusion, medical exposure and perinatal infection (*Families, Decision-Making and Human Development*). The authors define "voluntary" transmission of HIV as "behavior in which people are free to engage." In *Sex Respect*, the author writes: "Well, no one can deny that nature is making some kind of a comment on sexual behavior through the AIDS and herpes epidemics." *Facing Reality* posits: "Educators who struggle to overcome ignorance and instill self-mastery in their students will inevitably lead them to recognize that some people with AIDS are now suffering because of the choices they have made" (Parent/Teacher guide).

Inaccurate Information

The definitions of stages of HIV are inaccurate in both the Teen Aid and *Free Teens* programs. The stages in Teen Aid are listed as 1) acute illness, 2) latency phase, 3) AIDS related complex and 4) full-blown AIDS including AIDS dementia (*Me, My World, My Future*). *Free Teens* uses three of the above listed stages, omitting the "latency" category. While using ARC (AIDS related complex) may simply be outdated, the acute illness and latency phases are not official stages of the disease. The Teen Aid authors mention dementia over and over and state that: "Severe impairment of mind and nerve functioning occurs in two-thirds of those suffering from AIDS" (*Me, My World, My Future*). The authors list no documentation for this claim. . . .

Condoms and Other Contraceptive Methods   Fear-based curricula focus on contraceptive failure rates and exaggerate the risks associated with using birth control methods.

When any information about contraceptive methods is given, the possible consequences of using a method are distorted. In comparison, information about becoming pregnant and the risks of carrying a pregnancy to term are understated. *Sex Respect* mentions only one contraceptive method, the IUD, and provides this information: "The A.H. Robins Company has established a $615 million reserve fund to pay women suing the company over the next 17 years. Users are claiming the IUD made them unable to have children, gave them pelvic inflammatory disease, or even more serious problems." The text ignores that only the Dalkon Shield, which is no longer available, posed these risks.

FACTS mentions three contraceptive methods (condoms, oral contraceptives, and spermicides.) and offers only information about method failure rates. The failure rates provided include a 9-18% failure rate for the pill (Parent Guide). Studies place the actual failure rate for the pill for first-year users under 22 years old at 4.7%.

"Mixed Messages"

The approach abstinence-only curricula take to contraception is that information about birth control methods sends a "mixed message" to teens and will undermine the goal of adolescent abstinence. *Families, Decision-Making and Human Development* states that educators "send mixed messages by helping students to set high standards (i.e., premarital abstinence) and then undermining that standard with sub-optimal standards (i.e., instructions on using condoms)." Teen Aid justifies omitting contraceptive information with the argument: "Birth control is a personal, and in some cases a religious, issue and cannot be optimally presented in a group setting" (*Sexuality, Commitment and Family*). *Sex Respect* equates instruction about contraception with: "teens are being taught that they can act on any impulse and not have to face the consequences" (Teacher's Guide). . . .

Sexism/Gender Stereotyping   Gender bias is a common theme throughout the eleven programs. Curricula typically portray girls as nonsexual and boys as sexually aggressive and manipulative. Female anatomy is discussed primarily in reproductive terms and does not cover female sexuality. Likewise, women's developmental goals are limited to mothering. Finally, gender role stereotypes of mothers and fathers are common.

Boys are described as having uncontrollable sexual feelings and girls as having little, if any, sexual desire. For example, *Sex Respect* and *FACTS* include a chart which states that male genital feelings are aroused at the "necking" stage of arousal while female genital arousal doesn't occur until the petting and heavy petting stages. Sexual activities are listed in a straight line from "Being Together" to "End of relationship in its present form." Again, the idea that sexual progression is inevitable and unstoppable is underscored by the chart.

A strict gender differentiation in arousal is further supported by *Sex Respect* in a fictitious dialog between a TV host, Jane Bright, and Dr. I.M. Wise, a psychologist and marriage counselor on the topic of "male-female sexual differences":

> Wise: . . .Young males are tempted to provide sexual release for themselves while pretending they are having sex with a woman, or to aggressively seek sexual release with whatever person they can persuade or force to accommodate them.

The goal-oriented, sex for release construction of male sexuality is contrasted with female sexuality: "Boys tend to use love to

165

get sex. Girls tend to use sex to get love. . . . Females, when they visualize a sex partner—I should say love partner—think not of the male's genitals, but rather of his whole body as an instrument for giving them warmth, closeness, and security" (Jane-Wise discussion). Women are viewed as putting up with sex in order to get what they really desire, love. Women are thus confined to the role of "cop[ing] with the sexual aggressiveness of boys." These stereotypes of male and female sexuality reveal the sexist bias of the author and do a disservice to both the young men and young women who are presented with these messages. Also, while some physiological differences exist between male and female arousal, the curriculum does not attempt to describe sexual arousal in accurate or unbiased terms. . . .

Sexual Health

All people need and deserve accurate information about their sexual health. Students who choose to wait until marriage to have a sexual relationship will then need factual information to help them make decisions about their sexuality, and young people who are involved in sexual relationships need access to information about health care services. Although some people will have the benefit of receiving sexual health information from their parents, young people need opportunities to explore these issues with their peers and trained leaders.

Fear-based curricula not only fail in providing age-appropriate, necessary factual information, but foster a host of myths and stereotypes about serious topics including sexual assault, gender differences, sexual orientation, pregnancy options and sexually transmitted diseases. The curricula strive to provide a simplistic "just say no" solution to the complicated issues of teen pregnancy, STD transmission and sexual abuse. In the process, a variety of viewpoints about appropriate sexual behavior and effective public health strategies are ignored. In a pluralistic society, a curriculum that rests on the premises that every parent abhors premarital sexuality, promotes one type of family structure over another, and fosters particular religious beliefs is inappropriate. Worse, scaring adolescents about sexuality may have far-reaching implications for some students.

Periodical Bibliography

The following articles have been selected to supplement the diverse views presented in this chapter.

Peggy Brick	"Fostering Positive Sexuality," *Educational Leadership*, September 1991. Available from the Association for Supervision and Curriculum Development, 1250 N. Pitt St., Alexandria, VA 22314-1403.
Patricia Driskill and Robert L. DelCampo	"Sex Education in the 1990's: A Systems Perspective on Family Sexuality," *Journal of Sex Education and Therapy*, vol. 18, no. 3, 1992. Available from Guilford Press, 72 Spring St., New York, NY 10012.
Fidelity	"Guiding the Younger Generation," November 1991. Available from 206 Marquette Ave., South Bend, IN 46617.
Sol Gordon	"Values-Based Sexuality Education," *SIECUS Report*, August/September 1992. Available from 130 W. 42d St., Suite 2500, New York, NY 10036.
Michael E. Gress	"Sex Education in Schools: In Praise of Mystery," *Conservative Review*, December 1992.
Douglas Kirby	"Sexuality Education: It Can Reduce Unprotected Intercourse," *SIECUS Report*, December 1992/January 1993.
Elena Neuman	"The Birds and the Bees and More," *Insight*, October 12, 1992. Available from 3600 New York Ave. NE, Washington, DC 20002.
Anna Quindlen	"Parental Rites," *The New York Times*, September 25, 1991.
Phyllis Schlafly	"Sex Educators Must Stop Lying to Children," *Conservative Chronicle*, May 5, 1993. Available from PO Box 11297, Des Moines, IA 50340-1297.
Mark Sedway	"Far Right Takes Aim at Sexuality Education," *SIECUS Report*, February/March 1992.
Sharon Sheehan	"Why Sex Ed Is Failing Our Kids," *Christianity Today*, October 5, 1992.
Germaine O'Malley Wensley	"Condoms in the School: A Case of Educational Malpractice," *SIECUS Report*, February/March 1992.

How Should Teenage Homosexuality Be Treated?

**TEENAGE
SEXUALITY**

Chapter Preface

In the late nineteenth century, homosexuality was called "the love that dared not speak its name." Discussion of it was taboo in polite society, although society probably had as many gays and lesbians then as it does today. In recent decades gay activists have lessened the taboo. Discussions of homosexuality are often seen in books and magazines, on television, and in movies. However, homosexuality is still a sensitive topic for many people.

Among teenagers, many of whom are still unsure of their sexual identity, the topic often evokes fear and anger in those who wonder if they are homosexual and in their friends and acquaintances. Most gay teens agonize for years before they get the courage to openly acknowledge their homosexual orientation, if they ever do. They feel different from everyone else; envious that their straight friends are able to pair off with members of the opposite sex while they themselves often do not even know another teenager who is openly gay; frightened that someone will find out their secret; and frustrated that they cannot express their whole personality. Often they feel depressed.

What can be done to help gay and lesbian teens feel more comfortable about themselves so that they can be satisfied and contributing members of society? The viewpoints in this chapter address some of the controversies surrounding what schools, parents, and homosexual teens themselves can or should do about teenage homosexuality.

"Studies estimate that . . . young 'homosexuals of both sexes are two to six times more likely to attempt suicide than are (young) heterosexuals.' "

Gay Teens Should Be Treated as High Suicide Risks

B. Jaye Miller

In 1989, a government task force report estimated that a high percentage of youth suicides are committed by young gays and lesbians. This led activists to search for ways to understand and prevent such tragedies. B. Jaye Miller, a teacher of gay and lesbian history in California colleges, believed that society's attitudes toward homosexuality are a major factor in the desperate despondency often experienced by gay and lesbian youth. A homosexual, Miller lost his partner to AIDS in 1986 and himself died of an AIDS-related illness in 1991. In the following viewpoint Miller tells the story of one young gay suicide and points to some of society's traits that he says contributed to that death.

As you read, consider the following questions:

1. In what sense did Mary Griffith feel "deprived" of her son long before his death? What are some of the factors she blames for this deprivation, according to Miller?
2. The author concludes that "suffering in silence brings needless pain and tragedy." Do you think Bobby Griffith's life would have been saved had he voiced his fears and revealed his homosexuality to his mother? Explain your reasoning.

From B. Jaye Miller, "From Silence to Suicide." In *Homophobia* by Warren Blumenfeld. Copyright © 1992 by Warren Blumenfeld. Reprinted by permission of Beacon Press.

In the early, predawn hours of 27 August 1983, Bobby Griffith, who had just celebrated his twentieth birthday two months earlier did a backflip off a freeway overpass in the path of a semi-truck and trailer. He was killed instantly. Later that morning, his mother, Mary, was called from her workplace to receive the news. When she came down to the lobby and saw her older daughter crouched in the corner, crying uncontrollably, she knew that something horrible had happened. For four years, Bobby and his parents had been struggling with the fact of Bobby's homosexuality. Parental pressure, "Christian" counseling, and the antihomosexual attitudes of society had proved too heavy a burden to bear; suicide seemed the only way out.

The tragic story of Bobby and Mary has its own particular character, but it is by no means unique. Each year, many young gay males and lesbians commit suicide. Recent studies estimate that perhaps fully one-third of all completed teen suicides are associated with questions of sexual orientation and that young "homosexuals of both sexes are two to six times more likely to attempt suicide than are (young) heterosexuals," [as stated in Paul Gibson's 1989 "Gay Male and Lesbian Youth Suicide," a U.S. Department of Health and Human Services task force report]. We can only hope that, by retelling and remembering the story of Bobby and Mary, we can better face the situation with which gay, lesbian, and bisexual youths are dealing and learn how to support them. . . .

By all accounts, Bobby was a sensitive, bright, talented young man who had a tremendous love of life. But the burden of being gay in a nonaccepting church, in a nonaccepting community, in a nonaccepting family, proved more than he could bear. A mother, a father, and three siblings were deprived of a son and brother. The broader community lost an honest, sincere, and able young citizen. It is of course impossible to calculate the meaning and measure of those losses. The clear and immediate losses are so great that we are tempted to forget about, not even to ask about the more subtle, more hidden losses. But not to inquire further is a loss in itself.

Society's Nonacceptance Led to Suicide

Mary now argues that she feels deprived of her son, not just in death, but from the day he was born. Because of the narrowness and homophobia of the world in which she grew up, of the negative attitudes toward all deviation that she had internalized long before Bobby was born, Mary was unprepared to fully accept and productively support her special son: "I lacked the education. I lacked the knowledge." From early in Bobby's life, Mary found it impossible to relax and just enjoy her son. Instead, every instance of behavior or attitude that spoke of some deviation from the norm frightened her. She was intimidated by her mother's concerns; she was anxious about her neighbors' comments; perhaps most of all she was severely limited by the teachings of her church. . . .

Gay Youth at Risk

The Institute for the Protection of Lesbian and Gay Youth, an educational and advocacy group for youth in New York City with 1000 or more clients per year, reports that 21% of their clients (both male and female) have attempted suicide before the age of 20 years. The incidence of suicide attempts among gay males is reported to be between 18% and 20%. Clearly, these estimates represent more than an occasional youth.

Gay youth frequently are ostracized by peers, suffer verbal insults and threats, feel they have little support or no one to turn to, and find understanding and supportive counseling difficult—if not impossible—to obtain.

Linda K. Snelling, *JAMA*, June 5, 1991.

Mary is convinced that Bobby, even in early childhood, was able to detect her fears. He sensed that there was something about himself that his mother couldn't understand, couldn't accept. . . . By junior high and high school, he had learned to hide his inner feelings, often even from himself. When he could no longer keep his emerging sexual feelings from himself, he knew he could not share them with his family. The pressure grew to the point of explosion, and finally the secret, by now made horrible, came out. Bobby was gay. There was nothing within his upbringing that prepared Bobby for his life; the lack of acceptance within the family now infected Bobby himself.

At sixteen, Bobby wrote in his diary:

I can't let anyone find out that I'm not straight. It would be so humiliating. My friends would hate me, I just know it. They might even want to beat me up.

And my family? I've overheard them lots of times talking about gay people. They've said they hate gays, and even God hates gays, too.

It really scares me now, when I hear my family talk that way, because now, they are talking about me.

I guess I'm no good to anyone . . . not even God. Life is so cruel, and unfair. Sometimes I feel like disappearing from the face of this earth.

Homosexuality became a kind of dark cloud for Bobby. Somehow everything else about Bobby was forgotten. Nothing was important except his being gay. Society had only bad things to say about homosexuals: they are all perverts, sex maniacs, and sick. His church conspired by preaching that homosexuality is a moral sin and inspired by the Devil. Bobby was forced to forget about everything else in his life. During the last year and a half, he tried to find some self-acceptance, but the cards were stacked against him. Every step forward was matched by lingering doubts, by constant fears about the future, and above all by an overwhelming sense of failing his family and himself. In the end, the family was robbed of a son and brother, the son robbed of his family, and the child robbed of himself. . . .

Harmful Fear of Homosexuals

Bobby's and Mary's life stories reveal a fear of homosexuality that is common in our society. They are unique individuals, of course, but the issues they dealt with touch more people than we generally assume. It is widely argued that 10 percent of the overall population have exclusively or predominantly same-sex sexual experiences in their adult lives. Even if we halved that figure to make a highly conservative estimate, that still leaves a gay population of approximately twelve million in the United States alone.

During the last two decades, nothing less than amazing progress has been made by gay, lesbian, and bisexual people in building a sense of self-acceptance and pride. But, for gay, lesbian, and bisexual youths, the issues are much more problematic. Little if anything in most public schools hints at their existence, confirms their right to self-esteem. Even less is done for the parents of these young people. As Bobby's and Mary's stories make clear, suffering in silence brings needless pain and tragedy.

"Gay teen suicide is fabricated crisis, the excuse du jour for another binge of social engineering."

Gay Teen Vulnerability to Suicide Is Mere Propaganda

Don Feder

Don Feder is a conservative syndicated columnist whose opinion pieces are published in many newspapers and journals around the United States. In the following viewpoint, Feder maintains that the idea that gay and lesbian teens are more vulnerable to suicide than other teens is a falsehood promulgated by gay activists with a hidden agenda.

As you read, consider the following questions:

1. Feder states that the major support for the claim that gay teenagers are vulnerable to suicide is a biased 1989 government task force report. How can you tell that Feder is being sarcastic when he terms the report's sources "scholarly"?
2. What ulterior motive does Feder say gay activists have in promoting the idea of rampant suicide among gay teens? What kind of "social engineering" does he say gays intend?

"Gay Teen Suicide Is a Manufactured Crisis" by Don Feder, *Conservative Chronicle*, March 10, 1993. Copyright 1993, *Boston Herald*. Reprinted by permission of Don Feder and Creators Syndicate.

Homosexual activists have targeted the nation's school children. Militants are eager to use the schools to indoctrinate for acceptance, recruit when possible, all in the name of treating a social trauma.

In Massachusetts, the Governor's Commission on Gay and Lesbian Youth has issued a report that, given the panel's composition, was as predictable as the orbit of the planets.

To address the supposed scourge of gay teen suicide, homosexual issues must be integrated into all areas of public school curriculum, the commission pronounced. To provide "positive role models" for gay youth, history classes should stress the contributions of famous homosexuals. Like Brownshirt leader Ernst Rohm, no doubt.

Even Gov. William Weld, the most compliant of public officials when it comes to promoting the homosexual agenda, distanced himself from the report. Perhaps he was thinking of the fate of New York Schools Chancellor Joe Fernandez, whose head was served up on a copy of *Heather Has Two Mommies*.

In their coverage of the report, the Boston media didn't think it relevant to inform the unenlightened that Commission Chairman David LaFontaine is the lobbyist for the Coalition for Gay and Lesbian Civil Rights. Such a disclosure would have made the group's partisanship all too apparent.

Fabricated Crisis

Gay teen suicide is fabricated crisis, the excuse du jour for another binge of social engineering. In 1991, Gallup surveyed teenagers on the leading causes of suicide. Those who said they'd attempted or thought seriously about the act were asked what factors influenced them. Drug and alcohol abuse, grades, family problems and boy-girl relationships all figured prominently. Feelings of anxiety or alienation due to homosexual tendencies didn't even register in the survey.

The commission's claim that 30 percent of the teens who take their own lives are homosexuals comes from a 1989 paper published by the Department of Health and Human Services. The work of therapist Paul Gibson, it footnotes such scholarly sources as the *Philadelphia Gay News*, the *Washington Blade* and National Gay Task Force.

Bias aside, the monograph provides interesting insights—for instance, the movement's unremitting hostility toward religion, which, in the author's words "presents another risk factor in gay youth suicide because of the depiction of homosexuality as a sin and the reliance of families on the church for understanding homosexuality."

That being the case, surely the educational effort to eradicate bigotry should include a frontal assault on the principal purveyors of homophobia, traditional religion and the family.

The effort to combat this non-existent contagion is but one aspect of the homosexual educational advance. Through multiculturalism, homosexuals are presented as a minority worthy of respect. AIDS education courses cover the broad variety of homosexual acts, usually in excruciatingly explicit detail, described in value-neutral terms.

Gay Suicides Exaggerated

Gay activists . . . have often cited a statement in a 1989 report by the government's Task Force on Youth Suicide that gay adolescents may account for as many as thirty per cent of youth suicides each year. In my psychiatric practice I have found that the "government" statistics so frequently cited were not prepared by the government and are not statistics. They are estimates based on a projection in a paper prepared for the task-force report. The paper was never subjected to the rigorous peer review that is required for publication in a scientific journal. . . .

The procedure used in studying the characteristics of suicide is called the psychological autopsy, and involves interviewing the victim's relatives and friends and obtaining his medical, school, or police records.

My colleagues at Columbia University and I recently carried out such a study on teen-agers and children in the New York area. Patterns of sexual orientation are fluid in the teens, and experimentation is common, but nevertheless, only three of a hundred and twenty (2.5 per cent) were unquestionably known to be homosexual. Four others showed some behavior that could have been indicative of homosexuality. If all of the suicides who showed any evidence of homosexual behavior were indeed gay, then we would have had a total of six per cent gays in our study. Two other such studies have been done: in 1959, Eli Robins, in St. Louis, found no homosexuals in a group of a hundred and thirty-three suicides, and in 1986 Charles Rich, at the University of California, San Diego, found a homosexuality rate of seven per cent among suicides under thirty. No one can say with certainty whether these studies undercount or overcount the percentage of suicides that are gay, but by any measure it is clear that the figure of thirty per cent is far too high.

David Shaffer, *The New Yorker*, May 3, 1993.

Even without the implementation of the commission's recommendations, homosexuals are making significant strides in the state's schools. In December 1992, the Beverly, Mass., high school observed Homophobia Awareness Week, with mandatory assemblies and dispassionate advice from the Gay, Lesbian and Bisexual Speakers Bureau. In a letter to the principal, an indignant father complained that his 14-year-old daughter "had to listen to two deviant men describe how they have their niece bring cookies over to their house to be shared with their gay lovers."

Among the literature provided to students and faculty was What You Can Do: 10 Steps Toward Ending Homophobia in Your School. Step No. 7, "Reassess the curriculum," demands discussion of homosexuality in all areas of study.

Step No. 8 notes the importance of "extracurricular messages." Recommendations here include, "films, speakers and performance groups such as the Boston Gay Men's Chorus or the Triangle Theater Company. Perhaps a tasteful exhibit of Bobby Mapplethorpe's provocative photographs?

Blatant Bigotry?

My favorite is Step No. 10, "Do not assume Heterosexuality." Avoid such blatant bigotry as invitations to faculty members and their "spouses"—with the insensitive implication that male/female couples are the norm.

But do not imagine the program was entirely one-sided. On Friday, Father Mullen of St. John the Evangelist Church was brought in to present the religious perspective. After a week of indoctrination, the poor old priest was almost booed off the stage by well-conditioned students.

All of this is based on the totally unscientific assumption that a teenager who's confused about his sexuality (with an adolescent crush or two) was a homosexual from birth and will remain so for the rest of his life—and here's a list of bars and bathhouses for a little lifestyle adjustment. Given the diseases rampant among homosexuals and the violence that often accompanies these relationships, directing teens toward the homoerotic culture is nothing less than officially sanctioned child abuse.

3
VIEWPOINT

"One fact is undeniable: Gay students could use some special attention."

School Curricula Should Support Gay Teens

Del Stover

A former associate editor of the *Executive Educator*, Del Stover believes that educators must improve the school environment for gay and lesbian teens. Currently, he says, the educational atmosphere for homosexual teenagers is, at worst, hostile and threatening and, at best, unempathetic and aloof. If these conditions are not changed, he says, many more gay teens will be at high risk for suicide, leaving school, and succumbing to undesirable influences.

As you read, consider the following questions:

1. What does the often hostile school atmosphere do to gay teens, according to the author?
2. For what reasons, according to Stover, do schools avoid giving the problems of gay teens adequate attention?
3. How does Stover justify giving gay students special attention? What does he say is the *minimum* that should be done for gay students?

From "The At-Risk Students Schools Continue to Ignore" by Del Stover. Reprinted with permission from *The Executive Educator*, March 1992. Copyright 1992, the National School Boards Association. All rights reserved.

Even today, when AIDS has forced schools to tackle such controversial subjects as condoms and sexual behavior, homosexuality remains a sensitive—if not taboo—topic. And school executives are caught in the middle: Gay activists and some educators demand assistance for gay students at risk, while some community members oppose any action that smacks of condoning homosexuality.

One fact is undeniable: Gay students could use some special attention. Almost everywhere is the message that they are outcasts of society. In church, they may hear homosexuality described as a sin. They hear of people being fired from jobs for being gay. They learn homosexuals cannot serve in the U.S. Armed Forces. Even parents make their feelings plain: One counselor of gay youth knows a child whose parent said, "If I thought you were gay, I'd smother you with a pillow."

The typical high school is no less hostile. Dominated by a teen culture of marked intolerance for differences and strong homophobia, school is a place where "fag" and "queer" are everyday insults, where many older teens are vocal in their willingness to use violence against anyone suspected of being gay. Hostility is even found among some teachers and school executives themselves.

Society's Hostility Harms Gay Youth

This hostility leaves gay youths frightened and uncertain about their own worth. Their self-esteem plummets, and they quickly realize the necessity of hiding their sexual orientation. Terrified of being marked as "different," afraid they'll be rejected by friends and family, they grow up unable to reach out to others for help.

Isolated, forced to wrestle with their emotions alone, gay teenagers are highly vulnerable to bouts of depression, drug use, school failure, and suicide. Not all gay students encounter problems in adolescence, of course, but gay students, as a whole, are a high-risk population. Many end up on the street because they run away from home or are thrown out by parents. The U.S. Department of Health and Human Services reported in 1989 that 30 percent of all teens who commit suicide are gay and that gay teens are two to three times more likely than other teens to attempt suicide. Furthermore, some gay youth turn to sexual experimentation or seek companionship of adults without considering the risks, exposing themselves to the possibility of contracting AIDS.

All this is alarming, especially since the number of gays in our society is estimated at 4 to 10 percent, suggesting that a typical high school of 1,000 has 40 to 100 gay students. Clearly, the at-risk population isn't small.

But only a handful of metropolitan school systems offer special assistance to gay students, and school executives in rural areas and small towns show little sign of following suit. For one thing, the invisibility of gay students works against any response: Many educators are simply unaware of gay students in their schools. Also, many people aren't convinced gay students require special assistance: Aren't counselors there to help all students?

But advocates for gay students say ignorance is no excuse. They also point out that other at-risk student populations with small numbers (e.g., suicidal youth and pregnant teens) receive assistance, saying this is at odds with reluctance to single out gays for assistance.

Untrained Professionals

Also, failure to treat gay students as a unique population means school personnel aren't trained to counsel them. "When [gay] students bring their problems to school professionals, the professionals don't know what to do," says Gary J. Remafedi, University of Minnesota assistant professor of pediatrics and a researcher on teenage homosexuality. "When the issue is raised, the professional needs to know how to keep the door open, to detect the common problems in young gay people and get them the appropriate resources for help."

Another reason for inaction is fear of controversy. Any attempt to provide counseling to gay students is likely to spark accusations by some community members that the school is condoning homosexuality. Attempts to discuss homosexuality in sex education classes also can lead to community discord. Much of the opposition comes from conservative parents and religious leaders, who decry homosexuality as an abomination, a mental illness that should not be discussed with youngsters.

The political debate is muddied by misconceptions. Some parents fear any discussion of homosexuality will encourage teens to experiment sexually. Others are afraid that counseling gay students is sanctioning their homosexuality—at an age when, some believe, they could be talked back into heterosexuality.

Medical experts dismiss these ideas. Although the cause of homosexuality is undetermined, recent research suggests sexual orientation is set before birth or in the early years of life. "There's mounting evidence of a biological basis for sexual orientation," Remafedi says. "It's not realistic to think any of us have any impact on adolescent sexual orientation. People don't change their sexual orientation."

This view, widely accepted by the medical community, has helped persuade national organizations to speak out on behalf of gay students: The American Academy of Pediatrics has urged members to provide services to gay youth; the National Education Association says every school should provide counseling to gay students; and the Child Welfare League of America, a major children's advocacy group, urges efforts to help gay youth.

But this offers little comfort to a gay teenager—or a principal or superintendent battling the local community. Some opposition to helping gay students is not homophobic; it is based on a sincere belief that schools have no business discussing sexuality of any kind. "You have to remember, we as a culture don't deal with sexuality very well," says Jerald Newberry, Fairfax County (Virginia) Public Schools coordinator of family life education. "The fact that schools are going to talk about and take on the task of educating students on these issues isn't always going to be accepted."

Empowering *All* Students

When teachers have resources for creating an educational context that empowers students, great moments of learning and personal growth can emerge. . . . But transforming schools into places where all people feel accepted, not in spite of their differences but through acceptance of their differences, is a complex process. It not only requires individual educators to take the initiative to examine their own attitudes, behaviors, and relationships; it also requires development and implementation of systemic change that sets fair policies and practices. Thus, accountability for the process is in the hands of individual educators as well as with those in positions of leadership in our schools.

If educators choose to do nothing, they must be willing to be held accountable for supporting school environments in which lesbian, gay, and bisexual students often drop out, act out, commit suicide, or survive physically while losing self-esteem.

Richard A. Friend, *Independent School*, Spring 1992.

This political reality has taught many school executives to tread lightly. "No matter how you come down on this issue, you're going to create some ill will with a large percentage of the population," says E. Wayne Harris, an area superintendent on leave from Fairfax County Schools. "It's no different than issues about teaching family life—and teaching about condoms, abortion, sex education. These are issues we wrestle with all across the country."

In Fairfax County, school executives hoping to deal with homosexuality in the schools' family life program brought together a representative sample of community members to review the curriculum. When opposition arose to the proposal, a ready-made core of supporters was available to defend it. "We had very strong proponents," says Marie Sterne, Fairfax County Schools coordinator of health and physical education. "Parents spoke out for it. We had students speak for it, as well as counselors and mental health professionals."

Developing community support is important, but its absence doesn't relieve you of responsibility to take the lead on the issue, says Virginia Uribe, who founded Project 10, a Los Angeles school program that trains staff members on gay issues and counsels gay students. You mustn't let public opinion determine whether your schools offer counseling for gay students, she says—instead, you must mold public opinion to ensure such help: "We in the public school system are committed to providing for the needs of all of our students. If some kids demonstrate a need, we must try to respond to that need."

Guaranteeing a Safe Environment

At the minimum, says Harris, schools can ensure gay students the same safe environment they would ensure any other minority, protecting them from the verbal or physical abuse common against homosexuals: "As school administrators, we all have a responsibility to protect these youngsters. I'm opposed to [harassment of gay students], just as I'm opposed to harassment against anyone who belongs to a different ethnic group."

Guaranteeing *everyone* a safe school environment is a positive step toward helping gay students—and it leaves school executives on safe political ground. But it tiptoes around the central issue of responding directly to the risks gay students run.

A handful of school systems have met the issue head on. One response is staff training. In New York City, school executives have invited the Hetrick-Martin Institute, a nonprofit organization that serves the needs of gay youth, to provide training focusing on teacher and student prejudices and strategies to support gay students. Such training can make a big difference for gay students, says Frances Kunreuther, the institute's executive director. "Our biggest enemy is ignorance," she says. "A lot of teachers and counselors have never met a gay person. Nobody teaches them to work with these young people. One thing we give them is accurate information. We don't want them to tell a gay youth, 'It's just a phase you're going through.'"

The isolation of gay students needs to be broken, and a school's staff is a good place to begin. "I can't emphasize enough how one accepting voice can change a youngster's life," Kunreuther says. "[Gay students] just need to know there's someone they can talk to."

Another valuable response is to provide counseling in the school—or refer students to outside counseling. In San Francisco, each high school has a teacher or counselor identified to the student population as available to talk to gay students, called gay- and lesbian-sensitive adults.

Some gay advocates want schools to go further, calling for open discussion of homosexuality in health and sex education classes and recognition in English, history, and science classes of the contribution of gays to society. And some school systems have responded. In Fairfax County, a lesson on homosexuality is included in the schools' family life curriculum. In that program, ninth-graders spend a class period discussing homosexuality and watching the video *What If I'm Gay?* A homework assignment requires students to discuss the lesson with their parents.

Other Programs

One well-known program for gay students is New York City's Harvey Milk School, a small, alternative program jointly run by the city schools and the Hetrick-Martin Institute. Most of the school's 33 students are homeless, runaways, or chronic truants; providing them counseling and individualized instruction is con- sidered their only hope of graduation. "It's only for young peo- ple who cannot be mainstreamed back to the public schools," says Kunreuther. "Still, we try. But many have been so severely abused verbally or thrown out of their homes that they've found it impossible to go back to school. It's for people who have seri- ous problems."

Perhaps the biggest developed program for gay students in a traditional school setting is in Los Angeles, where Virginia Uribe, a counselor and science teacher, started a dropout pre- vention program for gay students at Fairfax High School in 1984. It has developed into an extensive undertaking involving teacher training, counseling for students, and discussion of gay issues in the curriculum. In recent years, the program has ex- panded to other city schools.

Among the most helpful features of the program are in-school discussion groups that let gay students realize they aren't alone, Uribe says. Such groups exist in 20 of the city's 50 high schools. Students can also get help on a drop-in basis, and Uribe's office serves as a resource center where students can find books and articles about homosexuality.

Still, despite a surge of media attention on the needs of gay students in recent years, such programs are rare. Uribe says prejudice is part of the reason: "Some [school officials] will sim- ply ignore the issue. The fact that this population is at risk doesn't seem to reach through to these people."

But few school executives are willing to abandon these stu- dents. "It's touchy, but I as an administrator wouldn't shy away from the issue," says Harris, of Fairfax County. "And I haven't found many colleagues to be reluctant to serve these youngsters or shy away from them."

Establishing special programs for homosexual students might not be in the cards politically. But until society resolves its own attitudes toward homosexuality, responsible school executives will have to try to ease the homophobia in many schools—and quietly help gay students find the help they need.

"The whole argument for the gay-driven curriculum is profoundly artificial—and dishonest."

School Curricula Should Not Provide Homosexual Propaganda

Joseph Sobran

In an effort to end discrimination, increase understanding, and reduce intergroup hostilities, many schools provide curricula that present a multitude of cultural histories, lifestyles, and values in a neutral way. While most people willingly accept classes that study African-American history, Asian traditions, and multicultural holiday celebrations, many do not accept the integration of information about homosexuality, homosexual families, and homosexual lifestyles into the classroom. Joseph Sobran, a conservative syndicated columnist, speaks out against the presentation of such information in the classroom and against the normalizing of what he perceives to be aberrant behavior.

As you read, consider the following questions:

1. What is Sobran's main objection to teaching about homosexuality in the classroom?
2. Sobran says that no matter what is taught, children will still perceive homosexuality as perverse. If so, why does he object to its inclusion in school curricula?
3. The author argues that schools falsely believe that children have no souls and that the educational system is "driving faith into the closet." What does he mean?

From "Faith in the Closet" by Joseph Sobran, *Human Life Review*, Fall 1992. Reprinted by permission of the author and *Human Life Review*, 150 E. 35th St., New York, NY 10016.

Our time, it's often said, outstrips satire. I'm beginning to think it even outstrips paranoia. None of the parents' groups who opposed sex education in public schools a decade ago foresaw, in their most hysterical nightmares, what has actually come to pass.

Consider the sex education program in New York City's public schools. The system now provides condoms to high-school students. Instruction on the use of condoms begins in the fourth grade. In the sixth grade, pupils are taught all about oral and anal sex. And this year [1992] the schools' chancellor, Joseph Fernandez, is pushing a curriculum that includes bizarre "story books" that would subject six-year-olds to homosexual propaganda. Yes, six-year-olds.

One story book is *Heather Has Two Mommies*. It's about a little girl named Heather who lives with her biological mother (via artificial insemination) and her mother's lesbian lover. Heather becomes confused when she learns that her little playmates have daddies. The concept of a "daddy" is foreign to her, until she meets a little boy who has *two* daddies.

Then there is *Daddy's Roommate*, a little boy's account of a weekend with his divorced dad and Dad's new male lover. "Daddy and his roommate live together, work together, sleep together, shave together. . . . Daddy and his roommate are very happy together, and I'm happy too."

This has caused some uproar, even in liberal New York. But Fernandez has staunchly defended the curriculum, saying: "If we're ever going to get this country together, we have to deal with these issues of hate. Kids learn biases from us, from adults. We have to teach them through education.". . .

Somebody should have explained to Fernandez that to disapprove of homosexuality is not the same thing as hating homosexuals. Most parents don't want their children to become alcoholics, but this isn't the same thing as hating drunks. This should be obvious to any schoolboy, let alone the chancellor of an education system. . . .

Amid today's nauseous explicitness, there are taboos. One simply must not suggest that there is anything *wrong* with homosexuality, morally or otherwise. Sophisticated magazines like *New York* and *Vanity Fair* cater to expensive consumer tastes, making fine distinctions among wines, perfumes, books, and operatic performances, but they would never dream of admitting that there may be certain qualitative differences, so to speak, between anal sex and the more conventional kind, between organs of procreation and organs of evacuation. It is impolite to notice such things.

Why Should Schools Favor Homosexuality?

If homosexuality isn't wrong, the question still arises, Why is it special? Why does it take precedence, among all the polymorphous perversities, over, say, solo sex, or sheep sex, or sex with the deceased? Surely these appetitive permutations have brought suffering and persecution on their votaries too; popes, priests, puritans, and Victorians have taken a stern view of all of them. Why don't accredited victimhood and its privileges attach to them as well?

© Hofoss/Rothco. Reprinted with permission.

Never mind. We are simply expected to observe the new customs around here, without asking too many questions. This is what happens when an ideology manages to establish itself as a code of etiquette. You don't ask *why* it's proper to use this fork rather than that to eat your salad or dessert; you just do what the others do. The rules are arbitrary, for all their moral pretensions.

In fact, it's very bad manners to raise moral and spiritual questions about sex. Physical questions are always welcome, the grosser the better, but metaphysical ones are considered unrefined.

That is to say, the real questions are being begged. Our very habit of talking of "sex" as an isolated thing implies that it has no dimension beyond pleasure and maybe romance. It may result in life or death, but these are by-products, generally to be averted by the technical means the modern world provides.

Gays Seeks to Impose Their Values

At first glance it seems odd that homosexuals should be concerned about what children are taught, since they are pretty much disabled from parenthood and few of them have children. But the answer is that gays (in the sense of ideologically committed homosexuals) crave public legitimacy, which requires a revolution in community morals, and this is a tall order. Having few children of their own, the gay "community," such as it is, can't transmit the new morality through the home, family, tribe, and tradition, as most of us transmit our moral attitudes. They have to *impose* it through official propaganda, now known as "education," or what the august editor of *Human Life Review*, J.P. McFadden, calls "artificial indoctrination." They have to control the schools—a chief channel of access to the young. For them, *more* than for parents, the schools are crucial.

Hence our story, which might be called "Gay Rights Meets Sex Education." Gays have become the shaping force in sex education, defining the lowest common denominator of sex as we, alas, know it. They have managed to make homosexuality the great test-case of the sexual revolution: after all, if the point of sex is not to procreate, why not sodomy? The rest has followed with dizzying speed as gays have perceived the corollaries of the concession they have extracted. Their fate and the fate of the sexual revolution are one. The campaign for gay-inclusive sex education has made its way under the language of diversity, tolerance, multiculturalism, pluralism, and simple realism (we can't bury our heads in the sand!). It admits that sex can have its little hazards, which leads us to "safe sex," free condoms, and, if necessary, abortions.

Gone is the language of purity, chastity, virginity, self-control, waiting until marriage. These are outdated terms, fraught with religious overtones, and we must always keep church and state separate. Even value-free "abstinence" flunks the test of realism, since today's kids are going to have sex, no matter what we tell them. The hard-nosed realists, as I say, expect hot-blooded boys always to wear their condoms. Well, not really. But the supposition that the boys will do so is a convenient fiction, one that relieves the sex educators of responsibility for what actually happens to the kids.

Kids Will Always Despise Homosexuality

Real realism might reflect that the kids are going to despise homosexuality, no matter what we tell them. The naïveté of all this sex education lies in assuming that adults who have thrown out any semblance of a demanding moral code are going to continue to enjoy moral authority. Whose conscience is really compelled by fake words like "homophobia"? . . . The only moral the kids will draw from the new morality is that they have the permission of their weak elders to do whatever they please.

The whole argument for the gay-driven curriculum is profoundly artificial—and dishonest. Nobody in his right mind thinks anal sex is sex, even in the debased sense of the term. Those who do prefer it only prefer it by default, because they

188

are incapable of enjoying the regular kind. The essence of what we call homosexuality is a sexual aversion to the opposite sex. It's a pitiful condition, but not one that commands respect. Many parents have hoped a son would grow up to become a priest, even though that means he'll be celibate and childless, but none has ever hoped a son would turn out homosexual. That it happens anyway is sad beyond words, but there is no point in pretending it's desirable.

Lessons on the Gay Curriculum

Lesson 1. "Love me, love my lifestyle" cannot be the foundation for the tolerance, respect, and civil rights that gays and lesbians want and deserve. "Live and let live" has been the genuine strength of the pluralism by which New Yorkers have long survived, just as a spirit of agreeing to disagree has moderated the city' s diversity of cultures, moral views, and life styles. Now we are seeing a new kind of pluralism, "enforced diversity." In a *New York Times* op-ed piece, Richard Vigilante argues, "Rather than asking us to live together in peace despite our deepest disagreements, enforced diversity asks us to surrender those disagreements, to pretend that our deepest beliefs do not matter and to shed them for a government-enforced least common denominator of values."

Lesson 2. Don't introduce moral conflicts into the classroom when adults themselves are deeply and honestly conflicted. Homosexuals want gay bashing to stop, they want discrimination in jobs and housing to end, and most Americans agree with them. But some homosexuals want more than tolerance. "Gay-rights groups, emboldened by the election of openly gay and lesbian candidates in New York and around the country but vulnerable because of political setbacks elsewhere, view the gay curriculum as a measure of acceptance" (*New York Times*). . . . In fact, the religious beliefs of most Americans still hold that homosexual acts are wrong. . . . No parents who honestly hold such a belief could responsibly allow their children to sit in a class where approval [of homosexual relationships] is promoted.

Lesson 3. Political correctness is a fatal barrier to open and honest debate about such moral disagreements.

Editorial, *Commonweal*, January 15, 1993.

Throw nature out the door, as the maligned medievals used to say, and she'll come in the window. Tell children that there is no important difference between the natural and the unnatural, and they will—naturally—decide you're too silly to heed. The sex educationists, like all propagandists, gravely overrate their own ability to manipulate their subjects.

What they *can* achieve, though, is confusion. They can obscure the all-important truth that we have souls, and that sexual intercourse involves the soul along with the body. . . .

What the sex educationists are really doing is burning the cultural bridges back to Christendom—the West's traditional ground of community and public morality. The sexual revolution is really a revolution in our conception of man, a denial of the immortality of the soul. Under color of mere instruction in sexual hygiene, a whole cosmology is being smuggled in. Parents have been as slow to recognize this as the sex educationists have been to admit it. . . .

Two views of man are contending for control of our public life. Education, beyond the point of training in simple skills, must adopt one view or the other. There is no real neutrality except uncertainty—and nobody who was truly uncertain would subject children to instruction in anal sex. . . .

And so, as homosexuality has "come out," faith has been driven into the closet. Parents who believe their children have souls have been told that they must argue from the premises of those who don't believe it. They will never recover their rights as parents until they learn to speak from their own depths.

*"You must stop . . . in your clinical analysis of
your gay child's sexuality. . . . You must love
them as the individuals you've always loved."*

Parents Should Support
Their Gay Children

Walter Fricke

Most parents, like Walter Fricke, travel through their offsprings'
childhood assuming that their children will grow up to be something like themselves—even in their sexuality. Some parents, like
Walter Fricke, are shocked when they discover that this is not to
be the case. They often do not know what to do when their child
announces that he or she is a homosexual. This happened to
Walter Fricke when his son, Aaron, was seventeen. After several
years of struggle to accept his son as he was, Walter Fricke agreed
to work with Aaron on the writing of a book—the story of the ups
and downs of their relationships after Aaron's "coming out." The
following viewpoint is an excerpt from that book, in which
Walter Fricke urges parents to be accepting and loving toward
their children who turn out to be not quite what they expected.

As you read, consider the following questions:

1. How does Walter Fricke suggest that parents try to make
   sense of and accept their child's puzzling sexual orientation?
2. Why does Fricke think acceptance and love are so important
   in dealing with a homosexual child?

"Accepting Your Gay Children" by Walter Fricke. In *Sudden Strangers: The Story of a Gay Son
and His Father* by Aaron Fricke and Walter Fricke. Copyright © 1991 by Aaron Fricke.
Reprinted by permission of St. Martin's Press, Inc., New York.

When a parent witnesses something threatening happen to his child, the incident will remain indelible in the parent's memory. I have permanent recall of one such threatening incident that happened when my son was four years old.

Aaron had been walking just inches in front of me as we entered the breezeway behind our local pharmacy. He reached for what he thought was the door to the pharmacy and in the blink of an eye was tumbling head over heels down into what was actually a darkened cellar. He fell so suddenly that I did not have a chance to grab hold of him. My brain was working a bit faster than my arms, because as I ran down the stairs, I projected calling an ambulance and perhaps applying splints to him before the ambulance arrived. By the time I reached the bottom of the stairs, however, Aaron was standing firmly upright, unscathed. This was the first time I had encountered the feeling of losing Aaron to a darkened unknown, but certainly not the last. . . .

That Aaron would be heterosexual was simply and indisputably taken for granted. When Aaron was about nine, a scene took place at the same local pharmacy. He had spotted a cute little girl exiting, so he made his way to the door, held it open, and smiled at the girl as she walked by. Later, when he turned to me confused about why he felt tenderness toward her, I explained that these were the first stirrings of appreciation of the opposite sex. He looked perplexed at this, and I did not expand on it at the time. Still, his actions served as confirmation to me of a budding nine-year-old's impending heterosexuality.

I saw that Aaron was never overly active like many other young boys were. He was always especially timid about engaging in sports. This did not seem to be cause for alarm, considering that as a child I tended toward the cerebral and was not overly active, either. Of course, our father and son relationship was headed for the test bound to occur in all growing parent/child relationships: adolescence.

Adolescence gives rise to a generation gap between parents and their children. Generation gaps do not merely imply a distance in years, however. If that were the case, generation gaps would occur between parents and their two-year-old children. Generation gaps invariably arise during the child's adolescence, that most memorable and classic period of life that so clearly establishes each and every one of us as distinct and separate identities.

Adolescent Alienation

Up until adolescence, Aaron never seemed to have any problems expressing his identity. Then, around the time my son was thirteen or fourteen, I noticed him withdrawing. He shut himself up in his room. No friends came to visit. He had no peer group to speak of. It was as if Aaron was expressing his teen rebellion through total apathy. . . .

I knew that something was wrong as I watched the identity that had been such an intrinsic part of Aaron's boyhood slip away. I saw him becoming secluded, but I didn't know how to break down the barriers. I searched for a possible explanation for what seemed like an out-of-the-ordinary problem, even for an adolescent. In my struggle to understand, I wondered whether Aaron's indifference might be caused by some form of drug abuse. At one point when I found him alone in his room writing on his bedroom mirror with a Magic Marker, I was sure he was having a bad trip. So he was placed in a juvenile center and given a battery of tests. The tests showed Aaron was not using any drugs. Homosexuality is not detectable through blood tests. . . .

Missing Out

Los Angeles, California—Six years ago, when Brenda Freiberg first learned that her son Brett, 26, was HIV-positive, she immediately got drunk. "I walked around depressed, feeling sorry for us all," says the 54-year-old business consultant. A year later, when her other son, Michael, then 22, broke the same news, Brenda decided to enjoy whatever time she had left with them both: "It was like a lightning bolt. Something inside me said, 'You're going to miss what's going on if you don't cut it out.'"

One day in 1991, Brenda sensed she should go see Brett at his home in San Francisco. That night, after they had spent the afternoon together, he died in his sleep. Now Michael has come home. "Our life may seem like it's closing down because of our tremendous loss, but it's opened up so much at the same time," Brenda says. "I wish parents realized the love they're missing by rejecting their sons because of homosexuality or AIDS."

Barbara Nevins, *Redbook*, May 1993.

Then, around the time Aaron was turning seventeen, he introduced me to his first new friend in years. This friend was so obviously gay that I felt compelled to warn Aaron. He said that he didn't really know the guy that well, so I let the matter rest. It was not so much later that Aaron began dieting to lose weight. Then he started trotting more gay friends into the house, too. When I approached him about these friends, he said he was aware that his friends were gay but that he felt sorry for them when other people picked on them. The mixture of emotions that this caused me should be obvious.

I had fears. I knew the libido of a seventeen-year-old boy is strong and I wondered whether these homosexuals might be availing themselves and taking advantage of the natural curiosity of Aaron's own seventeen-year-old libido. I thought it entirely possible that these boys could be plying my son with some sort of favors. Were they doing his homework for him? I wondered. (Aaron's grades were, after all, improving at this point.) My worst fear was that Aaron might be some kind of sexual puppet to these boys.

Then, just a year and a half after Aaron had introduced me to his first gay friend, he was sitting on the witness stand during his lawsuit to win the legal right to attend the senior prom with that same gay friend. As I sat in the courtroom the day Aaron gave testimony, I experienced a revelation. The identity Aaron seemed to have lost during adolescence came flooding back right before my eyes. He was becoming a man. He was standing up for something he really believed in. As I looked at Aaron from the back of that courtroom, I felt proud. Aaron was nobody's puppet. I could look at my son for the first time since his childhood and proudly say as a father, "That's my son . . . that's *my* son."

I certainly was not *proud* of the fact that Aaron was gay. . . . It was his ability to stand up for something he believed in of which I was proud. . . . I have a difficult time integrating Aaron's identity as a homosexual with Aaron's identity overall. I recognize this as a mental block, but one that most people will have when thinking of their own gay child. . . .

Don't Analyze; Accept

How are parents who are raised in a society that says even "normal" sex is something to be ashamed of supposed to understand what these kids go through? Perhaps the best way to start is by acknowledging that it very well could be that the gender attraction your children feel is as strong as the one you feel. If you take the intimidation and shame you felt about your own sexuality during puberty and then multiply it a thousand fold, you can probably get a clearer picture of how a young homosexual must feel about his or hers.

You must stop there in your clinical analysis of your gay child's sexuality. It may sound awful, but you must sanitize your thoughts of your gay children and separate them from your thoughts about homosexual acts. Up until you found out your child was gay, homosexuality was probably on the periphery of your concerns, and it is perhaps best that it stay there. It's true that being gay is bound to make growing up much harder for your children, but it really is their own personal challenge. Hopefully, they will understand, or come to understand, that as hard as it was for them to look at themselves while growing up gay and say "I am gay," it is a thousand times more difficult for you to look at yourself and say "My child is gay."

194

That doesn't mean you love them any less. You must love them as the individuals you've always loved, capable of every emotion you are capable of. If loving another person of the same sex is what they lean toward, then the least you can do is be thankful they are capable of love. . . .

Finding Out That Your Child Is Gay

Nothing can prepare you for the day when your child comes to you and says "I'm gay." Nothing in your consciousness will allow you to accept that your child could be that way and no words of advice can really cushion the aftereffects once you are told. . . .

You may go through a denial stage first, telling yourself that it isn't true, that it couldn't possibly be true. You may rush to your nearest calendar in hopes of discovering that it is April Fool's Day and this is just your heterosexual child's idea of a cruel joke. What will seem most cruel is if it is not a joke. Deluding yourself isn't going to change the situation. This is one you have to face head-on.

Keep in mind that your child would be gay whether or not you were told. And when you are told, it is with good intentions and innocence. To you, it may seem like a catastrophe, but to your child it is a metamorphosis. You can't be expected to understand that concept right away but you can make a start by accepting that your child has come to terms with a vital aspect of him/herself and *has* to share it with you. It would be unreasonable to expect you to share the enthusiasm, but it is not unreasonable to expect levelheadedness on your part.

When your child reveals his or her homosexuality, you and your child are facing a gigantic moment of truth. Your actions at this moment are bound to be unpredictable. The tragedy is when parents reject or disown their gay child for coming out to them. That act shows a lack of concern for the future. The enormous confusion you feel at the moment you are told is only normal, but there are two basic choices to fall back on in responding to this information: You can either react as you would to a homosexual stranger or you can react as you would to the child you have always loved and cared for. Granted, at the moment you are told, there will be a tendency to feel as though you don't know your child at all. The single most important thought to keep in mind at that moment is that this person is the same one you have always loved and nurtured. Your child will be looking for affirmation of that fact. A negative or violent reaction won't help.

Your parental instincts tell you to punish your children when they do something wrong and to reward them when they do something acceptable. That doesn't work in this case. Though you may have come to believe that homosexuality is not acceptable, your child has done nothing wrong in coming out to you. Punishing your child for this honesty will not change your child's sexual orientation. Just try to acknowledge that it is not realistic to reward the honesty and not sensible to punish it.

Appreciate Your Child's Honesty

In coming out to you, your children have enough confidence in themselves and in you to reveal their homosexuality. It is a major gamble for them because your response is unpredictable. Yet still they feel the need to share this with you. You may not really want them to share it, and may even believe they have done something to deliberately hurt you, but the unavoidable truth is that your children are simply expressing honesty with you. And they are taking risks in doing so.

Serious complications arise when a different scenario occurs. Some children take a malicious tack when coming out to their parents. Perhaps it will happen during an argument. Being informed of your child's homosexuality is never easy, but coming to this realization during an argument is infinitely more difficult. You'll feel struck down even if your child comes out to you in a civil manner, but under hostile circumstances the emotions are compounded. Yes, it is unfair for your child to make this disclosure with hostility. Yes, your child is playing a game with you and has just pulled the trump card. No, you never wanted to play this game, but you have been swept up in it and are now in trouble.

You must not play this game; you cannot win. Do not even attempt to continue the conversation, because your interactions will inevitably lead back toward antagonism. At this point you feel backed into a corner and ferocious. Your only defense, however, is to say nothing. Accept the situation and walk away. (Then you can look up the closest chapter of Parents and Friends of Lesbians and Gays for someone to talk to.)

On the other hand, when you are confronted in a civil manner, your child is in many ways displaying respect for you. He or she is being honest, and honesty is, after all, something you have probably always strived to instill in your child. He or she is hoping that you can cope with this truth. In effect, your child is trusting you with a great secret. It's only fair that you respect that trust.

Responding to your gay child is not an exact science. Even if it were, it is unlikely that many parents would care to study it. It is impossible to cover all bases in one chapter and describe the "right" way to respond to your child. The only responsible solution is to listen without rancor. Most of responding to your child's homosexuality relies upon love and intuition.

At age eighteen, Aaron took me aside and with a serious vocal intonation tried to set the stage for what he was about to say. I suspected it was something momentous, but I didn't expect to hear those words. I have always dealt with problems through my own rationality or turned to God for guidance. My reaction when Aaron told me he was gay was probably a combination of both influences. I cried. It was a spontaneously honest reaction, reminiscent of the same honesty with which Aaron had confronted me.

Days afterward, I overcame the initial shock and realized my son was the same son I always had loved. Because of this, I was able to take Aaron out to a restaurant and respond to his homosexuality by saying, "I never thought I'd be sitting in a restaurant with a homosexual telling him I love him."

Try it on your kid!

"If you will persevere and be there for [your homosexual children], there is hope that they will once again walk free to become all that God wants for them."

Parents Should Support Their Gay Children and Pray for Their Change

Stephen Arterburn and Jim Burns

Active in youth ministry and authors of several books on matters of Christian faith and youth problems, Stephen Arterburn and Jim Burns believe that parents can be supportive of their homosexual children and at the same time remain true to religious values that condemn homosexuality. By "condemning the sin but not the sinner," Arterburn and Burns believe, Christian parents can offer their children the kind of support that will bring them back to the right path and keep them from seeking love and solace in unacceptable places.

As you read, consider the following questions:

1. According to Arterburn and Burns, is there any room for homosexuality in a Christian life?
2. These authors, unlike some, do not suggest that all homosexual teenagers can change their sexual orientation. For those who cannot, what options do they have if they are to be good Christians, according to the authors?
3. How can parents help their homosexual children, according to the authors?

Reprinted, with permission, from *When Love Is Not Enough: Parenting Through the Tough Times* by Stephen Arterburn and Jim Burns. Colorado Springs: Focus on the Family, 1992. Copyright © 1992 by Focus on the Family. All rights reserved, international copyright secured.

An almost panicked feeling comes over parents whenever they must deal with their children's sexual identity issues. Parents hope and pray that their children will grow up "normal." They hope and pray that each child will find the perfect mate with whom to walk down the path of marital bliss. And most parents hope their children will in turn produce "Kodak-picture-perfect" children. Unfortunately this doesn't always happen. . . .

We have counseled many Christian parents who were broken-hearted over the "sexual-preference" decisions their children had made. The revelation to Christian parents that their child is having a homosexual relationship is perhaps more painful than any other problem they could face. Maybe it's because homo-sexuality involves the adolescent's entire identity. Or it could be because children who move into a homosexual lifestyle abandon so many values their Christian parents hold dear. . . .

This issue used to be simple from theological and psychological points of view. The field of psychiatry viewed homosexuality as a maladaptive lifestyle and treated it as a problem. Now many psychiatrists view it as nothing more than an alternative life-style, not an indication of underlying emotional problems. In many denominations, the church's view of homosexuality has also changed. Many denominations that used to interpret the Bible as condemning homosexual behavior now openly welcome homosexuals as ministers. This has produced a lot of confusion.

Major changes in the way homosexuality is viewed have also taken place in the political arena. In recent years, a strong pro-gay movement has emerged. Nearly every major city now cele-brates a "gay pride" day. Some state legislatures have considered bills that would grant minority status to homosexuals—making it illegal even for churches and church-run organizations to dis-criminate against gays.

These trends have left many parents asking important questions that affect how we raise our children: "Is a homosexual lifestyle normal?" "Are evangelical Christians lacking insight into this problem, or are they right in holding on to their biblical view of homosexuality?" "Is homosexuality just an alternative lifestyle?" "What exactly is a homosexual?" "If children have homosexual tendencies, should parents make them feel more comfortable with their feelings or try to change the way they feel?". . .

Separating the Issues

In looking at homosexuality, each of us must carefully differ-entiate between the person and his or her behavior. To do this, we must consider homosexuality and homosexual behavior as two separate issues.

Homosexuality is an inclination or desire for someone of the same sex to provide emotional intimacy, acceptance, and/or affection. It describes the heart—the identity—of a person who isn't attracted to people of the opposite sex. It doesn't always result in homosexual behavior.

Homosexual behavior, on the other hand, is the manifestation of that inclination and desire. The difference is significant. Lust is a sin, but inclination toward lust is not. The inclination toward homosexuality is not a sin, but the behavior, as outlined in Scripture, is. Scripture is clear that homosexual behavior is sin. It is one of several sexual behaviors that are unacceptable to God. We are not to have sex with our parents, children, brothers, sisters, with animals, with another person's spouse, or with a person of the same sex.

Faith Will Carry the Family Through

If you sense that your child is having a problem in the area of sexual preference or identity, I urge you to do possibly the most difficult thing for you to do—discuss it with your child. Bring it out in the open. Once you are able to talk about it, your child will know you will not reject him or her for it. Reject the behavior but not the person; then you will be in a position to help. . . .

Leaving the gay life is not something that happens overnight, and there may be many relapses along the way. Please be patient, and don't give up. Your son or daughter may not make it out of the gay lifestyle, but this is no cause for rejection. Continue to show your love and concern. Be sure that your child knows that you are available and willing to help. I know that this is a difficult problem to handle. I watched my parents struggle with it through the years as I struggled also. But through it all, my parents' faith brought them through it. I encourage you to go to your minister and seek his guidance, and don't forget the wisdom of the Scripture. God wants to help you and your child if you will call upon Him to do so.

Jerry Arterburn, *How Will I Tell My Mother?* 1988.

Through the years, a number of groups have asserted that sex is permissible with any and all of the above. One group tried to convince the world that it's good for children to have sex with their parents. "Swingers" tried to convince others that sex with someone else's spouse is liberating. Groups who want to be free from the standards of God's Word are not new. The Bible clearly acknowledges that some people will desire to have sex with others of the same sex. It also clearly states that people so inclined are to abstain. Many people today say this is unreasonable. We believe it's a tough reality.

Many individuals make a sexual decision based on their theological beliefs. Dedicated nuns and priests, for instance, choose to not have sex out of commitment to God. A Christian man attracted to a woman who's not his wife must abstain if he's to remain true to his beliefs. A woman who kisses her soldier husband good-bye must resist natural urges while he's away if she is to remain faithful to the God-ordained institution of marriage. Only an animal must give in to sexual urges. Human beings have the ability to make decisions that counter sexual urges.

When a married man is attracted to a woman other than his wife, that attraction isn't sinful. What the man does with that attraction, however, can become sin. Lusting after her—wanting her for sexual pleasure, fantasizing about her—is sin. Having sex with her is sinful. Sin comes from a decision to move beyond the attraction.

According to biblical standards, the same principle holds true for a homosexual. Sexual attraction to a person of the same gender isn't a sin. Heterosexuals don't lust after every person they're attracted to, and neither do homosexuals. But when homosexuals act on the attraction and sexualize it, according to Scripture they cross over a line into behavior that is not acceptable to God. As individuals, they are acceptable and deserving of our love. We must not reject them. It's their behavior that's sinful. . . .

Offer Hope, Not Anger

As parents, one of the biggest mistakes we can make is to say things that invite people with homosexual tendencies to feel their whole being is a mistake. We must separate the individual from the behavior if we are to be a source of hope for those who want to find a different way to live.

We must offer hope to, rather than heap more guilt on, people who struggle. If these people don't believe there's hope, they are more likely to deny their problem. They will cling to the homosexual behaviors that have helped them survive rather than give them up. In all we do, we must believe there is hope and offer that hope in love. If we react with anger, all our actions will be ungodly and distorted. . . .

As parents, we must fight the urge to reject, label, and make false assumptions. We must encourage our kids to develop their talents. We must give up our preconceived images of what a "real boy" and "real girl" should be and simply love the boys and girls we have. This is our greatest hope of raising kids who make sexual choices in line with God's best for them. And we can never forget that our children will—must—find somewhere the love and acceptance they need every bit as much as they need food and water. If we don't provide it, someone else will. . . .

Secular wisdom insists that homosexuals should explore the facets of their sexual orientation and seek ways to be comfortable with—even proud of—their sexual identity. But if we parents know that homosexuality is not a natural lifestyle (and biblically we know that), such an approach provides no hope or comfort.

On the other hand, many men and women have been able to leave the homosexual lifestyle through the grace of God. Christians can take heart in knowing they "can do every thing through him [Christ] who gives . . . [us] strength" (Philippians 4:13). But forsaking homosexual behavior is never easy and never instant. It takes time and ongoing accountability with others who are holding fast to the biblical mandate. Like any other problem, this one can't be wished away.

If your children are already involved in homosexual behavior and starting to identify with the homosexual lifestyle, they need your love and acceptance—now more than ever. Parents often withhold these out of a fear that their children will think they condone homosexual behavior. Don't let the conflict move your children further from you. The relationship may be rough, but if you will persevere and be there for them, there is hope that they will once again walk free to become all that God wants for them.

In working with kids who became involved with homosexuality, we have counseled their parents to pray, be patient, and show their undying love. We have watched many parents rejoice because their sons and daughters have decided not to follow a homosexual lifestyle. There have been great victories and times of emotional healing in numerous families.

Don't give up on your children. Show God's relentless love by loving them relentlessly, even when it feels like the hardest thing in the world you could possibly do.

"I believe [God] made you [homosexuals] . . . to be happy in a celibate condition."

Homosexual Teenagers Should Commit Themselves to Celibacy

Tim Stafford

The conflict between religious belief and homosexual practice is longstanding. Most Christians have traditionally believed that homosexuality is sinful and therefore not acceptable as a lifestyle. Tim Stafford, contributing editor to *Campus Life* magazine and author of several books for young people, concurs with this belief. However, he does not condemn the homosexual, only homosexual activity. He urges young people who believe they are gay or lesbian to choose a life of celibacy and remain true to traditional Christian values. The following viewpoint, excerpted from Stafford's book *Love, Sex, and the Whole Person*, is based on his column in *Campus Life* in which he responds to the questions of readers.

As you read, consider the following questions:

1. Why does Stafford say the idea that people must express their sexuality through sexual activity is bunk?
2. According to the author, why has Christianity traditionally condemned homosexuality?
3. Why does Stafford view celibacy as a "gift to homosexuals"? Do you agree with him? Explain.

Taken from the book *Love, Sex, and the Whole Person* by Tim Stafford. Copyright © 1991 by Campus Life Books. Used by permission of Zondervan Publishing House.

Q: I am gay. . . . I am also a Christian. . . . I don't even know if I want to change. What should I do? . . .

A: God has expressed his expectations regarding your choices. He is not ambiguous. God does not want you living a gay lifestyle.

The Bible considers homosexual actions wrong. There isn't a great deal of material dealing with it; in the Old Testament it simply is declared off-limits, and that is carried over in the New Testament. The only passage that gives a hint of why it is wrong is Romans 1:26-27. There Paul discusses homosexuality in the context of people that have turned their back on God and have succeeded in twisting far away from what is "natural." Paul probably was thinking of the story of creation in Genesis, where it is said that God made man in his own image "male and female." We're sexual people—that's what's "natural"—and sex was made to be between male and female. We learn something about ourselves and about God through the wonderful erotic attraction and interaction of male and female. We learn even if we never marry, for we take part in those interactions at other levels.

That is the basic threat—that you would lose out on part of your identity. Your true identity in Christ isn't homosexual. Some experts say nearly everyone has homosexual desires to some extent. But the sexual focus of our lives is meant to be the opposite sex, for that is how we discover more about ourselves.

It is important to distinguish between your personality structure and the way you live it out. In other words, there is a difference between homosexual tendencies and a homosexual lifestyle. Everyone has certain dispositions that lead to particular strengths and weaknesses. The Big Lie of the sexual-freedom revolution is that you have to follow your sexual preference (whatever it is), that you have no choice. If I fall in love with someone, it's inevitable we'll end up in bed—unless I am a repressed and unhappy individual determined to stay in an unhappy marriage. If you feel attracted to other men, you will either "stay in the closet," repressed and unhappy, or you will enter the free-flowering splendor of the gay community.

Humans Can Control Their Sexuality

But this is sheer nonsense. It's really just a variation on the old line a guy gives who wants to take a girl to bed: "Fate meant us to be together. It's bigger than both of us. It's chemistry." One difference between human beings and animals is that we can control our sexuality; it doesn't have to control us. If we all did everything we felt like doing, the world would be sheer chaos. Instead, as rational, thinking creatures, we take our many desires into consideration—desires for sexual release, for personal intimacy, for long-lasting friendships, for marriage and children, for many things—and we decide on a course. We choose a lifestyle that really suits us. We may need to say no to certain desires, but the overall result will be positive, fitting our personal needs.

First published in *The Spectator* (London) 1991. Reprinted with permission.

Scripture does not indicate that it is wrong to be tempted. In fact, temptations are normal. The fact that you are tempted to have sexual relations with other men may reflect badly on our sex-crazed society, which inflames our tendencies, or it may reflect badly on your family background, as some psychologists say. I don't see that it reflects badly on you. How you came by the desires that trouble you I do not know. I suspect that most people feel a certain amount of sexual ambiguity, some people more than others.

I get many letters from young people who are afraid they are homosexuals. They've never lived a gay lifestyle, but they feel some variance in their sexual longings—maybe the opposite sex does not attract them in the way they expect is normal, or maybe they have tender feelings for a friend of the same sex. The gay movement claims that one out of ten people is a homosexual and that if you are one you can't do a thing about it. So the question arises: "Am I one?" Once the idea is planted, it tends to grow. And if a person tries it out, he will probably find that, indeed, he can be sexually aroused by his own sex. Therefore, he thinks, he must be gay. In reality, he may merely be ambivalent. In another society, in another time, he would have channeled his sexual desires in a different direction. Sexuality is more fluid than the gay movement leads people to believe. Sexual attraction is as much mental as physical.

You Can Choose Your Lifestyle

You cannot choose your desires, but you can choose your lifestyle. Your feelings and desires for sex will still be there. But what does that prove? Mine are still there too, but I have chosen to focus them within the marriage relationship. That means saying yes to some desires and no to a great many others. Some Christians are single, and they live with continuing heterosexual or homosexual desires. Need they be unhappy? The Bible answers a resounding no! The single, celibate life is honored in the New Testament without reservation. Everyone is called to it for some portion of his or her life. Some are called to it permanently. Jesus was, Paul possibly was, and countless other great and inspiring Christians through the ages have been celibate. Jesus' words in Matthew 19:12 suggest that the call to singleness is not always based on great religious feeling. Practical factors enter: "For some are eunuchs because they were born that way; others were made that way by men; and others have renounced marriage because of the kingdom of heaven." All three causes are honorable.

I believe singleness is the healthy and blessed lifestyle for you at this point. It won't be sheer bliss—I don't know of any lifestyle that is, realistically. And because your struggles are less acceptable in our society than mine, you will suffer a special loneliness in them. Given the judgmental disgust that many people feel regarding homosexuality, you can't expect the sympathies of vast numbers of people. However, you can hope to find the help and support of some. . . .

You cannot change your lifestyle alone. That is why I strongly encourage you to begin today asking God to put before you one or more people whom you can confide in with complete confidence. You need them not just to listen to you and accept you, but to play an active, caring part in your life, meeting regularly with you for prayer and Bible study. You need to take the risk of revealing your inner thoughts so that you can quit living in lonely secretiveness and begin to develop satisfying, deep relationships. Jesus is the answer to all our problems, but he doesn't work in a purely spiritual way. He has a physical and relational reality, what the Bible calls "the body of Christ"—that is, the church.

I look for the day when Christians will get over their homophobia and realize that those with homosexual temptations differ very little from the rest of us. We all struggle with temptations, and the Bible never treats one sin as worse than another. In the fellowship of the Holy Spirit, which is the togetherness binding Christians, we come closest to grasping Christ's full and final victory over sin.

There is no mysterious, awesome power in homosexual temptations. Temptation is temptation—we all know how impossible it can be when we are in the wrong situation and how easy to resist when we leave that situation. You say you are not sure that you want to change. I think you do want to change, but you are not sure you can. The gay movement says that you cannot, that you can only repress your natural feelings. That is not so. It is most natural to follow Jesus. You were made to do that. . . .

Hope for Change Is in God

I don't doubt that you are unable to change yourself. If there is any hope for change, it is in Christ's power, not the homosexual's. I do know of many people who lived as homosexuals for years and were able through the power of Christ to convincingly shift direction. I am also aware that many homosexuals doubt the reality of the changes in these people's lives.

God, I am sure, is able to change a homosexual's orientation, or any other orientation. I have little doubt that he sometimes does so. However, I know the power of sexual patterns, and I know there is no automatic, magical way to change them. They usually change, if they change at all, through long, determined struggle and a lot of outside help. You don't ordinarily change your sexual patterns, heterosexual or homosexual, by praying alone in your room. . . .

You seem to think of [celibacy] as a punishment—a curse of abnormality and deprivation. I can understand that view: most people in America think of it that way. But Christians have never thought of it that way. They have, since the time of Jesus, thought of it as a privilege and an opportunity to serve God. If Jesus was celibate and Paul was celibate, it was obviously a good condition. I don't see that a person's free choice has anything to do with it, either. Paul calls singleness a gift in 1 Corinthians 7—a gift from God. God chooses what gifts to give his people. Our choice is how we receive and use those gifts.

I was celibate for twenty-seven years, and I regard those as wonderful, full, rich years. I do not regret them, nor do they make me feel sorry for my friends who are celibate now. These friends miss some great joys in not being married, but they can gain others. For me to say to someone who is homosexual, "You should follow Christ and be celibate," is not offering a message of judgment but of hope. I would say exactly the same thing to an unmarried heterosexual. (I would never, under any circumstances, urge someone to marry a person with whom he or she could never be happy. Just the opposite.)

Celibacy: A Gift to Homosexuals

One principal reason why I see celibacy as a gift to homosexuals is that I think promiscuity is a source of deep unhappiness, to them and to anyone else. The gay movement is highly promiscuous, as you know. Even now, while AIDS rages, surveys show that the average homosexual has several different partners per month. They risk their lives to do so. I don't understand why they do, but I wonder if there is something inherently unstable about homosexual relationships. Perhaps this is one reason why the Bible encourages people to leave them rather than try to make permanent relationships with them in a "homosexual marriage." The Bible regards all homosexual relationships (not persons) as being far from what God wants his people to enjoy.

I don't know why you are oriented the way you are. I believe, however, that God created you and intends good for your life. . . . I believe he made you to serve him, and to obey him, and to be happy in a celibate condition.

"Only when we're all free to be ourselves, open and proud of our way of loving, will the straight world see that gay people come in all shapes and sizes . . . and we really are everywhere. *"*

Homosexual Teenagers Should Feel Positive About Their Sexuality

Sasha Alyson

In 1979, Alyson Publications, a fledgling gay publishing house, published an Americanized version of the Australian book *Young, Gay, and Proud!*, first produced by the Gay Teacher and Students Group of Melbourne. Sasha Alyson, head of Alyson Publications, felt that this book and others like it were needed by many American teenagers who were puzzled and worried about their sexuality and who felt isolated from their heterosexual peers. The following viewpoint is excerpted from the 1991 edition of *Young, Gay, and Proud!* It explores some of the reasons homosexuality is looked down upon by many in American society, and it encourages young gays and lesbians to accept themselves.

As you read, consider the following questions:

1. According to the author, how common is homosexuality among teenagers and among the general population?
2. List three of the reasons Alyson says gays "get hassled."
3. What does the author think of efforts to change one's sexual orientation?

From *Young, Gay, and Proud*, edited by Sasha Alyson. Text of U.S. edition copyright © 1980, 1985, 1991, by Alyson Publications, Inc. Used by permission of Alyson Publications, Inc.

The people we *know* to be gay are just the tip of the iceberg. You can't always identify gay people from the way we look. Most of us look pretty ordinary, and some of us are in good disguise. For instance, many of us are married. According to one estimate, about one in three of all lesbians are married, and many are mothers.

We're spread across all social classes too. From movie stars to union organizers, from New York City to Dubuque, Iowa, from construction workers to the woman next door . . . we're everywhere.

If there are fifty teachers in your school, the chances are that about five of them will be gay. And about fifteen or twenty of them will have had some gay sexual experience. If there are thirty kids in your class, probably about three of them will like their own sex best.

Only a few gay teachers have let the world know they're gay. A few cities and states have laws against anti-gay discrimination, but in many areas, a teacher who came out would stand a good chance of getting fired.

Because we're so hard to pick out, one of our biggest problems is meeting one another. There are places where gays meet—clubs, groups, etc.—and gay newspapers and hotlines can tell you about these.

Telling people we're gay, starting with a few friends we can trust, is another good way to meet other gays. If they're not gay themselves, they often know someone who is. You'll be surprised at how many of the people who are shocked when they first hear that you're gay are telling you, five minutes later, about a gay friend they want to introduce you to.

Only when we're all free to be ourselves, open and proud of our way of loving, will the straight world see that gay people come in all shapes and sizes . . . and we really are *everywhere*. . . .

Why Are We Hassled?

As gay people, we are hassled by lots of Big Lies that are spread about us. Too many people believe the lies. Many don't—but not enough of them speak up.

Why do people believe the lies? They're often spread by ministers, doctors, politicians, judges, and newspapers, even teachers—and the man or woman on the street expects those people to know what they're talking about. Besides, it's easier—and safer—to believe what you're told than to think for yourself and ask thoughtful questions.

There have always been people who could see through the lies—but usually they kept silent because they were lazy, or scared, or had no say in things . . . or a bit of each. Until recently you weren't listened to if you spoke up about homosexuality unless you were a minister or doctor or lawmaker.

Then gay people started putting the record right. This started happening in the late 1960s. Since then there has been a lot more disagreement among ministers and doctors. And among ourselves too.

Being Gay Is Me

Two years ago, I tried to kill myself. I slit my wrists. I was OK with myself, but nobody else was. I didn't think I could go through life with everyone beating up on me, harassing me, hating me.

But now I know I'm going to be able to make it. I have a good network of friends, and I'm feeling good about myself. My experience has made me want to get active in the community, to fight homophobia.

The thing is that people think homosexuality is demented and perverted. They also think it's a choice. It's not. It's not like I woke up and said, Oh, I think I'll be gay today, like I think I'll wear my blue jeans today. If it was a choice, I would have chosen to be straight.

Being gay is just a part of me. There's also a part of me that likes the mountains, that likes to work on motorbikes, that likes country music. It's just a part of me, not all of me.

Gordon Diefenbach, interviewed by Lauren Tarshis, *Scholastic Update*, April 3, 1992.

You might wonder why the lies got created in the first place, and why they've persisted for so long. No one knows the exact answer to this, but here are some ideas.

Some people say that gays get hassled because we're different. People are often scared of what they don't understand, and instead of admitting they're scared, they attack whatever is different. This has happened to other people, such as immigrants. It's happened to Jews a lot, and it's even happened to left-handers. Did you know that people used to believe that left-handers were possessed by the devil? When things went wrong, the left-handers got the blame. And society tried to make them into right-handers. Sound familiar?

The Church

Another reason is the way our society treats sex. Most of the straight world's ideas about sex can be traced back to religious teachings, and Judeo-Christian religions get uncomfortable about sex. Around 700 B.C. the Hebrew church set up laws that made thirty-six crimes punishable by death, and half of these had to do with sex. The penalty for males guilty of homosexual acts was death by stoning, the most severe penalty imposed for any crime. There were no laws against lesbianism. Women's sexuality wasn't taken seriously then, either.

For centuries, the church has said that sex is only okay between married people who want to have children. If people enjoy sex in any other way—by themselves, with someone of the same sex, or with someone they're not married to—then the church calls them sinners and tries to make them feel bad.

For a while, the church seemed to be losing its grip in our society. But recently, right-wing fundamentalist churches have become more vocal about promoting so-called traditional values. Some have even started groups that they claim can convert homosexuals into heterosexuals.

These fundamentalists love to quote passages from the Bible that seem to condemn homosexuality. If you read these passages with an open mind, most of them say no such thing: these Bible-thumpers are really only interested in making themselves feel superior by putting you down. In one breath they will tell you the Bible is infallible, and in the next breath they'll tell you the devil can quote scripture for his own ends—in other words, that you can find a passage in the Bible to support *any*thing.

Don't let these idiots mess with your mind. If these silly, inaccurate claims about what the Bible says are worrying you, read the Bible's story of the love between David and Jonathan. This is the David who slew Goliath and later became King of Israel.

The Bible says: "The soul of Jonathan was knit with the soul ot David, and Jonathan loved him as his own soul . . . They kissed one another, and wept one with another, until David exceeded." Doesn't sound very disapproving, does it? Later, after Jonathan's death, David said, "Jonathan, very pleasant hast thou been unto me: thy love to me was wonderful, passing the love of women." The story of this great love affair is found in I and II Samuel.

Not all churches are against homosexuality. Gay people even have a church of their own now (the Metropolitan Community Church, or MCC), and most of the biggest churches have gay groups. But anti-gay church teachings still greatly affect the way our society treats homosexuals.

Mental Health Experts

School counselors, psychologists, and psychiatrists ("headshrinkers," or "shrinks," as people jokingly call them) are in the business of helping people deal with their personal problems. Many people still depend on their church for this, but there is an important difference between the church and shrinks. The church will try to get you to do things its own way, and try to make you feel guilty and "sinful" if you don't.

A good therapist will help you think clearly about your own problems and make your own decisions about them. They believe there are too many men and women who are grown but not mature because they don't understand their own minds.

"Know thyself," they'll say, or, "Take charge of your own life." Or they quote Plato (whose famous *Symposium* is simply the conversation at a gay banquet): "The unexamined life is a life not worth living."

Some people find psychological counseling an expensive waste of time. But others swear that at its best, it can be a voyage of self-discovery that changes one's life.

The trouble is that much depends on the therapist. A therapist who is fighting a battle against his or her own gay feelings won't be able to give you good advice.

The very worst thing a shrink can do is to betray your trust by telling someone what you have said in private. They say they never do this, but the fact is that many lesbian and gay students have been informed on by school counselors they trusted.

We're not saying you should always avoid counselors and other mental health workers. Sometimes, talking with one can be of great help. Just be sure you can really trust them. Find out what your friends think of them. In your first meeting with a counselor, *don't* talk about whatever is bothering you. Instead, feel them out. Get their opinion about all kinds of things, like cheating, school bullies, religious convictions, and gay people. Then give yourself a few days to think about what they've said. This way, you're more likely to make the right decision.

For many years, gay and lesbian leaders protested the homophobia of the mental health establishment. Finally their efforts paid off. In 1974 the American Psychiatric Association removed homosexuality from its official list of mental disorders. A year later, the American Psychological Association took a similar step.

Some psychotherapists still treat homosexuality as something to be cured, however, and even those who don't may believe some of the lies about gays and lesbians. But there are many therapists who are gay, and if your parents insist on sending you to one, tell them that you will only cooperate with a therapist who is comfortable with gay issues.

Many Are Screwed Up

It's no wonder that so many people today are screwed up about sex. If they haven't actually broken the church's and shrinks' rules, then they feel bad about wanting to!

[Human sexual behavior researcher Alfred Charles] Kinsey's figures show that lots of people have homosexual feelings, in-

213

cluding many who don't call themselves gay. People who don't like to face up to their gay feelings may be especially nasty toward gay people.

When people are afraid of their own feelings, something sometimes snaps, and they do some very violent things. If gay people can be picked out, we may become the target of this violence. The result is gay-bashing.

One reason we get picked on is that such a big deal is made about *men making it with women*. This is supposed to be *the* way of proving how much of a man or how much of a woman you are.

Self-Acceptance

When I was in my teens and thought of my homosexuality as a dirty little secret that I shared only with God, I prayed for change. I prayed that God would make me heterosexual. God answered my prayers in a more profound way than by making me heterosexual, however. I stayed true to my identity and God showed me a new understanding of the world in which that identity was grounded. And at those times when I feel that world leaves something to be desired, I do not pray for sweeping social reforms, because I believe there are some things one must pray to God for and other things that require a little personal sweat. In my opinion, sweeping social reform belongs to the latter category.

So before I ever pray to be heterosexual in order to be accepted, I remember that God accepts only those who are true to themselves. Before I ever equate heterosexuality with happiness, I remind myself that there are a lot of unhappy heterosexuals in the world. If my homosexuality is something that makes my father one of those unhappy heterosexuals, I do not pray to be heterosexual. Because I know that if I can show myself as the decent, hardworking person my father raised me to be, then his happiness is not something for which I will have to pray.

Aaron Fricke, *Sudden Strangers: The Story of a Gay Son and His Father*, 1991.

Men are supposed to act tough, get married, and boss their wives around. The feminist movement has made great strides in changing society's expectations, but in many quarters, women are still expected to be dependent on men.

Anyone who doesn't go along with these ideas, even if they're not gay, often still gets called a "dyke" or "fairy."

Any boy who doesn't want to play football or other rough games will often get called a "sissy" or a fairy.

Any girl who is good at sports gets called "tough" or a dyke and the other girls tell her that boys won't like her if she's too good at sports. Girls aren't expected to excel at anything unless it's sewing or cooking.

A woman who demands a better deal often gets called a dyke.

A man who's gentle often gets called a fairy.

You can see that the words *dyke* and *fairy* are used to make everyone toe the line! . . .

Getting By

The first thing we all have to do is find a way of getting by. A way to keep alive—and kicking!

At school most of us are terrified to think we're gay. Some of us decide to stay quiet. We try not to give anything away about ourselves. Some of us become bookworms. We bury ourselves in schoolwork so that we'll forget what we're feeling inside. Some of us push ourselves in other ways. Some get into sports, or drama, or we help teachers with this and that. Some of us put all our energy into acting more straight than the straights so that no one will guess.

If we act in any of these ways, we're often just trying to push our gay feelings to one side. That may work, but only for a while. Doing these things certainly won't help us if we're feeling uptight.

If you're finding life hard at the moment, you may sometimes wish you were straight. You may have heard of so-called cures for homosexuality. Some gay people even go so far as to marry because it's the straight thing to do. If your feelings are honestly talked out beforehand, such a marriage has a chance, but many are terrible disasters. Anyone who marries without telling their mate that they are gay or lesbian is creating a marriage based on deceit. Later, if the straight member finds out, they're likely to feel that their life has been ruined and that they can never trust anyone again. Children in such a marriage are likely to feel the same way. This kind of thing gives all gay people a bad name. The solution is so obvious that it shouldn't even need to be said: Give love to get love; give trust to get trust.

Well, there are as many kinds of homosexuality as there are homosexuals. Some people discover they are gay rather late in life, perhaps after getting involved in a straight marriage. A shrink might say of them that they once were straight, and became gay. Just so, a person who did not like being gay might, after years of struggle, start having sex only with the opposite sex. The reality is within the mind, and this person might be paying a terrible cost in frustration and self-deception.

On the other hand, the person might have always been more bisexual than gay, and have no trouble at all switching. "AC/DC" they are called (referring to the two basic kinds of electric current).

Some psychotherapists and religious cults claim to have "cured" gay people. They set themselves up to make lots of money from upset parents who want them to do the same for their kid. But can they actually deliver the goods? Not likely! Some people believe that not one such "cure" has ever been shown to work. While this can't be proven, we can certainly say that it *almost never* works. And the cost in mental anguish and disappointment is enormous.

Almost all gay people would strongly advise you not to go this route. Why waste your energy fighting your deepest instincts? You could be using that energy to cultivate your individuality.

Whether your difference is a blessing or a curse depends entirely on how you choose to think of it. Think of it as a blessing and you free yourself to experience a world more complex and beautiful than most heterosexuals know. Think of it as a curse and you are laying a curse on yourself worse than any evil wizard could cast.

There are lots of books you can read written by gay people about being gay. They'll give you useful information and make you feel better about being gay yourself. . . .

You can also find out what the gay groups in your city (or the city nearest you) are doing. . . . Write to them, or phone them, even if you feel you're not ready yet to mix with other gay people. Even occasional contact can be reassuring.

Most important, keep in mind that you are not alone. The world is full of other gay people, even if you haven't been able to connect with others yet.

Periodical Bibliography

The following articles have been selected to supplement the diverse views presented in this chapter.

Amy Cunningham	"Not Just Another Prom Night," *Glamour*, June 1992.
Midge Decter	"Homosexuality and the Schools," *Commentary*, March 1993.
David Gelman et al.	"Tune In, Come Out," *Newsweek*, November 8, 1993.
David Gelman et al.	"The Young and the Reckless," *Newsweek*, January 11, 1993.
Ellen Germaine and Alice Park	"Born Gay?" *Time*, July 26, 1993.
Paul Giurlanda	"What About Our Church's Children?" *America*, May 8, 1993.
Erica E. Goode with Betsy Wagner	"Intimate Friendships," *U.S. News & World Report*, July 5, 1993.
Stephanie Mansfield	"Gays on Campus," *Redbook*, May 1993.
Donna Minkowitz	"Wrong Side of the Rainbow," *The Nation*, June 28, 1993.
Katie Monagle	"Portrait of a Hate Crime," *Scholastic Update*, April 3, 1992.
Sassy	"It Happened to Me," January 1993.
Joseph P. Shapiro et al.	"Straight Talk About Gays," *U.S. News & World Report*, July 5, 1993.
William Tucker	"Revolt in Queens," *The American Spectator*, February 1993.
Ivan Velez Jr.	"Tales of the Closet." Eight comic books dealing with issues of lesbian and gay teens. Available from the Hetrick-Martin Institute, 401 West St., New York, NY 10014.
Donovan R. Walling	"Gay Teens at Risk." Pamphlet available from Phi Delta Kappa, PO Box 789, Bloomington, IN 47402-0789.

For Further Discussion

Chapter 1

1. The viewpoints by Catherine S. Chilman and Patricia Hersch both argue that the legacy of the 1960s has influenced teenage attitudes toward sexuality in the 1990s. However, they differ in opinion regarding the nature of that legacy. How do they differ? Who do you believe offers the more convincing argument? Why?

2. This chapter offers a wide range of opinions on what influences teenage sexual attitudes and development. Group the viewpoints into categories (for example, social influences, economic influences, religious influences). Is (are) there any category(ies) that you feel were not, but should have been, included in the chapter? Formulate your own opinion on the subject. Into which category would you place your opinion and why?

Chapter 2

1. Which of the first four viewpoints in this chapter do you find most accurate? Why? Can you think of other factors that might contribute to teenage pregnancy?

2. Some of the viewpoints in this chapter, Suzanne Fields's and Claire Brindis's in particular, discuss factors that both contribute to and result from teenage pregnancy, thus creating a vicious cycle. Examine their viewpoints and try to explain how this cycle works. What, if anything, do the authors suggest could interrupt the cycle?

3. If you or someone you know became pregnant as a teenager, did your or their experiences match those discussed in the viewpoints in this chapter? Are the authors' discussions of the causes of teen pregnancy accurate, in your opinion? Why or why not?

4. The viewpoint by Mike Males is slightly different from the others in that it discusses the actions of a group of people rather than a social phenomenon. How does the argument he presents differ from the arguments given in the other viewpoints in the chapter?

Chapter 3

1. In her viewpoint, Catherine O'Neill argues that providing the contraceptive Norplant to sexually active teenage girls will

help prevent them from becoming pregnant. In his viewpoint, Tom Bethell argues that providing Norplant will have little effect on teen pregnancy because many inner-city teenagers—those to whom Norplant would be offered—choose to become pregnant and would shun Norplant anyway. Whose argument do you find more convincing? Why?

2. Both Phyllis Schlafly and Howard Hurwitz contend that government programs have contributed to the rising incidence of teenage pregnancy in the United States. How are the arguments they present similar? Do the solutions they propose seem viable? Why or why not?

3. Stephen Chapman, like Suzanne Fields in the previous chapter, contends that dramatic changes in social conventions—marriage, divorce, and premarital sex, for example—beginning in the 1960s, have contributed to an increase in teenage pregnancy. He suggests that society should attempt to reverse such permissive trends in order to reduce the teen pregnancy rate. What methods does Chapman propose to accomplish his goal?

4. Douglas J. Besharov asserts that during the 1980s and early 1990s the federal government ignored the problem of teenage pregnancy. Besharov suggests that the federal government can play an important role in reducing teenage pregnancy. Describe some of the recommendations that he makes in his viewpoint. How does this viewpoint differ from those by Schlafly and Hurwitz?

Chapter 4

1. In the first pair of viewpoints in this chapter, both authors, Sol Gordon and Dana Mack, are scholars. Gordon states, "We owe it to our children and their children to provide them with the [sexual] information they need." Mack opposes teaching sex education in the schools, arguing, "The disparity between the sexual code propounded at school and that generally promoted at home has only grown greater." What do these two statements mean? How do the two authors' opinions differ?

2. The viewpoints by Debra W. Haffner and Haven Bradford Gow both discuss the relationship between sex education in the schools and religion. Which viewpoint do you find more convincing? Explain your answer.

3. The controversy over sex education has many factions. One believes that sex education of any kind in the schools is inappropriate. Another faction contends that comprehensive sex

education—including information about sex, contraception, pregnancy, and diseases—should be taught beginning at an early age. A third group asserts that some sex education should be taught but the primary focus should be on convincing teenagers to abstain from sex. This is the view Nancy Pearcey promotes in her viewpoint. To what does she object about many of the sex education programs currently in place in many schools? What does she propose instead? What are some of the objections that Leslie M. Kantor makes to the programs Pearcey promotes?

Chapter 5

1. The B. Jaye Miller viewpoint includes brief excerpts from Bobby Griffith's diary. Do you see any qualitative difference between the feelings Griffith expresses and the feelings many other teens experience? Do you think Griffith's ideas about society's perceptions of homosexuality are accurate? Do you think the consequences Griffith feared (being hated by his friends, for example) are realistic? In your experience, are gay teens more discriminated against than other teenagers? Explain.

2. Don Feder states that gay activists are using gay youth suicide as a lever to get their own agenda into schools. Which aspects of his argument do you find convincing? Which aspects do you find unconvincing? Why?

3. Joseph Sobran states, "*Real* realism might reflect that the kids are going to despise homosexuality, no matter what we tell them." Do you agree with him? Explain. If he is correct, will educational programs describing homosexuality as just another lifestyle, no better or worse than any other, have any effect on students' beliefs about homosexuality? On activities such as gay-bashing? Explain.

4. The viewpoints by Walter Fricke and by Stephen Arterburn and Jim Burns both suggest ways for parents to respond to their child's revelation of his or her homosexuality. List the similarities you see in the two viewpoints. List the differences. Is one view more compassionate than the other? More practical? Explain.

5. List three generalizations from each of the viewpoints of Tim Stafford and Sasha Alyson. Then list ways the authors support those generalizations (facts, statistics, quotes from authorities, etc.). Which viewpoint seems better substantiated? Does this affect your opinion about the issue they are debating? Explain.

Organizations to Contact

The editors have compiled the following list of organizations concerned with the issues debated in this book. The descriptions are derived from materials provided by the organizations. All have publications or information available for interested readers. The list was compiled on the date of publication of the present volume; names, addresses, and phone numbers may change. Be aware that many organizations take several weeks or longer to respond to inquiries, so allow as much time as possible.

The Alan Guttmacher Institute (AGI)
111 Fifth Ave.
New York, NY 10003
(212) 254-5656

AGI works to develop effective family planning and sex education programs through policy analysis, public education, and research. The institute publishes the bimonthly *Family Planning Perspectives* and the quarterly *International Family Planning Perspectives*.

Center for Population Options (CPO)
1025 Vermont Ave. NW, Suite 210
Washington, DC 20005
(202) 347-5700

CPO is an educational organization dedicated to improving the quality of life for adolescents by preventing teenage childbearing. CPO's national and international programs seek to improve adolescent decision making through life planning and other educational programs, to improve access to reproductive health care, to promote the development of school-based clinics, and to prevent the spread of HIV and other sexually transmitted diseases among adolescents. It publishes the quarterly *Clinic News* and *Options*, as well as fact sheets, reports, and resource guides.

Children's Defense Fund (CDF)
25 E St. NW
Washington, DC 20001
(202) 628-8787

The CDF promotes the interests of children, especially poor, minority, and handicapped children. It supports government funding of education and health care policies for children. In addition to its monthly newsletter, *CDF Reports*, the fund publishes many books, articles, and pamphlets, including *The Adolescent and Young Adult Fact Book* and *Adolescent Pregnancy: An Anatomy of a Social Problem in Search of Solutions*.

Concerned Women for America (CWA)
370 L'Enfant Promenade SW, Suite 800
Washington, DC 20024
(202) 488-7000

CWA lobbies Congress to pass laws that will strengthen the traditional nuclear family. It is opposed to government-funded day care and abortion. It publishes several brochures, including *Teen Pregnancy and School-Based Health Clinics.*

Couple to Couple League
PO Box 111184
Cincinnati, OH 45211-1184
(513) 661-7612

The league teaches natural family planning methods and opposes artificial contraception, premarital sex, and abortion. It publishes a bimonthly newsletter, *CCL News,* and *The Art of Natural Family Planning* manual. Also available is *The Springtime of Your Life,* a pro-chastity slide show for teens.

Eagle Forum
PO Box 618
Alton, IL 62002
(618) 462-5415

The Eagle Forum advocates traditional family values. It opposes any political forces that it believes are antifamily, antireligious, or antimorality. Its members believe that mothers should stay at home to raise their children. It publishes the monthly *Phyllis Schlafly Report* as well as various brochures.

Exodus International
PO Box 2121
San Rafael, CA 94912
(415) 454-1017

Exodus International is a referral network offering support to homosexual Christians who want to overcome their homosexuality. It publishes lists of local ministries and programs as well as bibliographies of books and tapes on homosexuality.

Focus on the Family
420 N. Cascade Ave.
Colorado Springs, CO 80903
(719) 473-4020

Focus on the Family is a Christian, conservative organization dedicated to preserving and strengthening the traditional family. It believes that the breakdown of the traditional family is linked to increases in poverty, teen pregnancy, and drug abuse. It produces several radio programs and magazines as well as family-oriented books, films, videos, and audiocassettes. Among its publications are the monthly magazine *Focus on the Family* and the booklet *Teaching Your Kids to Say 'No' to Sex.*

The Hetrick-Martin Institute (HMI)
401 West St.
New York, NY 10014
(212) 633-8920

The Hetrick-Martin Institute offers a broad range of social services to gay and lesbian teenagers and their families. It also sponsors advocacy and education programs for gay and lesbian adolescents. HMI and the Child Welfare League of America cowrote the booklet *Serving Lesbian and Gay Youth*. Its publications also include the newsletter *HMI Report Card* as well as articles, comic books, and pamphlets on homosexuality.

Homosexuals Anonymous Fellowship Services (HAFS)
PO Box 7881
Reading, PA 19603-7881
(610) 376-1146

HAFS serves as a self-help group based on Christian fellowship for individuals seeking "freedom from homosexuality." It seeks to help group members realize their true identity as part of "God's heterosexual creation." It publishes the bimonthly *HA Newsletter* as well as brochures and monographs.

National Family Planning and Reproductive Health Association
122 C St. NW, Suite 380
Washington, DC 20001
(202) 628-3535

The association works to improve family planning and reproductive health services by acting as a national communications network. It publishes *NFPRHA News* and *Report* monthly as well as various papers, including "The Effects of Sexuality Education."

National Gay Youth Network
PO Box 846
San Francisco, CA 94101-0846
(phone number unpublished)

The network distributes educational materials for and about young lesbians, gays, and bisexuals. Its publications include *Helping Gay Youth: Problems and Possibilities* and *We Are Here*, a listing of community resources and services for gay and lesbian teens. Interested youth can obtain information by sending a stamped, self-addressed envelope to the above address.

Parents, Families, and Friends of Lesbians and Gays (P-FLAG)
1012 14th St. NW, Suite 700
Washington, DC 20005
(202) 638-4200

P-FLAG is a national organization that provides support, education, and advocacy services for gays, lesbians, bisexuals, and their families and friends. It works to end prejudice and discrimination against gays, lesbians, and bisexuals. It publishes and distributes pamphlets and articles, including *Why Is My Child Gay?*, *About Our Children*, and *Coming Out to Your Parents*.

Planned Parenthood
810 7th Ave.
New York, NY 10019
(212) 541-7800

Planned Parenthood supports people who make their own decisions about having children without governmental interference. It provides contraceptive counseling and services through clinics located throughout the United States. Among its extensive publications are the brochures *Guide to Birth Control: Seven Accepted Methods of Contraception, Teensex? It's Okay to Say No Way, A Man's Guide to Sexuality,* and *About Childbirth.*

Project Reality
PO Box 97
Golf, IL 60029
(708) 729-3298

Project Reality has developed a sex education curriculum for junior and senior high students called Sex Respect. The program is designed to provide teenagers with information and to encourage sexual abstinence. According to the authors of the curriculum, "Sex Respect teaches teens that saying 'no' to premarital sex is their right, is in the best interest of society and is in the spirit of true sexual freedom."

Reconciling Congregation Program (RCP)
3801 N. Keeler Ave.
Chicago, IL 60641
(312) 736-5526

RCP is a network of United Methodist churches that welcomes and supports lesbians and gay men and that seeks to end homophobia and prejudice in the church and society. Its national headquarters provides resources to help local ministries achieve these goals. Among its publications are the quarterly magazine *Open Hands*, the book *And God Loves Each One*, and pamphlets, studies, and videos.

Search Institute
Thresher Square West
700 S. Third St., Suite 210
Minneapolis, MN 55415
(612) 376-8955

Search Institute is a nonprofit research organization dedicated to advancing the well-being of children and adolescents through scientific research, evaluation, consultation, and the development of practical resources. The institute has developed a values-based curriculum for the seventh and eighth grades titled *Human Sexuality: Values & Choices*. It publishes the quarterly newsletter *Source*, research reports, books, videos, curricula, study guides, and workbooks.

Sex Information and Education Council of the U.S. (SIECUS)
130 W. 42d St., Suite 2500
New York, NY 10036
(212) 819-9770

SIECUS supports the individual's right to acquire knowledge of sexuality and encourages the development of responsible standards of sexual behavior. The organization provides education, training, and leadership programs and is one of the largest national clearinghouses for information on human sexuality. In addition to publishing sex education curricula, SIECUS also publishes a newsletter, *SIECUS Report*, and the books, *Adolescent Pregnancy and Parenthood* and *Oh No! What Do I Do Now?*

Bibliography of Books

Paula Allen-Meares and Constance Hoenk Shapiro, eds. — *Adolescent Sexuality*. Binghamton, NY: Haworth Press, 1989.

Stephen Arterburn and Jim Burns — *When Love Is Not Enough: Parenting Through the Tough Times*. Colorado Springs, CO: Focus on the Family, 1992.

Shirley Arthur — *Surviving Teen Pregnancy: Your Choices, Dreams, and Decisions*. Buena Park, CA: Morning Glory Press, 1991.

Betty Berzon — *Positively Gay: New Approaches to Gay and Lesbian Life*. Berkeley, CA: CelestialArts, 1992.

Warren J. Blumenfeld and Diane Raymond — *Looking at Gay and Lesbian Life*. Boston: Beacon Press, 1993.

Claire D. Brindis — *Adolescent Pregnancy Prevention: A Guidebook for Communities*. Palo Alto, CA: Health Promotion Resource Center, 1991.

Susan Cohen and Daniel Cohen — *When Someone You Know Is Gay*. New York: Laurel-Leaf Books, 1992.

Gary David Comstock — *Gay Theology Without Apology*. Cleveland: Pilgrim Press, 1993.

William A. Dannemeyer — *Shadow in the Land: Homosexuality in America*. San Francisco: Ignatius Press, 1989.

Leon Dash — *The Urban Crisis of Teenage Childbearing*. New York: William Morrow, 1989.

John P. DeCecco and John P. Elia, eds. — *If You Seduce a Straight Person, Can You Make Them Gay?* Binghamton, NY: Haworth Press, 1993.

Joy G. Dryfoos — *Adolescents at Risk: Prevalence and Prevention*. New York: Oxford University Press, 1990.

Joy G. Dryfoos — *Putting the Boys in the Picture: A Review of Programs to Promote Sexual Responsibility Among Young Males*. Santa Cruz, CA: Network Publications, 1988.

Carolyn Welch Griffin — *Beyond Acceptance: Parents of Lesbians and Gays Talk About Their Experiences*. New York: St. Martin's Press, 1990.

Thomas P. Gullota, Gerald R. Adams, and Raymond Montemayor — *Adolescent Sexuality*. Newbury Park, CA: Sage Publications, 1992.

Karen M. Harbeck	*Coming Out of the Classroom Closet: Gay and Lesbian Students, Teachers, and Curricula.* New York: Harrington Park Press/ Haworth Press, 1993.
Janet B. Hardy and Laurie Schwab Zabin	*Adolescent Pregnancy in an Urban Environment.* Baltimore: Urban Institute Press, 1991.
Gilbert Herdt and Andrew Boxer	*Children of Horizons: How Gay and Lesbian Teens Are Leading a New Way Out of the Closet.* Boston: Beacon Press, 1993.
Gilbert Herdt, ed.	*Gay and Lesbian Youth.* Binghamton, NY: Haworth Press, 1992.
Marion Howard	*How to Help Your Teenager Postpone Sexual Involvement.* New York: Continuum, 1988.
Frances Hudson and Bernard Ineichen	*Taking It Lying Down: Sexuality and Teenage Motherhood.* New York: Macmillan, 1991.
Gary F. Kelly	*Sex and Sense: A Contemporary Guide for Teenagers.* Hauppauge, NY: Barron's, 1992.
Jeff Konrad	*You Don't Have to Be Gay.* Hilo, HI: Pacific Publishing, 1992.
Brian McNaught	*On Being Gay: Thoughts on Family, Faith, and Love.* New York: St. Martin's Press/Stonewall Editions, 1988.
Eric Marcus	*Is It a Choice? Answers to 300 of the Most Frequently Asked Questions About Gays and Lesbians.* San Francisco: Harper, 1993.
Robert Marshall	*Blessed Are the Barren: The Social Policy of Planned Parenthood.* San Francisco: Ignatius Press, 1991.
Jules Hymen Masserman and Victor M. Uribe	*Adolescent Sexuality.* Springfield, IL: Charles C. Thomas, 1989.
Steward Meikle, Jacquelyn A. Peithcinis, and Keith Pearce	*Teenage Sexuality.* San Diego: College-Hill Press, 1985.
J. Gordon Melton	*The Churches Speak on Homosexuality: Official Statements from Religious Bodies and Ecumenical Organizations.* Detroit: Gale Research, 1991.
Brent C. Miller et al.	*Preventing Adolescent Pregnancy: Model Programs and Evaluations.* Newbury Park, CA: Sage Publications, 1992.
Judith S. Musick	*Young, Poor, and Pregnant.* New Haven, CT: Yale University Press, 1993.

Constance A. Nathanson	*Dangerous Passage: The Social Control of Sexuality in Women's Adolescence.* Philadelphia: Temple University Press, 1991.
Les Parrott	*Helping the Struggling Adolescent: A Guide to Thirty Common Problems for Parents, Counselors, and Youth Workers.* Grand Rapids, MI: Zondervan, 1993.
Janice E. Rench	*Understanding Sexual Identity: A Book for Gay Teens and Their Friends.* Minneapolis: Lerner Publications, 1990.
Annette Rickel	*Teen Pregnancy and Parenting.* New York: Hemisphere Publishing, 1989.
Margaret K. Rosenheim and Mark F. Testa, eds.	*Early Parenthood and Coming of Age in the 1990s.* New Brunswick, NJ: Rutgers University Press, 1992.
Joelle Sander	*Before Their Time: Four Generations of Teenage Mothers.* San Diego: Harcourt Brace Jovanovich, 1991.
Tim Stafford	*Love, Sex and the Whole Person.* Grand Rapids, MI: Zondervan, 1991.
Tim Stafford	*Sexual Chaos: Charting a Course Through Turbulent Times.* Downers Grove, IL: InterVarsity Press, 1993.
Patricia Voydanoff and Brenda M. Donnelly	*Adolescent Sexuality and Pregnancy.* Newbury Park, CA: Sage Publications, 1990.
Andrea Warren	*Everybody's Doing It: How to Survive Your Teenagers' Sex Life (and Help Them Survive It, Too).* New York: Penguin, 1993.
Merry White	*The Material Child: Coming of Age in Japan and America.* New York: Lexington Books, 1993.
Constance Willard Williams	*Black Teenage Mothers.* Lexington, MA: Lexington Books, 1991.
Robert Williams	*Just as I Am: A Practical Guide to Being Out, Proud, and Christian.* New York: HarperCollins, 1992.
Laurie Schwab Zabin	*Adolescent Sexual Behavior and Childbearing.* Newbury Park, CA: Sage Publications, 1993.
Shepherd Zeldin, ed.	*Losing Generations: Adolescents in High-Risk Settings.* Washington, DC: National Academy Press, 1993.
Ann Creighton Zollar	*Adolescent Pregnancy and Parenthood.* New York: Garland Publishing, 1990.

Index

Orr, Donald, 107
Overbeck, Joy, 29

parenting, as difficult, 87
parents
    abdication of responsibility, 22-23,
        40
    as isolated from other parents
        support, 22
    as sex educators, 48, 49
        con, 39, 128
    teenage, 19, 55-56, 59
Parents and Friends of Lesbians and
    Gays (PFLAG), 196
Parrot, Andrea, 35
paternal child support, and
    unemployment, 122, 123
Pearcey, Nancy, 150
peer pressure and teen pregnancy,
    59, 78, 113
Perez, Rosie, 39
Perry, Luke, 39
Philadelphia Inquirer, 92, 93
pill, the, 108
Planned Parenthood Federation of
    America (PPFA), 40, 104, 109, 110,
    136, 148, 151
    "Teen Sex? It's Okay to Say No
        Way," 155
    see also ETR Associates
Planned Parenthood of Metropolitan
    Washington, 93
political correctness, as false and
    destructive value, 189
pornography, 47-49
poverty of youth, increase in, 58
Pratt, Jane, 113
Presbyterian Church USA, 145
Project 10 (Los Angeles), 182
promiscuity, 85, 208

rape, 31, 62
    of teens by adults, 60-61
    pornography's impact on, 47
Ravoira, LaWanda, 76
Reagan, Ronald
    poverty and, 58, 61
Remafedi, Gary J., 180
Remillard, James, 138
Rhode, Deborah L., 115
Rich, Charles, 176
Richard, Dinah, 147-148
right-wing fundamentalist religious
    organizations
    growing influence of, 159-166, 212
Ritter, Bruce, 48
Rivara, Frederick, 111-112
Robins, Eli, 176

Robinson, Holly, 39-40
Rodriguez, Patricia, 113
RSVP, 161-162
RU 486, 122

Santiago, Chile, study of teen
    pregnancy, 77
Schlafly, Phyllis, 94
school
    dropping out, 96
        reasons for, 66
    hours in
        cultural comparisons, 19
school-based health clinics, 44, 122
schools
    gay students and, 179-184
    gender treatment as unequal and,
        66
    homophobia and, 179
Schwartz, Michael, 26
sex, Christian view of, 48-49, 187,
    188, 190
    society's attitude toward, 211-212
sex education, 181
    as counterproductive, 138, 147, 148
    attacks morality and family life,
        136-137, 147-148
    compared to Sweden, 129-130
    contraceptive information and, 144
    counters teen pregnancy, 111
    fosters myths and stereotypes, 166
    has no impact on teen sex, 111-112,
        136
    homosexuality and, 131, 189-190
    increases teen sexual activity, 40,
        137, 148
    in the home
        is ineffective, 128-129
    in the media
        is countereffective, 128-129
    is a right, 131
    is given too late, 112
    is impotent against teen pregnancy,
        64, 104, 128, 139, 140, 148
    is inadequate, 111-112, 129-130
    is "perversion of nature," 136
    is shaped by gays, 188
    is too explicit, 134, 135-136, 186
    love and, 131-132, 136, 140
    parental opposition to, 186
    parental responsibility and, 132,
        138, 147
    should not be in schools, 147
    today, compared to twenty-five
        years ago, 134
    value-based, opposition to, 153
    vs. "sexuality education," 142
    what teens want to know, 130

University of Maryland study of teen pregnancy, 107
Uribe, Virginia, 182, 183

Vanity Fair magazine, 31, 55, 186
Vaughn, Tauscha, 70, 91
Vigilante, Richard, 189
violent crime increase, 58
virginity, loss of, 20

Washington Post, 70, 71, 90, 93, 151
Wattenberg, Ben, 96
welfare system
as devastating to young black males, 92
as fostering dependency, 91
reforms needed to deter teen pregnancy, 95-97
"whirlpooling," 44, 45
Whitehead, Barbara Dafoe, 55
Whitehead, K. D., 154
Williams, Lillian, 73-74, 75
Wilson, Susan, 154, 155

youth culture, 22, 23, 28
youth poverty statistics, 58, 61